You'll neve[r] m

write another letter

[fi]lled with doubt beca[use]

I'll never be doubtful

[i]f ever the time comes

I don't hear from you [&]

[th]at seems like a life[time]

[i] just read your lett[er]

[ag]ain & felt confiden[t]

within a cou[ple]

[da]ys time. I['d] receive [&]

everything & [th]at ele[ment]

Royko
in Love

Royko in Love

Mike Royko

EDITED BY DAVID ROYKO

The University of Chicago Press | Chicago and London

MIKE ROYKO, columnist for the *Chicago Daily News*, *Chicago Sun-Times*, and *Chicago Tribune* from 1963 until his death in 1997, was syndicated in more than six hundred newspapers. Along the way, he picked up the Pulitzer, Broun, Pyle, Mencken, and National Headliner awards, among others, while his now classic book, *Boss: Richard J. Daley of Chicago*, has remained in print since 1971.

DAVID ROYKO, son of Carol and Mike Royko, is a licensed clinical psychologist, director of the Circuit Court of Cook County's Marriage & Family Counseling Service, and author of *Voices of Children of Divorce*. He has written about music, autism, and divorce for a variety of publications, including the *Chicago Tribune*, *Parents* magazine, *Chicago Reader*, *Bluegrass Unlimited*, and the *New York Times*.

The University of Chicago Press, Chicago 60637
The University of Chicago Press, Ltd., London
© 2010 by The University of Chicago
All rights reserved. Published 2010.
Printed in the United States of America

19 18 17 16 15 14 13 12 11 10   1 2 3 4 5

"A November Farewell" by Mike Royko was published in the *Chicago Sun-Times* on November 22, 1979. Reprinted courtesy of the *Chicago Sun-Times*.

ISBN-13: 978-0-226-73078-3 (cloth)
ISBN-10: 0-226-73078-6 (cloth)

Library of Congress Cataloging-in-Publication Data

Royko, Mike, 1932–1997.
  Royko in love / edited by David Royko.
    p. cm.
  ISBN-13: 978-0-226-73078-3 (cloth : alk. paper)
  ISBN-10: 0-226-73078-6 (cloth : alk. paper) 1. Royko, Mike, 1932–1997—
Correspondence. 2. Royko, Carol, 1934–1979—Correspondence. 3. Love-letters.
I. Royko, David, 1959– II. Title.
  PN4874.R744A4 2010
  070.92—dc22

[B]

                                        2010000258

♾ The paper used in this publication meets the minimum requirements of the American National Standard for Information Sciences—Permanence of Paper for Printed Library Materials, ANSI Z39.48–1992.

For Karen   I know how he felt.

CONTENTS

Photos follow page 106.

ACKNOWLEDGMENTS

I know she is already covered by the dedication, but the importance of my wife (Dad's beloved daughter-in-law), Karen Miller Royko, to the publication of the Royko letters cannot be overstated. Quite simply, if it weren't for Karen, these letters would still be packed tightly in their box, a wonderful but little-seen family heirloom. It was Karen who became worried at the letters' fragility and vulnerability—floods and fires happen—and took it upon herself to transcribe them all for safekeeping. I loved the letters, but didn't trust that my own reaction would be shared by others not so directly involved in the story (after all, I probably owe my existence to them). But every day, as Karen typed the contents into text files, she kept telling me over and over, "These are incredible—you really have to do something with them. People will love them, fans of Dad's of course, but anybody who loves a great love story."

Finally, after talking about it with close friend (to Dad as well as us) Rick Kogan, I sent some of the files to Dick Babcock at *Chicago Magazine*, who agreed with Karen. Thanks to Dick, in March 2009 *Chicago* published my story about the letters with enough of a sampling to entice John Tryneski, editorial director at University of Chicago Press, to call and say, "We want a book!" Carol Saller, U of C's assistant managing editor, is somebody I believe Dad would have appreciated working with—she is that good.

Don ("Chris") Karaiskos, Dad's air force buddy in Blaine, Washington, has been a wellspring of firsthand tales of Dad's base days as well as warm memories from the friendship that continued with Mom and Dad through their lives. And the photos! I can't thank you enough, Don.

Thank you to Dad's surviving siblings, Uncle Bobby and Aunt Eleanor, and Dad's niece (Aunt El's daughter and Dad's one-time sister-in-law), Aunt Barb, for answering questions and helping to fill in my many knowledge gaps.

Thanks also to actor JoBe Cerny for helping Rick and me present the letters at a benefit for Family Service (Lake County, Illinois), an event which only reinforced our belief in these letters' power to move.

And thanks, finally, to Mom—for being the kind of person who would inspire Dad to write letters like these—and to Dad, for not letting her slip away.

Acknowledgments

The envelope arrived in May 1997, the week after my father, Mike Royko, died. Unopened, it blended in with the scores of other cards and letters that had been coming, which meshed with the daily radio, TV, magazine, and, of course, newspaper tributes. But this one felt heavier, and as I opened it, several snapshots tumbled out. They were from someone who knew my father before he became a one-namer, before he was ROYKO. Don Karaiskos had been my father's roommate and buddy in the air force while they were stationed in Blaine, Washington, where my dad had been sent after serving overseas during the Korean War. The photos had been taken with an old camera that leaked light, which meant the pictures were on the dark side, and also had faded a bit in the intervening forty-three years. But they were wonderful, showing my father back in the days when he was a skinny twenty-one-year-old in a uniform. One of the pictures had my father standing in front of a car on a mountain road, and on the back was written, "Mt. Baker, Easter." I made a mental note to find Mt. Baker on a map.

After a few minutes, I put the pictures back in the envelope and began looking through one of the many boxes that my father had left behind. I was just beginning to realize he'd saved everything—photos, canceled checks, paintings, costume jewelry, clothing, knickknacks, everything. As I moved things around, I uncovered a smaller cardboard box containing letters, maybe a hundred or more, all neatly packed. I pulled one out and looked at the postmark: Blaine, Wash., April 22, 1954. As I began reading, the words described a day trip to Mt. Baker on Easter Sunday. It provided the story to the photo I had just seen.

That degree of serendipity should have floored me, but it took a back seat to my astonishment over something else: These were the letters. THE letters. The holy grail of my nuclear family. The place where it all began. My mother had told me about them, but I had come to doubt they still existed; I had even begun to wonder whether they ever had, at least in the way my mind had held them. But here they were.

My father was born September 19, 1932, and my mother, Carol Joyce Duckman, November 21, 1934. By the time "Mickey," as he was then known, was ten, he was secretly in love with my mother. She liked him, but not in the way he loved her. His feelings only deepened with time, but he could be painfully shy, especially in the area of romance.

She grew up to be a stunning beauty, five feet nine inches, blonde, and possessing an intelligence and gentle charisma that attracted men in droves. He, on the other hand, was a skinny guy with a large Adam's apple and a larger nose. That his already huge wit and mind dwarfed these physical attributes did little to boost his self-image, and he suffered the torture of being her close friend and having to listen to her talk about the positives and negatives of the various "boys" she dated. Carol had no idea how he really felt about her.

In 1952, my father enlisted in the air force, and as he was about to head to Korea, he received the terrible news that Carol was getting married. His dreams of what might someday be were over. She was seventeen, and Larry, the man she was marrying, was a few years older, one of the many neighborhood guys who adored her.

When Dad returned from Korea, he stopped in Chicago before going to Blaine. Even though a visit to the Duckman house would have been expected—the entire family enjoyed him—he couldn't bring himself to confront the reality of Carol's new life. He stayed away.

Once in Blaine, he wrote a letter to the Duckman family. It was lighthearted and witty, betraying none of the anguish he felt. My mother wrote back. In her letter, she gently chided him for not stopping over during his leave. Carol also wrote that she and Larry had separated and were planning to divorce. The marriage, lasting little more than a year, had been a mistake.

My father was about to try to correct his own mistake. And he would do it with his pen.

The next letter could not be more different from the first. In one short page, in a single burst, he told her the truth. I can only imagine the fear he felt as he waited for her reply, and the heart-in-the-throat as he opened it—and the joy when he read that, if she did not reciprocate his feelings in full, she did not reject them either. The door was open. It was time for Cyrano.

Serious fans of my father know of his love for the tale of Cyrano de Bergerac, the man with the big nose and brilliant way with words. Cyrano wooed his beloved with prose that he provided to a callow but handsome suitor, watching her fall for a dolt because of the words Cyrano put into the other man's mouth. Cyrano could say what he felt only when hiding from her sight.

He was my father's hero, and Dad would now follow suit, wooing Carol from two thousand miles away. To read his letters is to watch the die being cast as he applied, for the first time, his wit and facility with the pen to a practical purpose. My father was always pragmatic, and these circumstances brought his writing and pragmatism together for the biggest challenge of his twenty-one-year-old life. In the process of wooing the woman he loved, he would also make writing a habitual part of his life. Writing, and my mother, would become the most important parts of his future.

The letters are a mix of sweet seduction, sarcastic observations of military life by a nonconformist, a Chicago kid's wry view of rural folk, and the pain of self-doubt and the fear of losing what is finally so close, but literally so far. His only weapons against Carol's many suitors were his pen and his brilliance. And they were enough.

This is a different side of Mike Royko from what the public has seen, or at least a side seen rarely. I have little doubt, however, that he would have approved of the letters' publication—as long as he was dead. More than once in his later years, our private conversations dipped into what might be said or written about him posthumously. More precisely, we talked about how he felt about the inevitable postmortems. "You can write a *Mommie Dearest*—I could care less. As long as I'm dead." He said something similar to Pam Cytrynbaum about the journal she was keeping during her tenure as his assistant in the 1990s: "Just wait'll I'm dead, kid." He laughed like hell when I proposed, instead of *Daddy Dearest*, a posthumous biography titled *Daddy Putz*. I was joking then, but now I might suggest *Daddy de Bergerac*.

He saved these letters, through moves and major life changes, keeping them packed precisely in order. Any professional writer, particularly one as well read as Dad, knows what that means, after you're gone. He had already hinted at the story in one of his most famous, requested columns, "A November Farewell," and gave away the ending. These letters are the beginning, in full.

Mom had died suddenly, tragically, and prematurely of a cerebral aneurysm, at age forty-four, on September 19, 1979, my father's forty-seventh birthday. "A November Farewell" ran in the *Chicago Sun-Times* on November 22, 1979.

As was typical, my father wrote the column the day before. What few people realized, and he didn't announce it, was that November 21, 1979, would have been my mother's forty-fifth birthday. When I opened the *Sun-Times* on the twenty-second, I expected to find the paper "column-less," assuming that Dad would have been unable to get one done on Mom's birthday, only two months after she had died. But this was Dad: not only did he do a column, he made it about her, and he made it one of the greatest he ever wrote. The memories and feelings he shared with readers about my mother moved many to tears. Though my father wrote with sensitivity, this part of himself he laid bare only when shaken and moved by the end of their great love.

Or, in the letters, at the beginning.

And about her beauty: Recently, Don Karaiskos sent me some photos I hadn't seen before, taken in his backyard a few years after Mom and Dad were married. I commented to Don how gorgeous Mom looked. Don said, "Yes, your mom was gorgeous. And she had all the other attributes—considerate, kind, thoughtful, patient—all those things that make up a wonderful human being."

It reminded me of what Dad said about Mom, in the short piece he addressed to his readers a couple of weeks after she died, before he resumed writing the column:

People who saw her picture in this paper have told me how beautiful she appeared to be. Yes she was. As a young man I puffed up with pride when we went out somewhere and heads turned, as they always did.

But later, when heads were still turning, I took more pride in her inner beauty. If there was a shy person at a gathering, that's whom she'd be talking to, and soon that person would be bubbling. If people felt clumsy, homely and not worth much, she made them feel good about themselves. If someone was old and felt alone, she made them feel loved and needed. None of it was put on. That was the way she was.

It was all true. When her parents entered a nursing home, my mother became an adored presence. She got to know the other residents, regularly stopping into rooms to say "hi" to those who didn't have family or friends who visited or were going through a rough patch, bringing little gifts for everyone around the holidays, doing what she could to brighten the waning moments of often lonely lives. In her last few years she created and successfully launched with her friend Sue the I Care collection, greeting cards designed for people with chronic or terminal illnesses, a population for whom, in the 1970s, nothing else existed.

Yes, she was gorgeous, and we are lucky to have the photographic proof. But Don's comment hit me hard. Mom was an exceptional person, and Don knows that because he knew her, and there aren't many left who did. If Mom had been beautiful, but not a bright, kind, thoughtful, wonderful human being, Dad, who was never impressed by the superficial, would not have written these letters. As much as they display Mike's brilliance at an early stage, they are as much a testament to their inspiration—Carol.

BY MIKE ROYKO

CHICAGO SUN-TIMES   NOVEMBER 22, 1979

The two of them first started spending weekends at the small, quiet Wisconsin lake almost 25 years ago. Some of her relatives let them use a tiny cottage in a wooded hollow a mile or so from the water.

He worked odd hours, so sometimes they wouldn't get there until after midnight on a Friday. But if the mosquitoes weren't out, they'd go to the empty public beach for a moonlight swim, then sit with their backs against a tree and drink wine and talk about their future.

They were young and had little money, and they came from working class families. So to them the cottage was a luxury, although it wasn't any bigger than the boat garages on Lake Geneva, where the rich people played.

The cottage had a screened porch where they sat at night, him playing a guitar and her singing folk songs in a sweet, clear voice. An old man who lived alone in a cottage beyond the next clump of woods would applaud and call out requests.

One summer the young man bought an old motorboat for a couple of hundred dollars. The motor didn't start easily. Some weekends it didn't start at all, and she'd sit and laugh and row while he pulled the rope and swore.

But sometimes it started, and they'd ride slowly along the shoreline, looking at the houses and wondering what it would be like to have a place that was actually on the water. He'd just shake his head because even on a lake without social status, houses on the water cost a lot more than he'd ever be able to afford.

The years passed, they had kids, and after a while they didn't go to the little cottage in the hollow as often. Something was always coming up. He worked on weekends, or they had someplace else to go. Finally the relatives sold the cottage.

Then he got lucky in his work. He made more money than he ever dreamed they'd have. They remembered how good those weekends had been and they went looking at lakes in Wisconsin to see if they could afford something on the water.

They looked at one lake, then another. Then another. Cottages they could afford, they didn't like. Those they liked were overpriced. Or the lake had too many taverns and not enough solitude.

So they went back to the little lake. They hadn't been there for years. They were surprised to find it was still quiet. That it still had no taverns and one grocery store.

And they saw a For Sale sign in front of a cedar house on the water. They parked and walked around. It was surrounded by big old trees. The land sloped gently down to the shore. On the other side of the road was nothing but woods. Beyond the woods were farms.

On the lake side, the house was all glass sliding doors. It had a large balcony. From the outside it was perfect.

A real estate salesman let them in. The interior was stunning—like something out of a homes magazine.

They knew it had to be out of their reach. But when the salesman told them the price, it was close enough to what they could afford that they had the checkbook out before they saw the second fireplace upstairs.

They hadn't known summers could be that good. In the mornings, he'd go fishing before it was light. She'd sleep until the birds woke her. Then he'd make breakfast and they'd eat omelets on the wooden deck in the shade of the trees.

They got to know the chipmunks, the squirrels, and a woodpecker who took over their biggest tree. They got to know the grocer, the old German butcher who smoked his own bacon, the little farmer who sold them vine-ripened tomatoes and sweet corn.

They were a little selfish about it. They seldom invited friends for the weekends. But they didn't feel guilty. It was their own, quiet place.

The best part of their day was dusk. They had a west view and she loved sunsets. Whatever they were doing, they'd always stop to sit on the pier or deck and silently watch the sun go down, changing the color of the lake from blue to purple to silver and black. One evening he made up a small poem:

The sun rolls down
like a golden tear
Another day.
Another day
gone.

She told him it was sad, but that she liked it.

What she didn't like was October, even with the beautiful colors and the evenings in front of the fireplace. She was a summer person. The cold wind wasn't her friend.

And she saw November as her enemy. Sometime in November would be the day they would take up the pier, store the boat, bring in the deck chairs, take down the hammock, pour antifreeze in the plumbing, turn down the heat, lock everything tight and drive back to the city.

She'd always sigh as they pulled onto the road. He'd try to cheer her up by stopping at a German restaurant that had good food and a corny band, and he'd tell her how quickly the winter would pass, and how soon they'd be there again.

And the snow finally would melt. Spring would come, and one day, when they knew the ice on the lake was gone, they would be back. She'd throw open all the doors and windows and let the fresh air in. Then she'd go out and greet the chipmunks and woodpeckers. And she'd plant more flowers. Every summer, there were more and more flowers. And every summer seemed better than the last. The sunsets seemed to become more spectacular. And more precious.

This past weekend, he closed the place down for the winter. He went alone.

He worked quickly, trying not to let himself think that this particular chair had been her favorite chair, that the hammock had been her Christmas gift to him, that the lovely house on the lake had been his gift to her.

He didn't work quickly enough. He was still there at sunset. It was a great burst of orange, the kind of sunset she loved best.

He tried, but he couldn't watch it alone. Not through tears. So he turned his back on it, went inside, drew the draperies, locked the door and drove away without looking back.

It was the last time he would ever see that lovely place. Next spring there will be a For Sale sign in front and an impersonal real estate man will show people through.

Maybe a couple who love to quietly watch sunsets together will like it. He hopes so.

A/2C Royko
759th A C & Sgd.
P.O. 548 - Box 236
Blaine Washington

BLAINE, WASH.
MAR 16
9-AM
1954

Carol Wozny
5408 N. Central Ave
Chicago Ill

Carol

Writing this letter is going to
be the toughest thing I've ever done.
In answer to your note — Yes, I did
plan on writing once a year — or less
Naturally a statement like that warrents
an explanation I'm in love with you
Surprised? Well I am and the result
has been mental hell For a couple
of years I've been wondering when I'd
stop thinking about you every day. I've
come to the conclusion that I won't.
So as long as I have to keep going
this way you may as well know
about it I've been in love with you
for so long, I don't remember when
it started but when I decided to
do something about it it was too late

"Another year and another letter"

Dad's letters speak for themselves, but when necessary, I have added some brief commentary, including references based on my own knowledge and any information I have learned from those close to the story, including Mike's surviving older sister Eleanor and younger brother Bob; Don Karaiskos (Mike's barracks-mate, referred to frequently in the letters as "Chris," derived from "Karaiskos"); and Mike's niece and future sister-in-law Barbara (she married Mom's brother, Bob Duckman), who as a one-time close friend of Mom's provided some insight into the brief marriage and subsequent breakup of Mom and Larry. I also provide some brief historical background when needed. For the sake of readability, I opted to correct the rare spelling mistake.

Unfortunately, Mom's letters to Dad do not appear to have survived. She did keep—very sporadically—a diary of the "A Line a Day" variety, and I have included several of her entries in my comments where they offer insight into Carol's thoughts or feelings about Mick.

I have included postmark dates as they appear on the envelopes, as most of the letters are undated, though the day of the week is often noted. According to the 1954 calendar, these days usually correspond to the day preceding the postmark date. The stamps are always airmail, and were six cents.

As I looked for pictures to include in the book, digging through boxes I hadn't opened in years, I realized that I had far more than the book had space for. I have posted some of this additional material on my website (http://www.davidroyko.com) and on the University of Chicago Press website (http://www.press.uchicago.edu/).

Dad wrote 114 letters to Mom. They are preceded by a letter he wrote not to Carol but to the whole Duckman family, to whom Dad was close.

Mike and Carol both had brothers named Bob, and this letter refers to Bob Duckman. At the time, Bob was an undertaker.

POSTMARK: FEBRUARY 1, 1954
ADDRESSED TO: DUCKMANS

Hi Folks,

Another year and another letter from the bad penny. I'm now stationed in Washington, seven miles from the Canadian border. It's great up here. They have weekly barn dances and during our time off we can chase rabbits or carve our names in redwood trees. Nothing like a social life. The next time I get a leave, I'll probably arrive home wearing buckskins and carrying a flint lock rifle. The air force seems determined to keep me separated from civilization. The local farmers are very friendly tho, they probably reckon that I'll give em a mite of help with the spring plowin.

I guess I should apologize for not coming over during my leave, but I lost so much weight in Korea that I thought Bob might not recognize me and toss me in a pine box. I had a pleasant leave but it flew by so quickly that I didn't get around as much as I would have liked to and I spent a big part of it traveling back and forth from Washington.

Needless to say, I left Korea somewhat gaunt but still intact. The first condition I attribute to the bully beef and dehydrated potatoes we lived on and the second to the fact that on guard duty, when sighting a Korean I yelled "help" instead of "halt." All in all it was pretty interesting, but if they ever want me to go back there again, three of us will arrive at the dock. Me and the two cops who will have to escort me.

I'll probably take another leave this summer so you can expect me to pop in then. I've been here four days now and I haven't let the family know where I am so I'll close now and give them a buzz on the phone.

When you have time, drop me a line.

"Mountain Man" Mick

Carol wrote back, apparently chiding Mike gently for not stopping over and not writing. She also revealed that she and Larry had separated and would divorce. The marriage had been a mistake.

Carol was nineteen years old and Mike was twenty-one.

POSTMARK: MARCH 16, 1954

Carol

Writing this letter is going to be the toughest thing I've ever done. In answer to your note—yes, I did plan on writing once a year—or less. Naturally a statement like that warrants an explanation. I'm in love with you. Surprised? Well I am and the result has been mental hell. For a couple of years I've been wondering when I'd stop thinking about you every day. I've come to the conclusion that I won't. So as long as I have to keep going this way you may as well know about it. I've been in love with you for so long, I don't remember when it started but when I decided to do something about it, it was too late.

I was home for 30 days and at times the urge to go to you was over-powering. I drove by your house time after time but couldn't stop. I can't write anymore. Anything else I say would be a futile attempt to elaborate on a complete statement. I love you. I don't harbor much hope but please answer or I'll be forced to call you on the phone. I don't want to do that until I hear from you.

Love

Mick

In our day of cheap cell phones and e-mail and instant communication, it's hard to imagine the torture my father must have felt as he waited for his letter to cross two-thirds of the continent and hers to return. But when her reply came, the message was clear: Even if she did not reciprocate his feelings in full, she did not reject them either. In fact, they seemed to be just what she needed—her diary entry of March 18 says, "Got a letter from Mick today, telling me he loves me. I can't believe it's actually true. I'll start living again."

Stanley Steamer was one of Mike's nicknames for his car.

Dear Carol,

You haven't received any of them but in the past week I have written you dozens of letters. All have ended up in the waste basket. Nothing I write sounds right. Night after night I've sat here writing 'til my roommate is suspecting me of having a few loose screws. When I unfolded your artistic endeavor this afternoon, he just shook his head in a confused way and left the room mumbling in an undertone. Seriously, I feel guilty and sorry for putting you in the position of encouraging me to write. Your letter had such an exhilarating effect on me that my section chief gave me three days off, hoping I would come back to earth. I guess I've read your letter until the ink is practically worn off but I haven't been able to put together a reply so I'll just sit here and write whatever comes into my mind. I didn't know until last week that you had cried when I left. I'm glad that I didn't. My year in the land of rice would have been a lot tougher than it was. As it was I had an occasional day when I didn't think of you. Not often, but once in a while. Then I'd take a look at those pictures you gave me and my peace of mind would be shattered. One night, after consuming a goodly amount of distilled morale booster I came to a hazy conclusion that your pictures were doing me more harm than good. So you now have the unique distinction of having your image carried all the way to Korea for cremation services. I regret it very much.

Sorry to have upset your apple cart, but it's better to have an upset apple cart then to feel like a dog. I realized when I wrote that I wasn't going to help uncomplicate your life but I kept my feelings bottled up for so long that I had to share them with someone and you seemed like the logical person. I haven't kidded myself into thinking that you might feel the same as I do. This isn't the first time that a love has been one sided. No matter what happens, in feeling the way I do I've experienced something that most people have missed. I feel sorry for them. I realize that you've had a rough emotional experience. I can't help feeling that I'm partly to blame. I've felt this way for a long time and I should have said so long ago. It might have been different. But remember you're young and though you have had a

5

bad break, you have your whole life ahead of you. Life is similar to a card game. You're dealt so many cards and you have to make the best of them. I've seen good card players have a bad night and from then on they are wary and afraid to take a chance. The smart player bounces right back, forgetting the bad breaks and making the best of the good ones. You've been dealt good cards. You're young, attractive and intelligent. All you have to do is forget the unhappy things and take what's good out of life. I'm an optimist. To have loved you all this time, I can't have been anything else. I just want you to remember that no matter what happens, I'm going to be on call. I've been quietly hopeful for a long time. I can continue the same way for a long time to come.

It's getting late and I want to get this to town so I guess I'll go warm up my Stanley Steamer. By the way, when you write, please don't tell me about sitting on actors' laps. I'm hard enough to live with now and my roommate is a bundle of nerves.

Love

Mick

POSTMARK: APRIL 8, 1954

Wednesday

Dear Carol,

A half hour ago I returned from a two day trip to one of the other bases to pick up some radio equipment. When I walked into my room, your letter was on my desk. The letter was wonderful, the pictures are wonderful and right now it feels pretty good to be alive. An hour ago I was so tired it was an effort to keep my eyes open. Whatever the speed record is for 300 miles in a '42 Oldsmobile, I must have shattered it tonight. It's 1 AM but I want this to go out tomorrow so my roomy will have to endure the light in his eyes.

Your pictures are going to be a problem. My room is the hangout for most of the guys in the barracks, and I know exactly what their reaction will be. "Who are you kidding, you don't know her." I guess I'll just have to keep the pictures locked up.

The '42 Olds I mentioned is the car I recently bought. While I was home I bought a '50 Ford but the weather made it impossible for me to drive back in time so I sold it before I left. The main feature of the Olds is that it continually provides me with laughs. Last week the horn decided to blow. I was on a quiet country road when it happened and it took five minutes for me to find the cause. While I was looking, the farmer whose sleep I had disturbed arrived on the scene fully armed. He stood there yelling "Turn it off!" and his dog sat on the ground and barked. When I fixed the horn he told me to "git!" I gitted. It was probably the first time he had talked to anyone in years. The people out here are comparatively backward but the country itself is beautiful. From my window I can see a snow capped mountain range and the base is right on a bay. The weather is mild but rainy. It's not a bad base but the thought of two more years is pretty rough. I've already used up 60 days leave so I've got 60 more to go. I'll probably be able to get three weeks leave in September. How much time will we be able to have together? You asked me that question. I'm taking the leave for only one reason. To see you. My last leave was spent just killing time and thinking about you. When I arrive in Chicago in Sept., I'll stop at home long enough to say Hi, then I'm going to establish squatters rights on your doorstep. I had hoped to get home sooner then September but no leaves are being given right now. Five months seems like such a long time to wait so I've decided that I can't wait that long to talk to you. I'm going to call you up. When can I get you? You seem to have a pretty heavy schedule so if you can figure out a good time for me to call, let me know in your next letter.

This is my last piece of stationery so I'll have to cram a lot on it.

I was glad to detect a more cheerful spirit in your last letter. If my letters have done anything in the way of boosting your morale then I feel it's the most worthwhile thing I've ever done. You said that I'm wonderful. I'm not, but nothing anyone ever says to me will mean as much as that. Two months ago I was all set to volunteer for overseas duty again. Right now it would take a dozen men to get me on a ship. Since I've been in the service, the hardest thing for me to do has been to spend a night in the barracks writing letters but lately the only time I feel relaxed and happy is when I'm writing to you. As long as you enjoy hearing from me, the letters are going to keep coming.

I hope you never meet a multi millionaire or even a millionaire because I'd probably be converted to communism. Don't ever worry what people say. The world is full of unhappy people who have messed up their lives by being affected by what people say or think. Nuts to people. They aren't that important.

I'll probably be a bit more wide awake tomorrow and make a little more sense.

So until then

Love—

Mick

Dad went to Chase, a Chicago public grammar school.

POSTMARK: APRIL 13, 1954

Monday

Dear Carol,

I just checked my mail box and was greeted by the unhappy sight of emptiness so I'll have to try to salvage some pleasure out of this evening by writing a letter instead of reading one of yours.

Because it's raining I've managed to get a free evening. I'm on the base golf team and play a practice round each evening. When I finish playing I work 'til midnight in the clubhouse bar. The job helps compensate for the frugality of the AF but it doesn't leave much time for writing. The main benefit of a full schedule is that it keeps my mind occupied and facilitates the passing of time. September seems years away and 3000 miles seems like a million.

One of my favorite pastimes lately has been thinking about my leave, or, to be more correct, day dreaming about it. Mentally, I've been dancing, driving, I've proposed, and been accepted, and rejected. I guess it sounds corny, but literally, you're the girl of my dreams. I guess a cynic would doubt that I could love you because, as you've said, we've never even held hands but my concept of love differs slightly with that of other people. I love you, not because you have blond hair, a beautiful face and look good in a bathing suit, but because you have certain undefinable qualities that to me are unique in a person. A person isn't just so much flesh and bone put together in a certain way, but a creature with a soul and the beauty inside a person is the beauty that attracts love. If you were plain or even homely I couldn't feel any differently.

Some of the things I've said could probably be considered as being too forward to say to a married woman. I wouldn't have said them three months ago because then I thought you were happily married. What I should have just said was, because I thought you were married, because as far as I'm concerned, a marriage can't be a marriage unless it's happy. All the religious, and civil ceremonies in the world can't create a marriage unless both people are happy. I just looked back and discovered that I've been spelling marriage "marraige." It seems Solomon P. Chase didn't fulfill its responsibility.

Easter Sunday I'm taking a drive up to Mt. Baker. For the last 3 months I've been looking out my window and seeing this mountain and wondering what it looks like close up so I've made up my mind to find out. I'll probably take a few pictures so if any of them are worth seeing I'll send them. I never cease to be amazed at the beauty of the country around here. After living in Chicago and then seeing the drabness of Korea, this mountainous country is fascinating. When I look out the window in the morning, the mountains have a blue white color. When I was a kid, I'd look out the window and see the blue white color of the Pabst sign.

What kind of quartet do you sing with? Is it a hobby or do you have professional ambitions? Three of the guys who wait on tables where I work decided that we should organize a quartet. We practiced a few songs, then tried them out on the customers. The two songs we sang set music back 500 years and did more to further prohibition than the temperance leagues. The owner of the place has been giving us dirty looks ever since. Nothing sounds as terrible as everyone singing harmony. In order to hold our jobs we have disbanded.

It's time to go serve beer for the local lushes so I'll finish this up.

Whenever I read my letters I regret all the times I ignored my English teachers. When I hit the sack tonight, it will be with the hope that I receive a letter tomorrow. For two years I've been indifferent to the mail deliveries. Now when the mail arrives I'm the first one in line. I don't know if I mentioned it in my last letter, but I'll be able to get 24 days leave. You know, we never have had a date so how about leaving the first Saturday in Sept. open. I guess I'm the slowest worker in history—know a girl 10 years before I ask her for a date.

Love,

Mick

At the time, one of Carol's jobs was as an assistant to Dr. Eugene Marks. A holocaust survivor, Marks would remain Carol's doctor, and once we were born, our pediatrician, until his retirement in the late 1970s. It is likely that Mom was already confiding in him, and that he encouraged her to take Dad seriously.

Carol's mother, Mildred, turned out to have multiple sclerosis.

The 'heroine' of the movie "The Juggler" (1953) was played by actress Milly Vitale (born 1932).

POSTMARK: APRIL 15, 1954
Wednesday

Dear Carol,

The doctor you work for is obviously an astute, brilliant, talented, gracious, congenial old gentleman and is, without a doubt, wisdom personified. Compared to him the Mayo brothers were quack horse doctors and Plato was a babbling idiot. Why isn't he president of the National Medical Association? I'm going to write a letter to the White House condemning the country's ignorance of a man from whose lips comes that which is the pinnacle of wisdom. I will drink a nightly toast to the doctor.

The mailroom doesn't open until 11:30 so lately I've been phoning the mail clerk at 10:30 to see whether I received a letter. When I called this morning he told me I didn't receive any mail so I slumped down at my desk in as deep a mood of depression as I've ever been in. A few minutes later the phone rang and he said "I was only kidding, you have a letter." The things I said to him will be left unmentioned, but I'm sure that for the sake of his right ear he won't joke anymore. I dropped what I was doing, hopped in my car and violated half the base traffic laws in driving to the mail room. Thirty pages. The library has lost a customer. By three this afternoon the officer in my section asked me if I was trying to memorize every page so I showed him the picture you enclosed. That shut him up. I've worked out a pretty good schedule for reading your letter. I read it before and after lunch, while I'm working, before I go to the golf course, before I start my evening job and before I go to bed. The schedule changes in the morning because I usually oversleep and only have time to look at your pictures and bid you a telepathic "good morning."

Your letters have not only made me the happiest guy alive, but they have actually improved my golf game. This afternoon I came down from cloud nine long enough to shoot the best game I've ever had. If your letters continue to have such an inspirational effect on me, I'll challenge Ben Hogan. Right now I feel that nothing is impossible, nothing unattainable. I once read an article by a graphologist in which he said that the slope of the lines of a persons writing indicates the mood the person is in. If this keeps up I'll be writing vertically.

Do me a great favor. Don't stay up late writing me letters. Don't misunderstand me. Your letters are the greatest thing that's ever happened to me but your schedule sounds so grueling that I don't want you losing sleep because of me. Write them but do it when it won't keep you awake. No one is completely indefatigable and you're the one person in this world who I want to remain alive and healthy. Look, I love you and when I come home in Sept. I want you to be walking around, not in bed suffering from overwork.

Did you see a movie called "The Juggler"? It's at a local movie and the reason I mentioned it is because of something that happened overseas. The fellow who used to show the movies at my base in Korea lived in my barracks so each night he would show the movie to us before he ran it off for the base. One night I stretched out on my bunk, relaxed and prepared to enjoy the picture. I did, until the heroine appeared on the screen. (Actually it was a moth eaten sheet.) She was tall, blonde, and had bangs. Needless to say, she reminded me of someone. I'll always remember that night because I think I reached as deep a despair as a person could. At the time my morale was low but that night it was non-existent. If we had been overrun by gooks I don't think I would have cared. I don't know why I mentioned that now. Maybe because it exemplifies that no matter how hopeless a situation may seem, there's always a solution. Three months ago I was on a boat coming home and feeling no eagerness at all. Now I'm stuck up here, rusticating, 3000 miles from the closest civilization and amazingly enough, I'm happy.

I've just had a good idea. When I get home the weather should still be warm. Let's go on a picnic. For two years I have been living in a crowd. Barracks, work, planes, boats—always a crowd of people. Let's go to some quiet place where there isn't another human being in sight. You can sit in the shade, relax, and I'll sit and tell you how wonderful you are. Deal?

Were you eight when we met? It doesn't seem that long ago. I guess I'm the most haywire suitor that ever lived. When we were kids I used to cut my own throat by bringing you boyfriends, then I just stayed away, now when I'm across a continent I find my voice. Some people must be destined to do things the hard way.

I hope your mother's illness isn't serious. Because my folks are about as unparental as two people could get, I've always had a high regard for people who are capable parents and your mother created in my mind a standard that most people could never attain. Most people just don't impress me but your mother is one of the people I've known who have seemed outstanding. She must have sat through a million of our crazy "drink-chug-a-lug" games.

You said that you aren't getting married for years. How many??? It would be ridiculous, impossible in fact, to love a girl and not hope to marry her. If this sounds like a proposal, it is, and I'm having a heck of a time writing on bended knees. You'll probably refuse, so as long as you aren't going to marry for years, I have no alternative but to keep proposing for years. Anyway, they say a girl's morale is raised when she gets a proposal, so this will serve some use. If your answer is negative, don't say "no" period. Say "not right now," "maybe later," "we'll see," or something to that effect, unless of course, you actually mean "irrevocably no." In that case, just send a rope, 10-floor building, or a short plank so I can take a long walk. Do I sound facetious? I'm not. I'm completely serious. I love you, want you to be happy and want you to be my wife. I know I could make you happy because happiness is something that's contagious and being married to you would make me the happiest person ever so it would have to rub off on you. If you refuse, I'll make like a rubber ball and bounce back. I'll be as regular as taxes and K.P. If you say no now then I'll just try again later. I guess it's only fair to warn you.

It's 3 AM now so I'll have to close. I'll say good night to you now, say good night to your pictures in a few minutes and say good morning to them in a few hours.

Good night and I love you

Mick

Enclosed in the envelope is a smaller envelope with a flower card that says "Easter Greetings," signed "Mickey."

At some point for Carol and Mike, "September Song" (Anderson & Weill) was to become "their song." At this point, the lyrics might have simply reminded Mike of how long it would be before he would be able to see Carol.

Carol's concern over "the Indochina situation" most likely stemmed from the nascent conflicts that would eventually become the Vietnam War.

The "saying" Mike uses to close this letter is from the French writer Duc de la Rochefoucauld (1613–1680).

POSTMARK: APRIL 22, 1954

Dear Carol,

Today I discovered that anything is possible in the service. For two years I have been getting extra time off by conjuring some of the most fantastic excuses imaginable. This morning my mind was a blank so I did what every good airman knows is the wrong thing to do—I told the truth. I told the woeful creature who is my boss that I wanted the morning off to write a letter. The ridiculousness of my request must have dulled his little brain because he said OK. That's twice in the last two days that I have told the truth in the so called line of duty. Yesterday it had the opposite effect. I met a promotion board (a group of men whose IQs range from idiot to moron, gathered together to determine whether my mind has become stagnant enough to assume the lofty title of "sarge") and flunked with flying colors. I spent one full hour answering questions correctly. This was easy because they don't use any specific list of questions. They ask only what their limited knowledge allows them to ask. Finally one sly little sergeant created my downfall. He asked me if I would order one of my friends to shine his dirty shoes in the event that I were promoted. I've established a reputation for being non military so every man on the board knew that I couldn't give such an order. I spent a full minute debating with myself whether to tell an obvious lie or the truth. I said "no" quite emphatically. That ended my interview and also my chance for promotion this month. In the afternoon the results were posted and I was bypassed because of "Inability to assume responsibility." This caused the officer in charge of my section to feel that I had put a black mark on his record so he gave me a long winded lecture. I took the lecture OK but when he asked me if I planned on reenlisting I blew my stack. The profane eloquence of my answer rocked the building and unnerved him completely. Apparently he was still "shook up" when I asked him for the morning off.

What did you do Easter? All the while I was driving up Mt. Baker I kept trying to imagine what you were doing. Your time is three hours ahead of ours so when we started our trip I imagined you having dinner. This put me into a fine frame of mind, then some half wit disk jockey played September Song and ruined the whole day. On the way up we took three rolls of pictures and I'm pessimistic about the results. I think the camera we used is the granddaddy of all cameras. It passes more light through the cracks in its sides than through the lens. The only thing that made the trip worthwhile was the effect we had on the skiers at the lodge. Everyone up there was dressed in ski togs so when we entered the lodge dressed in suits & white shirts we stood out like sore thumbs. After dinner we returned to the car, took out our golf clubs, strolled casually to the edge of a cliff, teed up the balls in the snow, hit them, and walked back to the car. Everyone stood around looking bewildered so before they could summon the men in the white suits, we departed.

I just dropped my pen and ruined the point. This just isn't my day.

I wouldn't worry about the Indochina situation, at least not about me going over. There is a regulation that prevents my being involuntarily sent overseas for 18 months after returning so I doubt very much that I'll have to go. The thing that worries me is the possibility of my brother ending up there. He's 18 so by the time the fighting would get into full swing he'd be just the right age for the draft. He's starting college in September so he may get a deferment, at least I hope he does.

In answer to your question, I get up at 6:30 but because of the time difference, it's 9:30 in Chicago. The first thing I do when I wake up is roll over and look at your pictures. I've got them on my wall so that I see you before I fall asleep and when I awaken. It's really a wonderful way to start and end a day.

Something that has always bothered me is the complete conflict of thought between the two sayings "absence makes the heart grow fonder" and "out of sight—out of mind." I've finally found something that settles the issue—

Absence lessens half hearted passions and increases great ones, as the wind puts out the candles and yet stirs up the fire.

Love,

Mick

The Green Hornet was a popular series of comic books, radio serials and eventually, a television series.

Moe was a girlfriend of Carol's.

Mike's letters were usually written with a fountain pen, which he damaged while writing the previous letter. 1954 was the year the Parker Pen Company offered what is widely considered the first mass-produced quality ball-point pen.

An all-star cast movie version of "Julius Caesar" was released in 1953.

Sunday

Dear Carol,

I guess I'm the only person who ever received a negative answer to a proposal and walked around with a big silly grin on his face.

Someone in the mail department "goofed" because the letter you wrote Easter didn't arrive 'til Thursday. In fact, five minutes after mailing my last letter I received yours. Since then, every moment I've had has been occupied. When I get back to the base at night, my mind actually feels numb. I was out at the golf course all day today having the debatable pleasure of playing in my first tournament, other than Air Force. I always enjoy playing golf but I never enjoy losing and today I lost. What bothered me most was the fact that I hadn't written since Thursday. I was never so happy to finish a round of golf as I was today. For the first time in five years I've found something that I'd rather do than play golf. I'd rather write to you.

The pictures we took didn't come out. Actually they did but they were over exposed so badly that I looked like something out of Uncle Tom's Cabin. Come to think of it, it must have been under exposure plus the fact that the sun wasn't out, plus the important fact that none of us knew anything about photography. I have one picture that I took mainly to preserve the sight of what is laughingly referred to as the "green hornet"—alias, my car. The ornament on its hood is partially glass and at night it glows with a ghostly green light. This plus the unusual noises emitted from its engine give it a supernatural appearance at night. Sometimes, when returning to the base, I floor the gas pedal, causing it to reach its maximum speed—50 to 60. This sends the local rustics fleeing to their cabins to tell their bonneted wives that the spirits are prowling. The people up here are, by Chicago standards, pretty backward. The idea of a lively Sunday is to go clam digging. Our base is surrounded by farms and recently we had what would be called a "shotgun wedding." Everyone is still laughing. Due to the pressure applied by his new father-in-law, the young airman involved now arises at 3:30 to milk cows and perform other chores before coming out to the base.

He is from New York and had never seen a cow until his marriage. That last sentence sounds ridiculous.

You don't ever have to wonder if I'm thinking about you. Unless I am asleep, you are all I think about. I'm glad you're planning where we'll go because I haven't given it much thought. I've never been to many of the so called better places in Chicago because I wasn't old enough as a civilian (what a wonderful word) and during my leaves I lacked the desire. Where we go is all secondary to me. The main point is that I'll be going with you. I'd be happy just sitting on your porch munching grape ice cubes.

Tell Moe to keep her cynical astrological observations to herself. There are no "Vampire Moons"! If I remember correctly, the last time I saw Moe was about four years ago. I remember being very elated over the fact that I was an inch or so taller than you, when Moe appeared on the scene and shattered my masculinity. After years of looking up at you, it will be very refreshing to have the situation reversed.

You're right. These ball point pens are unmanageable.

I promised some of the lads that I'd drive them to town to see Julius Caesar so I'll close now. I should never had made that promise because I'd much rather write. I'll post this and start another when I get back. So for a few hours,

Love
Mick

P.S. I found a photo that didn't come out too dark, so I'll enclose it.

POSTMARK: APRIL 28, 1954
Tuesday
Dear Carol,

It's midnight, everyone's asleep, my radio is softly playing, cigarette's burning, so I'm all set to write. It's about four in Chicago so you're asleep right now. I sort of like the idea of writing when it's late because then I know exactly what you're doing and I can visualize you very vividly. This may sound crazy but do you curl up when you sleep? Hug the pillow, or what? I seem to always write this time of night so since I know that you're sleeping I want my vision to be as realistic as possible.

Your letters and pictures are alike in one respect. They always seem better than the last until I compare them. Then I realize that it's all a toss up. The pictures made things perfect. Now I have some on my wall, carry one in my wallet and keep one in my desk at work (no photos allowed on the desk). The dress is beautiful, but as I said, I'm completely prejudiced. You'd look great in a gunny sack. My friends are starting to get slightly peeved at some of my attitudes. When we go to a movie they generally discuss the physical attributes of the heroine, usually favorably, but all they ever get from me is criticism and sneers. I can't help it. They just seem to look drab to me. I guess I'll have to give up movies completely. That's ok. Most people go to movies just to escape reality and spend a few hours in a different world but since reality and this world include you, it's much more appealing than vicariousness.

It's been said that G.I.s can't be satisfied. I guess that there's quite a bit of truth in that statement. I read your letters, see you in your pictures and yet I'm not satisfied. I want to talk to you so Friday I'm calling. I'll go to town after work so I'll try to get the call through about 9 or 9:30 Chicago time. I'll probably sound tongue tied and if I have lapses of silence bear with me. I'll probably break out in a cold sweat when I'm making the call but I've got to hear your voice. I find it hard to believe but in the last 3 years we've seen each other once. January 16 to be exact. For a long time I looked back at that day with displeasure to say the least. During a twenty four hour period I managed to meet the husband of the girl I love and then board a plane, a rickety one at that, to begin my trip to Korea. Undoubtedly there are tougher hard luck stories than that but while I was flying along I would have been pretty hard to convince.

Do you remember a kid named Ed Helinka? He went to good old Solomon P. and must have graduated about the same time you did. I met him while I was in Japan and we came back on the same ship. We spent many an interesting night on deck (there was nowhere else to go) discussing the delinquents we knew and he seemed to have kept in touch with everyone though he now lives in Glenview. According to him everyone went to jail but I think he exaggerated a bit. About half way through the trip he accidently put an end to our reminiscing by asking me if I remembered that tall, blond girl named Carol. I guess I mumbled something before I walked away but I don't remember what. I went down to the absolute bottom of the ship (my home for 2½ weeks) climbed in my rack and asked myself what I was going home for. I didn't receive much of an answer.

I've decided to quit the golf team. It's cutting into my letter writing time too often and our chances of being an outstanding team are pretty slim. We have two officers on the team playing because of their rank instead of their skill, which is practically nonexistent and they manage to lose most of our matches for us, so instead of playing golf in the evening I'm going to do more writing.

This letter is short but my roommate is demanding darkness so I'll close and write again tomorrow. Give my regards to the Doc.

Love,
Mick

POSTMARK: APRIL 30, 1954
Thursday

Dear Carol,

When it rains it pours! After quitting the golf team to have more free time, I was ordered to give up my off base job. Now I have all the spare time in the world. It happened this morning. I was sitting at my desk, head in my hands, thinking about what a pleasant deal it is to be in this God forsaken place. The next thing I knew I was being carried bodily down the road to sick bay. Apparently, I fell asleep and refused to be awakened. They said they shook me, yelled and even slapped me across the face, all to no avail. I was told to quit my job and get some sleep, so I've been sleeping for the past ten hours. When the good Captain told me to quit my job, I raised quite a row and questioned his authority to give such an order but as usual the Air Force has a regulation to cover everything. He dug out an old reg. that stated that any job that interferes with Air Force functions must be given up so he told me that sleeping on the job interferes with my duties. What a laugh. My job is so ridiculously simple, I could train a 6-year-old kid to do it. He also said that during the last month or more I've been walking around in a daze. I had to laugh when he said that. If my being in a daze is detrimental to the AF then you are undoubtedly the prettiest saboteur around. So in the future I will go-to fresh as a daisy and give my all for the good old A.F.

If and when you make those records, by all means send one. Your mentioning records was really a coincidence because I was thinking how nice it would be to have a record with your voice on it. One of the fellows in my barracks has a player so there is no difficulty in playing it. I enjoy hearing music in the morning so I could start off each day with your pictures and your voice. What a way to start the day off!

You know, I can't really describe the way I feel when I receive and read one of your letters. All the words I know are inadequate. I just feel that everything else is petty and unimportant. Nothing that anyone has done has ever affected me the way that you do. Being in the service can get pretty depressing and frustrating at times. A person feels as though the world is passing them by and most personal ambitions seem far away and sometimes even impossible. That's the worst part about it. There are guys my own age already starting out and getting ahead as civilians. Naturally, I've got certain ambitions, some of them pretty big, and being out here makes me feel as if I'm in a vise and can't do anything about it. Then I read one of your letters and do I get a shot in the arm! Or maybe I should say the heart. Suddenly I'm Mr. Big and the whole world is my own personal oyster. No, you can never write too many letters. Not if you wrote 24 hours a day. My whole life has been rotating about you and what you write. I'll probably repeat this a thousand times between now and September but repetition will never make it any less sincere. You're wonderful. At times you seem too good to be true. Just knowing you makes me luckier than most people but being in love with you makes me about the most privileged guy alive. Some of the things I've nearly done seem pretty frightening now. When I got here I planned on putting in for overseas duty. Then we began writing. If I were faced with not seeing you for two years, as I would have been had I gone over again, I'd probably wind up in a padded cell. Right now it seems as though I haven't seen you for years. Four more months is all I could take and even that is too long.

I've checked with the post office in Blaine and now I know exactly when the trains come through and pick up the mail. Not often enough. The next one comes at seven thirty and it's a quarter to now so I'm going to drive into town.

You'll read this letter after I call you on the phone. The thought of that call makes me jumpy as a cat. Why can't they have a television hook up on the phones. Hey, only 22 more hours and I'll be talking to you.

Tell the Doc that when I get home the drinks are on me. I've never met him but he's the best friend I've got.

Love,
Mick

The song "Secret Love" was a hit for Doris Day in 1954.

The movie (Dad disliked the word "film") "From Here to Eternity" was released in 1953; "The Caine Mutiny," in 1954.

When Mike writes about Larry's "leaving" in the following letter, it is in reference to something Carol mentions in her April 27 diary entry: "I was lying on the bed reading Mick's letters when Bernice called to say Larry packed up and left town. Good bye divorce—'til next year anyway. Damn Him!" Carol must have told Mike about this in the phone call. Her diary entry of April 30 makes it apparent that she enjoyed the conversation: "Mick called me on the phone tonight. Was it wonderful to hear his voice. We talked for a ½ hour. Poor guy'll wish he didn't call when he gets the telephone bill." He had a different reaction, but it wasn't the cost that bothered him.

POSTMARK: MAY 3, 1954
Saturday

Dear Carol,

I'm going to stop berating myself long enough to write this letter. On second thought I won't even stop now. When I hung up the phone last night I was never so disgusted with anyone in my life as I was with myself.

If I sounded like an idiot it's because I am one. The one time in my life that I should have been eloquent, or at least normal, I was at a loss for words. While I was driving the 35 miles back to the base I must have used every derogatory expression I know to describe myself. I didn't make it to the base for many hours because I decided I needed something to settle my badly shaken nerves so I stopped at the quietest, most deserted place I could find. I was in there five minutes when Chris, the best friend I have in the service, arrived. We were in Korea together, rode the boat and both got stuck out here. He's a sawed off little Greek with the usual little man's complex. Most people avoid getting him mad and even talking to him because he has a sarcastic wit that is priceless but by fighting fire with fire I handle him OK so we get along. We greeted each other in our usual way. Criticized each other's clothes, appearance, choice of drinks and moral character—then he asked me what was wrong. He knows that I've been writing to a beautiful girl because he's seen your pictures and noticed the amount of letters I receive but that's where his knowledge ends. After a few drinks he pried the fact that I called you out of me and after many more he found out that I'm completely in love. This surprised him because I've never mentioned it or talked about you since I've known him. When I told him that I froze at the telephone he made me feel pretty good by telling me that the same thing happens to him every time he calls his girl so I'm not the only idiot on the base. I told him I was going home in September and that was all he needed. He went over to the juke box and played September Song five times and Secret Love at least a dozen times during the evening. By the time the place closed we had convinced everyone there that we had virtually won the Korean War single handedly which of course led to immeasurable free drinks, joined a choir and a quartet by demonstrating our vociferous talents, and in general made ourselves completely obnoxious. That was the first time in many moons that I've been on the receiving side of a bar and considering the way I feel now, it will be a long time before it's repeated. Chris had noticed your letter in my mail box so he had it in his car when we met in town.

What does Larry expect to accomplish by his actions? When you told me he left I was too stunned to think clearly but later when I read your letter I gave it a good deal of thought. My first reaction was rage— my second, pity. I really feel sorry for him. When he married you he automatically became the luckiest guy alive. For a man to do what he's done is completely beyond my understanding. As far as I'm concerned being married to you would be an ascension far above normal happiness and to have such an opportunity and discard it is an act of self deprivation as foolish as I could possibly imagine.

Being able to use your maiden name in my letters would have been a more than pleasant surprise but all in all it remains in my mind an unimportant detail. I think I mentioned before that I consider marriage a state of mind. Naturally in a so-called civilized state certain laws are required but since mutual love is what usually creates a marriage, the lack of it is the only thing that can really terminate it.

The last mail delivery just left the base so I won't be able to get this letter to the post office until tonight. I'm working late this evening writing up some ridiculous reports that will be sent to various people who will glance at them and then file them away and later burn them. I think I'll write a book someday exposing the numerous flaws in the Air Force. I'll call it "From Here to the Golf Course," or "The Blaine Mutiny."

I'll probably phone you again but next time it will be done extemporaneously. I like to surprise people too and I'll surprise you by doing more than stuttering and lapsing into silence. Did I sound gruff when I said good night? Attribute that to the self hatred I felt at the moment. Nothing I've ever heard sounded as beautiful as your voice when you said good night. Picturing you and hearing your voice nearly caused the telephone to melt in my hand. You'll probably read this in the evening so for now, a little softer, Good Night.

Love,
Mick

Tuesday

Dear Carol,

Hey, let's knock off this business of late hours, burned hands and bruised shins. It's much more appealing to think of you polishing your nails and wearing your best perfume than trying to catch pneumonia at 3:30 in the morn.

Saturday night at midnight I was sound asleep. At 12:05 I was being rudely awakened. When I was informed of the time, I told the culprit to go turn into a pumpkin but it seemed my wee friend Chris was in town, his car stalled and needed transportation. By the time I picked him up, had a bite to eat and returned it was 3:30. I slept all day Sunday. It was the first time in months that I've slept more than 5 hours at one time and I actually planned on sleeping right through to Monday but as usual my room was overrun with people having inspirations on how to spend Sunday evening. All that their ideas lacked was transportation and since they were courageous enough to ride in my "demon of the roads" I couldn't refuse. We eventually ended up in Vancouver Canada trying to find a place that served pizza. We were the most unlikely bunch of pizza eaters I've ever seen. A Greek, Syrian, hillbilly, and whatever I am all looking for an Italian restaurant. We finally found one in a very remote part of town. Most of the local clam diggers have never heard of pizza and when we asked one where we could find a place that served pizza pie he thought we said "piece of pie" and directed us to a soda fountain. This trip turned into another all night affair and I was my usual self at work Monday—present in body only. The base is marching in a parade next Sat. I'm not sure what the occasion is—be kind to dumb farmer week or something—so after work yesterday we spent three hours trying to tell our left foot from our right. By the time this was over I wasn't fit for anything but sleep. I hate myself for not answering your letter immediately but in the state of mind I was in yesterday, anything I wrote would have been seeped [*sic*] in hatred of the Air Force and I'd prefer not to expound on all the reasons I'm bitter. They all add up to the fact that you're in Chicago and I'm here. As far as I'm concerned that justifies anything short of treason.

This afternoon a bunch of us had a lengthy discussion on the repercussions of going AWOL. Every time I read one of your letters the idea comes into my mind. In fact I usually get the urge to tell all these unimportant people to "drop dead," and hop the next plane for Chicago but then the thought of spending a couple of months breaking large rocks onto small ones discourages me. When I left the States last year I decided to keep in my mind the fact that eventually the whole thing would end and I'd come back. At times it seemed so far off that it didn't seem possible that I'd ever leave Korea but naturally time passed and it all ended. That's what I keep telling myself now. These four months will end and I'll leave this place. Right now it seems so far off that at times it doesn't seem real. I'd give anything to be able to be with you for just a few minutes. When I read your letter today I felt that I was penned in like a prisoner. I took off in my car and drove around for about 4 hours until I felt a little more normal. Every second I was driving I was thinking about you. When I remembered that you burned your hand I nearly put my foot through the floor boards. I thought about the many nights we used to sit at your house playing those goofy games. Did you know that I used to be terribly jealous of Dave and Woody? I used to wish I was taller because how could a guy have a girlfriend that was taller than he was. I guess I was a victim of late growth. When I came back to the base tonight I thought I'd feel a little better but all I can think of is four months. Four long months. Four months 'til I can be with you and actually tell you how I feel instead of groping for words with a pen. Some day I'll look back on this part of my life as being two people. Wondrously happy because you finally know how I feel and haven't rejected me and completely miserable because I can't be with you. I'll always be miserable when I'm away from you so that's something I'll have to learn to live with. As you said, the whole world could fall apart and it wouldn't matter. I love you.

Mick

"Ike" was the nickname for Dwight D. Eisenhower, president of the United States 1953–1961.

POSTMARK: MAY 7, 1954
Thursday

Dear Carol,

About twenty minutes ago my phone rang and the mail clerk said "letter." About 5 seconds later I had my hat on and was out the door. Two minutes was all it took to pick up your letter, fly upstairs to my room. Just as I opened it the phone in the hall rang. I picked the phone up & yelled "What!" A familiar voice said "I hope you realize that you quit work 20 minutes early." There I stood, your letter in my hand waiting to be read and that fool was bothering me about an unimportant twenty minutes. The things I wanted to say would have cost me a stripe so I told him to dock my pay and hung up. I fell into my bunk, my head 10 inches from your pictures and started reading. The door flew open—"Borrow your hair oil?" I don't think that lad will ever return to this room again. He came in for hair oil and had to duck a shoe. I finished reading your letter and started to relax in my bunk. By the way, my bunk is 7 feet long, 2½ feet wide, 2 feet high on the edges, 1 foot high in the middle and is covered in the latest in olive drab. If I had a dog he couldn't sleep with me because there isn't room and I doubt if any self-respecting dog would go near it. As I was saying, I remembered suddenly that the last train for the day comes through in about two hours so I brought myself back to reality and this letter. I want to finish this and drive into town before the train arrives.

Today was the warmest day of the year so far and I tried every excuse and angle possible to get off duty but it seems that everyone has my number. During my lunch hour I drove down to the golf course, played 4 holes and dashed back to my dark little corner. I doubt if I could have made it if I had stayed cooped up all day. When I returned I was greeted by a brand new airman, fresh out of basic training. The poor guy has 46 months left in the service. My job consists of assigning guys like him to different jobs, outlining a training program and compiling background info in order to determine how stupid he is. After I interviewed him I felt like writing a letter to Ike. His home is 50 miles from here. Two months after he enlisted he was stationed right in his own back yard. He told me that he has a date with his girl so tonight he's driving home. When I asked him if he had any special job preferences he casually said no. I don't blame him. With his deal I'd gladly scrub floors 10 hours a day. I decided that no one has the right to have it that good so I assigned him to the chow hall where he will spend the rest of his time at this base slinging hash.

I'm sitting in my car now. This is a heck of a place to finish a letter. Only so many men can leave the base and it's first come first served so I had to get off in order to mail this tonight. Naturally the car is full of guys all wanting to go somewhere. If the writing seems scribbly it's because the car is going. Chris is driving and I'm having a ball trying to coordinate my writing with the bumps in the road. We're going to town to see a movie. Unless they let me get my job back I'll probably see so many movies I'll become a screen expert. Ah, the car has stopped. The "crew" is inside having a beer and I've got about 10 minutes before the mail is picked up. I just remembered that I've got some rotten pictures in the glove compartment that we took out at the course last week. The water in the background is Birch Bay and the cottages are all part of a fair sized resort that caters to Canadians who want to spend a few weeks in what they consider the U.S.

The boys are done with their beer, the mail is leaving so I'd better close. I still feel like writing. I always feel like there is much more to say than I actually do so when I get back to the barracks tonight, I'll write another letter. Why shouldn't I write two in one day?

Be with you again in a few hours.

Love,

Mick

Carol was part of a barbershop quartet called the Honey Gals.

"The Glenn Miller Story," starring James Stewart, was released in 1953.

Opened in 1916, the Edgewater Beach Hotel was among Chicago's most spectacular nightspots.

Otsie, a dachshund, was first animal I knew—he was around well into my young years. I was born in 1959.

POSTMARK: MAY 7, 1954

Dear Carol,

As I was removing this paper from my drawer I was thinking about the name of your quartet. I sat down and before I realized what I was doing I started the letter "Dear Honey Gal." The way my mind's been working lately, some colonel is liable to receive a report with "Dear Honey Gal" in it.

I just left the theatre and I don't remember seeing a picture I enjoyed more. The Glenn Miller Story finally worked its way up to this neck of the woods and tonight it opened at the local one aisle dump. A fine picture but not as good as the one I have in front of me right now. The more I look at the picture the more beautiful you look. That picture is my favorite because I like to think that when it was taken, you might have been thinking about me. It's the one you took Easter while sitting down. As I was looking at the picture I was trying to imagine how it would look if I were sitting next to you. It wouldn't improve the picture but it surely would improve my already lofty morale. One of the most impressive features of that picture is your left hand. That was one of the first things that caught my eye when I first saw it. You have the most beautiful hands. I just had what I hope is a bright idea. If I'm not mistaken, there is a place outside Chicago called the Venetian Village or something to that effect. When I'm home let's go there and ride in one of the gondolas. I just stopped writing for a minute while I sat back and pictured us riding along with soft music while I was holding your hand. I was wrong. The idea isn't bright—it's brilliant.

My roommate just rolled over and asked me if this is the same letter I was writing earlier. When I told him that it was another one he just moaned and went back to sleep.

I've never been to most of the so-called better places in Chicago because there has never been anyone that I wanted to go with, but now I sit for hours at work picturing us dancing at the Edgewater Beach. Doesn't it have an open air dance floor? Or just strolling along the lakefront in the evening. All these thoughts are great and I only have to wait 118 more days.

For the last two weeks I've been investigating a golf tournament that is going to be played tomorrow. It's an officers–enlisted man deal with 5 men on each team. The prize is a steak dinner and umpteen drinks to be bought by the losers tomorrow evening. Ever since I quit the golf team I've had a few of the officers feeling very unfriendly towards me so it will give me a big kick to eat a sirloin that they pay for. The scores from tomorrow's play will also determine who will go to Seattle this summer to play in the Northwest AF Tournament. If I do go my chances of winning are negligible but I just want to get away from here for a week. Two of us will be able to go so tomorrow I'll write & let you know how it turned out.

It's after midnight and I better get a little sleep. I play much better when my eyes don't look like road maps.

Give my regards to Doctor Marks and pat Otsie on the head for me. What's this about a "dog's life?"

Until tomorrow,

Love,

Mick

The Logan Square Drum and Bugle Corps, of which Carol and her brother Bob had been members, was a legendary outfit, at one point winning more than one hundred straight competitions. Though Mike refers to the Logan Square Corps as "we," I do not believe he was ever a part of the group, and meant "we" as a fan.

POSTMARK: MAY 9, 1954
Saturday

Dear Carol,

I'm sitting in the club house at the golf course, the place is nearly empty and as usual I feel depressed. The only other person in here has been feeding coins into the juke box and playing the slowest, most romantic songs.

We had our parade today and it really brought back memories. We were one of the first outfits to step off and after we finished I stayed for a while and watched the bands & drum corps come by. By Logan Square standards none of them were any good but I got a big kick out of watching them. One of the drum corps had uniforms very similar to the ones we used to wear and when they came into sight it startled me momentarily but when they started playing I realized that the only similarity was in the uniforms. I stayed around for about a half hour but seeing the majorettes and drum corps was getting to be too much to take so I found the rest of the troops at a local cafe. When I got there I discovered that the hot sun & the cold beer that they were consuming had combined to create what could have easily passed for a riot. The place was full of airmen and sailors, a very bad mixture. The bantering that had probably started out in fun had evolved to blunt insults and it looked like the bottles, chairs and fists would start flying any minute. Chris, all 5' 4" of him, was leading the vocal battle and more than holding his own but I saw that once the battle got started his hide wouldn't be worth 2 cents so I eased him out of there and back to the base. When we got to the base we discovered that the full quota of men had taken off so if we went on we couldn't get off again. Luckily, I had my stationery in the car so we came to the golf course where I planned on playing a round, then writing. After two holes I gave it up for the day and came in here. Chris is still out there and as soon as he finishes we're driving back to town to see a movie and eat and in all probability start working on another painful Sunday morning.

The little tournament I mentioned, the one between the officers & enlisted men was played yesterday and I'm happy to say that in the end it cost the good captains the price of a steak and many, many drinks. The party didn't break up 'til 3 AM so I didn't get a chance to write last night.

When I couldn't go on the base this afternoon I called up the mail clerk & talked him into bringing my mail off to me. Somehow the mail delivery must have got delayed because there were two letters from you, written on successive days. When I read the one with the earliest postmark I nearly did cartwheels. I let out a whoop that made Chris think someone had died & left me a million. How fast can a situation change? I've been sitting around trying to figure out the future and trying to figure out what Larry planned on doing. I had come to the conclusion that everything was in a mess but after that my mental powers failed me. When I read that the divorce was actually becoming a reality, naturally I felt elated but then I began trying to picture your reaction. If you should start feeling depressed about having things turn out that way just remember that in time it was only a small portion of your life. You deserved a heck of a better deal than you've had but the best way to react to it is the spilt milk and water over the bridge outlook.

Why weren't you invited to the party? There was no party. When I got home El told me of her plans to have a big get together and that you were invited. I gave it some thought and decided that the best thing to do was not have a party in order to avoid seeing you. That doesn't sound like something a person in love should be saying but at the time it was the best thing to do. I wanted to see you, I wanted that more than anything in the world, but to see you married to someone else, as you were when I left, would have completely shattered a mental condition I was trying to create. I was doing my best to forget you and I remembered what happened the last time I saw you. I didn't want to spend another year like that. What else could I do? The picture of you and Larry walking in, the polite how are yous, maybe a handshake, and me sitting around trying to be witty and jovial, was more than I could take. Rather than have to go through that I told El that I didn't want to be around crowds, which was true, and that I'd get around to see everyone. As the leave passed my resistance nearly broke down but every time I was on the verge of going to you I'd tell myself to forget you and at the time that was the best thing to do, but of course I realized the impossibility of it. At times the changes that have occurred in the last few months seem too good to be true. For a long time I felt that I was the most woeful person alive. Now—as I've I said, it's too good to be true.

Chris just walked in and is telling me to hurry up. He doesn't realize that he's walking on thin ice. I guess I'll humor him and go so until tomorrow,

Love,

Mick

Heartbreak Ridge was the site of one of the most famous, and brutal, battles of the Korean War, stretching from September 13 to October 15, 1951.

Joyce was a friend of Mom's.

Eleanor worked for Yardley Home Products, which her daughter (Mike's niece and future sister-in-law) Barb recalls "produced Everything in Plastic—including curtains, raincoats, garment bags, plastic covers for small appliances. Mom was the head of the sales organization. She hired about two hundred women to sell the products. Mom put on about seven demonstrations a week and made a lot of money. She, in a sense, was self-made and a natural saleswoman."

POSTMARK: MAY 11, 1954

Monday

Dear Carol,

At last. The AF has finally consented to give me enough time to write a letter. Six hours ago, as I was sitting down to write, sirens started wailing all over the place. It seems that someone decided that we should have a practice alert. That was at 4. It's 10:15 now and I have finished my little tour of guard duty. When I got down to the guard office I was assigned the job of guarding a little building that contains nothing. To assist me in this important mission were two apple cheeked young lads of 17, both of whom joined the AF 2½ months ago. When the three of us reached our little line of defense, I explained to these boys in my best old soldier manner that we must have a system. This system consisted of their staying on the outside and watching for any people that might be snooping around and me staying in the building as a one man reserve unit. When I explained to them that this was the system used in the battle sectors they readily complied so I entered the building, found a comfortable table and curled up for a six hour siesta. Just as I was dozing off, one of them came in and asked me what he should do if an enemy approached. Yell "halt" I said. Naturally he wanted to know what to do if the "enemy" didn't halt so I told him to engage in hand to hand combat. When the sun went down it became very dark outside since we were at the remotest part of the base. Apparently they were afraid of the dark because every little while they would enter and tell me that they see something moving in the shadows and want to go have a look. To help ease their minds I told them pleasant little stories of guards being found with slit throats and that if they kept a constant vigil they had nothing to worry about. When we were relieved both these "heroes" looked like they had been through an attack on Heartbreak Ridge and I can imagine the grizzly tales that will be written to their families this evening. One of them was so impressed with everything that he kept calling me "Sarge" and talking like one of the characters in an old war movie. Three months ago they were flighty young high school boys. Now they are hardened, calloused veterans of a harrowing combat mission.

Yesterday I had planned on spending the evening writing but as usual my plans were ruined. I was driving to town in the afternoon and the mail clerk asked for a lift so I made a deal with him. I'd take him to town if he'd check the post office for a letter for me. The mail gets to town Sundays but we don't pick it up 'til Monday. There were two letters for me. One from you, and one from El. I've been so wrapped up with my own affairs lately that I haven't written home for quite some time. Longer than I had realized, and they were getting a little worried so I spent the entire evening getting caught up on writing home. El kind of caught me off balance with one of her questions. It was very short and direct and exemplified the insight she has into my mind. When she closed her letter she mentioned you and asked "Serious?" The amazing part of it is that I've never mentioned you in any of my letters and when I was home she knew that I didn't see you. I guess El knows me better than I know myself. Pretty sharp gal. Her company had their convention and at the dinner at Tam O'Shanter the President, Mr. Yardley, gave away trophies to the outstanding dealers. The final trophy & naturally the largest went to the outstanding area manager of the year. There are 90 such managers and when he announced that it was El, everyone stood on their chairs and applauded wildly. At times she even amazes me. Naturally I had to answer her question because if I didn't she would have asked it again. My answer was as simple as her question. "Serious."

I tried keeping your pictures put away but every time I come into the room I immediately took them out so I decided to save myself all this effort by putting them in the most convenient places.

Chris just came in full of vim, vigor, and chatter. It's nearly midnight but he's hungry and suggests that we go to town for a clam burger. Just what I need to make me sleep well.

According to what you wrote, your divorce situation seems a mess but there must be a loophole somewhere. I can't see what he's trying to accomplish but most likely he doesn't know either. It would seem that you have reached a stalemate with the conflicting desertion charges but I don't believe that such a thing exists in law. Something has got to give. What does your lawyer think? You can't possibly be left in a position where his desertion charges prevent you from filing the same therefore making a divorce impossible. The law is full of angles and little loopholes and your lawyer should be able to find one. What about Larry's lawyer? Has he given any reason for Larry not showing up? One thing that might happen is the pressure of lawyers' fees plus the restrictions that come with being married, despite the separation, might eventually make him see the light. Something's got to give. I hope it's Larry and much sooner than the year that you're worried about. I think it will be.

Why aren't those shaggy haired friends of Joyce in the service? I don't object to their hair too much, it's their reference to you as "cool." Very inadequate description. If you do date (and the thought doesn't put me into a fit of gaiety) don't date creeps like that. I'm very unsympathetic to long haired cool cats. Shaving their heads and putting them into nice new khaki uniforms and sending them on a long long boat ride would soon clear their thoughts of "cool" ideas. The injustice of their being able to see you and talk to you causes me to wish heaps of misfortune to fall upon their undeserving heads.

Only 110 more days (only).

Til tomorrow,

Love,

Mick

The McGuire Sisters (covering the Spaniels' version) had a hit in 1954 with "Good-night Sweetheart, Goodnight."

Wednesday

Dear Carol,

In 20 seconds it will be 11:15. That's what the man on the radio said, so in 45 minutes I can scratch another day off my calendar. I'm getting to hate that calendar because of the time it represents. Here it is the middle of May and already, to use the favorite GI expression, I'm shook. I know that I'll make it through the next 3½ months but I've got doubts whether some of my acquaintances will. Whenever I'm not doing anything and even when I'm occupied, I think of you. If I'm left alone everything is OK but if someone unwittingly interrupts my thoughts he generally retreats, red eared, wondering if I'm crazy or just hard to get along with. This afternoon I was approached by a non com who offered me a place on the base drill team. I should have been honored because it is a crack outfit and never exceeds 28 men but instead I told him that he, the drill team, and the AF should all crawl in a hole. Luckily he's good natured so he came back later and I was a bit more cordial so now I'm a member of the drill team. This afternoon at lunch, I had just finished your letter and was dreaming of candle light, wine, soft music, and you. I turned around and what did I see. Two hundred silly looking airmen shoveling food into their cavernous mouths. The things I felt like doing would have resulted in my being shot at dawn.

Chris just walked in loaded down with sandwiches and beer. He was in town and figured that I'd still be up so he apparently bought out the town.

Chris has left, I've polished off my third sandwich with beer to match and it's 12:30. A new day in the longest summer in history.

I feel like calling you right now but that would mean waking you and knowing your schedule I don't want to deprive you of any sleep. What would I say if I called? I don't know. I guess I'd say I love you. Maybe I should be content with just writing it and wait 'til we can be together before I say it. Maybe as you said, people can fall out of love but the only way I could stop loving you would be to stop breathing. I've felt this way for so long I don't remember when it started. I felt this way when there was no hope and then I learned that there is always hope. How could I ever stop. Maybe if I knew I would so I could find out what it's like to live and feel normal. Other people don't seem to react the way I do. One fellow I work with met a girl two months ago. Since then he's been cheerful and easy to get along with. They're getting married next month. I envy him for the beautiful simplicity of his life. He met a girl, their love was mutual and they live happily ever after. It sounds too easy but I guess it's possible. I must have been one of the people who were born to live a complicated life. Come to think of it, you are too. In fact I shouldn't be complaining. You have more troubles than it's fair for one person to have. Fate's been pretty unkind but it can't continue that way.

The radio is playing "Good night Sweetheart" so until tomorrow,

Good night,

Love,

Mick

Bob in this case is Carol's brother Bob, who always liked Mike, and whom my father adored.

POSTMARK: MAY 15, 1954

Friday

Dear Carol,

I just finished reading your latest letter and if I'm not mistaken that's the 12th letter I've received in the last 11 days. I'm on my lunch hour and since the drill team is marching tonight I'm going to try to finish this before they send the hounds out for me.

I started my membership on the drill team with a bang. We practiced for three hours and then drove to a baseball game to put on an exhibition. Most of the movements are very complicated and when we started I was sure that I'd fall on my face or find myself marching alone. To make matters worse I was marching in the front rank and any error would have been doubly noticeable. We drilled for 15 minutes and somehow I made it through

OK though I had a few bad moments. The uniforms are sharp. White helmets, gloves, scarves & belts over the blues with the pants bloused into black boots. We're practicing again this afternoon and tonight we're marching in a horse show in Vancouver, before the horses I hope.

So the lady is a card shark and we both like the same game. When I was overseas I was pretty much of a black jack fiend. Since there was nothing to spend money on, the games ran pretty steep at times. I haven't learned canasta though I did play it once. I played for an hour or so and when I finished I discovered that I knew less about the game than when I started so I gave it up as a loss. Back to black jack again, I've never seen anyone but GIs play black jack and when I read your letter and visualized you dealing the cards and all the women playing the thought had me laughing out loud. When a bunch of good blackjack players get together there isn't a facial expression in the bunch and I've always connected that type of appearance with the game so naturally when I thought of all of you playing I also pictured the dead pans and it sure struck me funny.

After spending a couple of weeks with nothing but time on my hands I'm beginning to get swamped with activities. The drill team will occupy a lot of my time and today a guy I work with started the ball rolling for a base humor magazine, something like one of the college magazines. The fellow who thought of it worked for a newspaper before he came into the service and he brought the idea before the C.O. who O.K.d it. When our first copy comes out and if it's any good I'll send the first one that comes off the press to you (barring an abundance of profane G.I. humor of course).

This morning a Colonel from another base came around for an inspection and I provided him with the perfect example of how not to act around a Colonel. When he walked into the office, I was sitting at my desk, feet propped up, hands back of my head, gazing out into space. He walked over to me and stood there expecting me to react in the usual way—leap to my feet, bustle around and all that. What he didn't know is that I was in Chicago dancing with you at that moment and I didn't even notice him there. He said something, I still don't know what, and I came to. Then I stared at him for a few seconds, mumbled "yes sir" and then he left, probably wondering what the A.F. is coming to.

The picture you sent is in complete conflict with your description of it. Like all the rest, it's wonderful. I looked at it before I read the letter and my first impression was amazement at the size of Joyce. Of course I didn't know who she was but knowing that you're 5'9" I was stunned for a moment at seeing a girl who was 6'1". Then I examined the picture and realized that for her to be that long she'd have to have impossibly long legs or standing on something so I decided that she must be standing on something—at least I hoped so. I said my first impression was amazement at Joyce's size. Of course that was after I stared at you for a couple of minutes. Then I noticed that there were other things in the scene.

Tomorrow I have the entire day off so I'll probably sleep late, jump out of bed, run to the mail room and I hope find a letter there. Whether I receive one or not, I'll spend the afternoon writing, that is if I don't get kicked by a horse tonight.

It's nearing noon so I'll have to join the rest of the club foots for marching practice. Careful with those glue brushes, but if you're thinking about me results in a ruined cup of coffee I'll gladly send a barrel of dimes.

Tell Bob that when I get home the drinks are on me. All allies are appreciated.

Love,

Mick

Xavier Cugat, who performed easy listening and Latin dance music, was popular from the 1930s through the 1950s.

The Villa Venice was a nightclub in Northbrook, a suburb of Chicago.

POSTMARK: MAY 17, 1954

Sat.

Dear Carol,

I'm in the car again, parked outside the base club. As usual, I had to leave early to avoid spending the evening in my room.

We marched in the horse show last night and we stole the show from the horses. After it was over a rich Canadian took the team to a bar and bought a few rounds expounding all the while on how proud he was to meet a fine bunch of pilots such as us. We explained to him that we were airmen in name only but he wouldn't be swayed. We couldn't take his imaginary flights through the wild blue yonder so we left for the base. That's when the party began. On the way back we spotted a lively looking place so we stopped the bus and all 28 of us invaded. When we walked in I noticed the frightened look that appeared on the bartender's face. Then I saw why. The place was crawling with Canadian sailors. The usual result of such a gathering is a riot and the idea didn't appeal to me since win or lose we'd spend the night in the local jail and that definitely wouldn't appeal to the base C.O. I decided to avoid such a situation by buying a round of drinks for the nearest bunch of swabbies. They returned the gesture and in a little while we were singing God Save the Queen and they were singing the AF song. (Some of them were confused so it was interspersed with the Marine hymn.) A feeling of good fellowship prevailed and the bar stayed open much longer than the owner expected. This afternoon my roommate got around to waking me after letting me sleep through breakfast & lunch so here I am. I'm not dressed up and have nowhere to go. Someone suggested a round of golf but I doubt if I could make it around the course. I'm hoarse from the last dozen choruses of whatever we were singing and my nerves are still trying to recover from the trip back. We were in a large bus that was made to travel on the ground but our driver, his senses dulled, somehow got the idea that the thing could fly. Some of the big, new cars that we roared by on the road looked like they were standing still. From now on the bus driver is going to stick to cokes.

When I finally made it to my room last night I went to sleep with the light on because I was laying in bed, face to the wall, looking at your pictures. The first thing I saw when I opened my eyes this afternoon was you, smiling at me. The sun was shining on the picture and you looked radiant. Chris came in full of suggestions for the day but I couldn't see any way that I could enjoy myself more but finally he got me up and here I am. The doors to the club are open and I can sit here and listen to the music from the juke box while I write. It's pretty pleasant. Nothing like sitting in a car writing to you while there is 2500 miles between us. I better be careful, I'm starting to feel bitter again. Whenever I start to do something, play golf, march, perform my petty duties, and begin to get interested in whatever I'm doing I suddenly think of you. Then everything seems totally unimportant. It all seems like a waste of time and effort because you're there, I'm here and anything I do that has no bearing on you lacks meaning. Whenever this feeling gets overpowering I just tell myself to calm down because if I didn't I'd probably blow my stack. Whenever I start feeling that way it must show all over my face because the "wild eyed look" I sometimes have has been commented on by some of the people I work with. I'm half crazy now. I hate to think how I'll be in October when my leave is over and I'm confronted with many more months of not seeing you. I guess it would be better not to even think of that. It'll be rough enough then so there's no use worrying about it now.

I received another letter from El and as usual she was full of good news. She bought a '54 Packard so it looks like we'll go to the Edgewater Beach in style. Just mentioning the Edgewater brings thoughts which are becoming very familiar into my mind. I'm sure we'll be lucky and avoid the Cugat type music and the weather will be great. The government, the AF, and at times, it seems the whole world is against me so the law of averages says the elements can't go against me too. No, the weather will be warm, the sky full of stars, the music slow and soft and I'll be so happy I'll be in a daze.

I've thought about the Villa Venice for a long time. While I was overseas I used to think about going there with you. The fact that you haven't ever been there makes it a little better. That plus my having the pleasure of taking you there makes me feel confident that it will be great. In fact I don't see how any part of my leave could be anything but wonderful except, of course, the unavoidable hours when we'll be apart. I'm going to keep my presence a secret from everyone but the immediate family because I can't see wasting any time with my aunts, uncles and all the rest when I could be with you. If it sounds like I'm planning on monopolizing all your time—I am. For twenty some odd days I'll be haunting you. I'll be as relentless as an ace detective. The only way you'll be able to get rid of me is with a gun and I'm not sure that would do the trick. Just giving you fair warning.

Chris has been yelling "Let's go" for the last ten minutes. I don't know where we're going but that's none of my business—I'm just driving.

Until tomorrow

Love,

Mick

POSTMARK: MAY 19, 1954

Tuesday

Dear Carol,

I just picked up your letter and after checking my schedule, I've decided to write this during my lunch hour.

The last two days have been as hectic as any I can remember. Sunday four of us drove 100 miles to Seattle to play a golf course we've heard a lot about. The course was fine but my car wasn't. Apparently it's beginning to feel its years because it didn't cooperate when we started back. By the time we had it fixed and drove back the sun was starting to come up so for the first time that I can remember I made it to work on time on a Monday. Instead of feeling tired I felt fine and during drill practice I was patting myself on the back for my recuperative powers. After work I decided to relax in my bunk for a few minutes before writing. I must have over relaxed because the next thing I knew it was dawn. My room mate claims that he tried to wake me but I was in a death like trance. At times Chris has resorted to tipping my bunk over or throwing water in my face to get me out of these trances.

After work I'm going down to the golf course to settle a bet. Chris and I generally make small bets as we play and lately we've been betting scotch and sodas. I've run him up to ten so tonight we're playing 18 holes, double or nothing. I'm not sure if I want to win or not because I know him, he'll try to make me collect all at once. I'd prefer to collect them slowly over a long period of time but if he insists I'll accept immediate delivery.

I wish my dreams were as good as yours but I generally have nightmares or at best a complete blank.

If you and Chris are to become a couple I think it would be better for him to wear the 3 inch heels. His girl is 5'5" and she towers over him by an inch. He and I were in a bar one night and an obnoxious female drunk came over and asked me to dance. Trying to be polite I told her I suffered from webbed feet and couldn't dance a step. She asked Chris and I thought he'd run for his life. She must have stood 6 ft with her high heels on and besides that she had huge shoulders, and hair that reminded me of a forest dweller. He looked a little frightened and mumbled a refusal. Undismayed, she grabbed him, swept him off the bar stool and with a loud yell he landed on the floor. I would have helped him but I was convulsed with laughter as was everyone else in the place. He got up and for a minute I thought he might slug her but I guess he looked at her size and changed his mind. He hasn't lived that episode down yet. No, if he saw Moe he'd probably remember his embarrassment and come out swinging.

The weather (what a dry subject) has been sensational. Between the drill team and golf I've already picked up the best tan on the base. About the 2nd or 3rd of September a dark, sinister figure is going to come running into your house. Call off the hounds—it's me. I spend at least 3 hours a day in the sun and usually a lot more. In a week some of my very dark comrades will be calling me "cuz."

When I finished the account of your date a few minutes ago, I lit a cigarette, leaned back and was surprised to find that I wasn't overwhelmed with rage or turned green or anything. Maybe I should have been, but after spending the last two years in a state of hopelessness I can't get worked up over a date. I expect you to date so it came as no surprise. Now that I'm done telling all those lies you should know that I turned a deep shade of red, flew into a wild fit of jealousy and completely "lost my cool." Of course that's not true either (not much). Actually I just felt a little envious of him as I do of anyone who is around you. All these lucky people you work with. All they have to do is get up in the morning, go to work and there you are. Why can't it be me?

Sure it's possible for two people to fall in love that fast. Three months? I fell in love with you in three minutes and I couldn't have been more than twelve.

Would I stop loving you if I could? I doubt it but if I had to spend another year like 1953 I'd darn sure look for a way to forget you and that's the truth. I could never stop loving you. No matter what happens I'll always feel the way I do now. But there were times when I wished that we had never met. That was last year. 1954 is a brand new year and I have a brand new outlook and a brand new hope.

I keep thinking about the dream you had and that accounts for some of the shakiness in my writing. I close my eyes and see you standing before me, then I think about deserting. The time seems to be dragging. I wish I could go into one of my deep sleeps and wake up in 3½ months. I just had a terrible thought. When I get back from my leave I'll have 18 more months in the AF and at least 6 or 7 before I can take another leave. I'll make it but I'll hate the A.F. 'til my dying day. And I'll love you 'til the same day.

Too bad about that fellow's Chrysler but those are the ups and downs of life. He had a date with the most wonderful girl in the world then he ruined his car. Can't have all good luck. I'd gladly see my car torn into little pieces just to spend five minutes with you.

Love

Mick

POSTMARK: MAY 22, 1954
Friday

Dear Carol,

The first thing I am going to do is explain the recent lapses in my writing. Tuesday after writing my last letter Chris and I went to the golf course to settle our bet. Chris is a fair golfer but he hasn't been playing as long as I have and usually I can beat him without much trouble. Tuesday he shot like a man possessed and I had to break my back beating him. As I expected he demanded the right to pay off his debt immediately so we went to the local lounge and I consumed more scotch than I should have, at his expense. After work Wednesday I was stuck with the base paper that I told you about. Two of us comprise the entire staff and since my partner is married we went to his house to start work on it. It took up half the night and after writing what I hope will be received in good humor by the troops I couldn't write a thing when I got back to the base. Last night the base KV club, that stands for Korean Veterans, had a party. It's a fine club, its only function being the consumption of vast amounts of liquor. They usually end up in town, with most of the local citizenry fleeing for their lives. Last night we finished the party at the international café which is the closest thing to a night club that they have up here. We succeeded in winning many enemies for the AF and particularly our club. One of the boys who fancies himself a great lover kept staring at a woman with a very soulful look on his face. She stared back. Her husband stared at both of them. The lover asked her to dance and the husband blew his cork. We separated them, took the manager's advice and left. From there we went to one of the less elite places. This dump, Bill's Tap, has an aged female pianist who plays the piano and drinks beer by the gallon and sings at the same time. Her piano is next to a window that is usually open so we crept up on the window from the outside, slyly positioned ourselves beneath it and leaped to our feet screaming like Indians. She screamed also but for a different reason. She also dropped her glass, turned white and came very close to falling off the chair. Naturally the bartender didn't welcome us with open arms. If there is anyone left in this part of the country who we haven't alienated then they weren't out last night. This morning when I arrived at work, late as usual, I was told that I was receiving some extra duties as a reward for my fine record of seldom getting to work on time. There is a large field near the base. In that field there is a large hole. The hole wasn't there this morning. The blisters on my hand weren't there this morning either. I'll make it a point to be on time from now on.

Did El mention anything about us! She said and I quote "I can see what you see in her, but what can she possibly see in you?!" Good question but I'm afraid I haven't got a good answer. I think El always knew the way I felt but since I never said anything she kept quiet also. Whenever I had a date El would question me, try to detect a romantic interest and the lack of enthusiasm must have been apparent because the opinion at home was that I had many years of bachelorhood before me. Maybe I have, but it's against my will.

There won't be any problem with the folks when I'm home on leave. They saw so much of me during my last leave that I imagine they won't even notice my absence. Telling your friends that you're leaving town is a great idea. I've got things to say that have been accumulating for years and I can't say them if we're to be bothered by people. If there is anything the service has developed in me, it's a great appreciation of privacy and a dislike for crowds of people. If I came home and saw no one but you it would be a perfect leave. When I look at your pictures the thought of wasting time talking to people and answering their questions and wasting time makes me want to sneak into Chicago, wear dark glasses and avoid everyone between here and Central Ave. I think I will.

I had planned on letting you know the exact time that I'd be home but after thinking about it I've decided that a surprise would be more fun. I might even pull the stunt that a friend of mine did. On second thought that wouldn't be too good. When he came back from overseas, he went home, had his sister call his girl and pretend to be the telephone operator with a call from Seattle. He told his girl that he was in Seattle and would take the next plane out. Then he jumped in his car, took 5 minutes to get to his girl's house, ran in the door & yelled that he came by jet. Very funny fellow.

I told Chris that he'd have to stop bothering me when I was writing so he gave me an ultimatum. "This is the crossroads of your life—choose between us." Chris has got to go. I guess he does it as a form of revenge because there are times that he's writing his girl that I pop in, flop on his bunk and start saying "When I get home in Sept. etc." He'll listen for a minute then tell me to go AWOL so he can write his letter.

I found out while I was home on leave that my "little" brother is no longer little but I didn't realize how fast he is growing. As I may have told you, he's as big or bigger than I am and growing fast. The latest surprise that he's provided me with is his dancing. I knew that he cut a wicked rug but according to El's last letter he & Barb have specialized in the Tango & are good enough to have hopes for the harvest moon festival. At the time I enlisted he was a sawed off squirt who got in my way, now he's a youthful Gene Kelly. I regret missing his transition from squirt to young man. According to everyone at home, he's a darn good athlete and I know from experience he has a sharp wit. He kept me in stitches during my leave. Whenever I talk about him, I get carried away with enthusiasm and could go on all night so I'll talk about someone who I have much more enthusiasm for.

I like your remedy for a cold. I'm not sure it will cure a cold but it will make the cold much more interesting.

So I've never had it so good. Look, I could be living in the hotel Waldorf, drink Haig & Haig by the gallon, eat pizza all day, have a stream of dancing girls chasing me and I'd still complain. You're there—I'm here! That's it. I've never had it so bad. My evenings are free but I can't share them with you. I look for some way to kill time so I can knock off another day on the calendar. I sleep late on Sunday but I'd much rather get up early and go to church. That is, if I could go with you. In about three months you can tell me that I've never had it so good. Then I'll probably agree. It's getting late and I don't want to spend tomorrow displacing dirt again. So until tomorrow,

Love

Mick

Mike was a Virgo; Carol a Scorpio.

POSTMARK: MAY 25, 1954
Sunday

Dear Carol,

It's late afternoon, the rain is pouring down, the wind is blowing, it's dark, gloomy and as sad a Sunday as I've ever seen. My room is littered with empty beer cans, cigarette butts, and the remains of what appears to be a piano bench. Six of us slept through all three meals today so rather than drive 35 miles to a decent restaurant, we went to a local grocery store, filled a huge bag with food & beer and came back here for our combination breakfast, lunch & supper. Some of the sandwiches we made were works of art. Two kinds of cheese, four types of meat, an awful looking sandwich spread, a dill pickle, and beer accompanied by green olives. For variety we vary the arrangement of the meats. After everyone finished I dropped subtle hints that suggested they leave. A subtle hint in the service is one that excludes physical violence. I told them to leave, get out, depart, beat it and hit the road. Finally they caught on and left, nobly leaving me two cans of the beer I paid for as a reward for cleaning up this mess.

Last night I dropped into the bar at the golf course and within five minutes I was behind the bar serving beer to thirsty golfers and hoping none of the officers would walk in & discover I had defied their decree. It's a Canadian holiday week and so the place was crawling with American hating Canucks. They disgust me. They come across the border to find recreation then when they get here they spend all their time running us down. Usually I keep my mouth sealed for an hour or more before I blow my stack but last night I blew my cork early. One particularly obnoxious clam digger sat at the bar and kept harping on the fact that their dollar is worth more on the world market, our resources are depleted, theirs are growing, we're immoral, crooked, high pressure, and finally he broke the camel's back with the statement that the Canadians contributed more to the Korean war than we did. It took all the will power I had to keep from throwing him out bodily. Instead I told him that he was cut off and refused to serve him. He sat and continued to run off at the mouth receiving a lot of help from some of his countrymen. Finally I could take no more so I told them that as long as they didn't like this country they should return to their own *%+$ country. Once I got going I was carried away and before I was done I had completely insulted everything connected with Canada. There was one other airman in the place. A Chicagoan also, who is nicknamed Moose. In a loud voice he asked me if I had heard the rumor that the Queen of England had to get married. I told him in an equally loud voice that I thought it was true. The Canadians all glared at Moose but the fact that he is 6–4 and about 250 deterred them from any violence. The owner finally came over and calmed me down. That happens every time a bunch of Canucks get together. They must have a national complex or something because all they can talk about is what's wrong with the U.S. I'm not overly patriotic but I get peeved at some of their comments. According to statistics that this base has reviewed, this area of the country, Northern Washington and British Columbia, has got the largest communist population in North America so that could have something to do with it.

After finishing work at the course I stopped in at the base club and as usual the place was jumping. Some civilians had been admitted and one of them was attempting to do battle with an airman. He must have consumed a great deal because he was accusing the airman of making a pass at his wife. His wife looked like something from another planet and no self respecting airman would have gone near her. The gendarmes were summoned and peace was restored. On a Saturday night our club is the most interesting place in Washington. Civilians can come in and they add to the confusion. I usually get off in a corner with a drink and watch the human comedy unfold. Within two hours I saw the fight I mentioned, a man carried from the club by his massive wife, an airman slowly topple from his bar stool and fall flat on his face, the bartender go berserk and start serving whiskey by the water glass and finally the air police come & tell every one to go home. My sides ached from laughing when I left. When I reached my room I found a poker game going on so to be sociable I joined them. My luck was awful so I threw them out, looked at your picture for a while, tried to write and discovered that I was drunk so I went to bed. The last thing I thought about before I fell asleep was that it's 100 days to go as of today. One hundred more days. That doesn't seem like much. When I was overseas the big day was when you had 99 to go. Usually we had a party if liquor was available. Tomorrow I'll have 99 but I doubt if I'll do any celebrating.

First chance I get I'll check my horoscope. I've never paid much attention to it but it sounds pretty stable. How can I lose if I have the stars on my side? The last time I read a horoscope was in January and according to the one I read this was the year that Virgo 21 year olds would have romantic interests with "childhood sweethearts." At the time I thought it pretty depressing but after reading your observations and remembering the one I read I've come to the conclusion that it's 100% accurate. Carol, how can you fight the stars? Lately even the philosophers are on my side. I've been reading the works of Schopenhauer and he states that nature, in trying to create a balanced effect of color has created a greater attraction between blondes and brunettes than between people of similar coloring. I'm probably guilty of twisting everything I read to pertain to us, usually in an encouraging way, but you must admit that the stars and the philosophers can't be wrong.

Next week I'm going to return to radio work, my original AF job and that will mean working nights. I'll welcome that because it will give me a lot more time to write. I'll be going to work at midnight and I'll have 'til 8 in the morn to sit and write.

This won't make today's mail delivery and it bothers me to think of it sitting in the post office for another 12 hours. The outgoing mail system here is slow. A train picks the mail up in Blaine, takes it to the Billingham Airport which is a one horse airport, if there is such a thing. From there it's flown to Seattle where it is transferred to another plane and then to the east. Too slow.

It's getting pretty late in Chicago right now and unless you've gone out, you're probably going to sleep. I'm trying to picture the moonlight flooding your face, hair and pillow with a glow. If I sit back, close my eyes I get a realistic picture of you. After all these months of dreaming and planning, I'll probably fall flat on my face the first time I see you. On second thought, that would be impossible because I'll be floating along on cloud nine and couldn't fall.

I'm going to take the chance on a train coming through tonight and run this into town. I hope your dreams are as pleasant as my day dreams are. A hundred more days to dream.

Love,
Mick

Mike mistakenly refers to Carol's dog Otsie as Adolph.

POSTMARK: MAY 26, 1954

Tuesday

Dear Carol:

There was a mix up in the mail deliveries somewhere along the line and as a result I received the letter you wrote Sunday in the morning delivery and the one written Thursday in the afternoon delivery. This confused me no end. In the morning I read that you would be with my family Sunday. That was all. It sounded so casual that I felt that I was expected to know more but I couldn't remember being told anything about it. After reading the next letter my problem was cleared up. I hope you're not frightened by the wild eyed group that is my family. At times they even scare me.

We're having a party in the barracks. It's a special type of party known as a G.I. party and required special equipment such as mops, brooms, brushes, soap and other cleaning utensils. This morning the lad who was assigned the job of cleaning the halls, windows and such did a 2 hour job in ½ hour then dashed off to the golf course. The inspecting officer decided that the job was incomplete so we were confined for the evening. Now everyone is calling the negligent airman names and accusing him of causing them all this work. An evening in the barracks will do them all good. By the way, I was the guilty party.

Yesterday was as bad a Monday as I can remember. In the morning I saw a letter in my box and was all smiles as the mail clerk handed it to me. My mood was short lived. It turned out to be an invitation to a wedding from a friend of mine in N.Y. I told myself "maybe this afternoon." In the afternoon I saw another letter in my box and was smiling from ear to ear. It turned out to be a notice from the library that a book is overdue. The rest of the evening I sulked and snarled at everyone who was foolish enough to try to be friendly. I finally went to the club for a drink and hit the sack early after writing you a long letter that was so filled with depression I ripped it up.

This evening the mess hall served liver (ugh) so Chris and I drove to town. We went to a restaurant we frequent quite often and as it turned out I should have eaten at the base. While I was drinking my coffee, the waitress, a girl of 16 or 17 came over, turned deep red and stammered out the request that I take her to her senior prom. I nearly choked on my coffee. Whenever I go in there I kid around with her but I never bothered to find out her name. I was completely stopped. Chris just sat and enjoyed my plight. Finally I told her that I work nights and couldn't possibly go, thanks and all that. She said "oh" and just stood there. I couldn't think of anything else to say so I asked her for more coffee. Luckily some people came in and while she was waiting on them I came back here to join the clean up detail. Chris didn't let up once on the way back. He kept repeating in a falsetto "Lover, take me to the prom." By tomorrow I'll be getting it from everyone. I've never been to a prom so it's kind of late to start now. When I graduated I confined my celebrating to a couple of solitary drinks.

I can promise that in September you won't be submitted to any of our wild and wooly family gatherings. Maybe I'm selfish but I'll only have 3 or 4 weeks and I don't see any point in sharing you with anyone (except Adolph of course). Every time I think of my leave I see us in some quiet place dancing slowly to soft music. I'd be happy if I could spend my whole leave that way.

Shall I lie and say that I'm sorry you were stood up. OK. I'm sorry you were stood up. Now for the truth. Don't think I'm cold hearted and begrudge you a date and an evening's entertainment but being this far away the only way I can fight competition is with the power of the pen, which when wielded by me isn't very powerful, and luck. Luck seems to be with me when it provides competition in the form of complete idiots. The man has to be an idiot to stand you up. It's no wonder he smashed up his car. He's blind. He had a date with a girl in a million and apparently couldn't see. Fool!!! The day I stand you up will be the day I don a form fitting strait jacket and take up residence in a well padded cell.

I think about you so much while I'm awake that my mind refuses so conjure any visions while I'm sleeping. I dreamt of you once and the dream was brief and disheartening. I don't remember the details but when I approached you, you said hello in a loud way, got in a car and drove off. Rather than have such nightmares, I prefer my mind to remain blank. I refuse to have anything to do with any other girls so stop pairing me up with strange females even if it's only in a dream.

The G.I. party is over and we just finished being inspected by a young lieutenant who fancies himself to be quite a wit. When he inspected my room he pointed to the row of pictures on my wall and said "Who is that?" I said "my mother." He pointed to your picture and said "her?" so I pointed to the picture of my mother and said "no—her." He gave me what he thought was a wilting glance and dramatically strolled out. Two months ago he was a college ROTC student. Now he thinks he's a hero.

It's nearing the hour of ten so I'll run this into town so it will leave on the early train.

I think I neglected to mention it in my last couple of letters but I love you.

Mick

The Bob referred to in this letter is Dad's younger brother, born in 1935.

POSTMARK: JUNE 2, 1954

Monday

Dear Carol,

I've been sitting here for an hour grasping for the right words to explain why I've been writing so seldom and I'm meeting with very little success. Maybe if I just start writing the words will come. Actually, it seems silly for me not to be able to write more often because every minute of the day, no matter where I am or what I am doing, you're on my mind. Then when I try to write, everything I put on paper sounds so weak and inadequate I usually tear it up and give up for the evening. Then I spend 24 hours worrying. Believe me, I worry. Never before have I been in such a paradoxical situation. I'm happy and miserable at the same time and you're the cause of both. Just knowing you and loving you makes me as happy as I could ever be but when I think of the future and try to get it unsnarled in my mind, I get as dizzy as a little kid on a merry go round. Sure, things take care of themselves. The happenings in the last three months prove that, but it's impossible to use that as a philosophy. I've always tried to plan the future and usually I've done OK but now I'm having troubles planning things from day to day. When I left for overseas I had the next six or seven years of my life mapped out and when I returned my plans were nearly in a blueprint stage. The one thing that could have caused a change was a romantic interest and feeling the way I did, that was an impossibility. When I got here I looked forward to two years of playing golf, living a free and easy life and just waiting patiently for my discharge. Now the only pleasure I have is thinking about September and my greatest source of misery is the thought of the months that will follow my leave. When I think about the 18 months I'll have left after my leave, I'm not fit to talk to anyone and I definitely am in too depressed a mood to write. Lately that's been on my mind so much. I just haven't been able to write. Not writing creates new worries. I'll be driving somewhere and suddenly I'll think "If you don't write more often she'll think you don't love her." Don't ever think that. If a few days pass without a letter, think anything but don't ever think that I could have stopped loving you. The possibility of your thinking that unsettles the heck out of me. Sometimes I sit and day dream about my leave and I'll be feeling as full of hope and confidence as can be. Then those 18 months come into my mind and I'm forced to face things realistically. I'll be stuck here for all that time and anything could happen. If I come out of my little shell of daydreams I'm confronted with all sorts of possible occurrences. The most terrifying is that you could meet and fall in love with someone. No matter how many ways I try to argue myself out of that possibility I can't do it. It could happen. In your jobs you meet a lot of people and one of them could be a guy you could fall for. Being 2500 miles away and having a pen for my only weapon doesn't put me in much of a competitive position and I'd just be hiding my head in the sand if I didn't realize it. I started out in this letter trying to explain why my writing has fallen off and after reading it over I see that I haven't accomplished that. It all adds up to the fact that I walk around in a depressed mood most of the time and if I wrote when I feel that way my letters would all sound gloomy and depressed and rather than write something like that I wait until I'm a little more cheerful which isn't too often. Right now I'm breaking my rule because I'm far from being in a happy mood. Maybe I should tear this up and write something gay, saying I'm having a great time and wish you were here (that's partially true) but what would that accomplish?

Sunday and the graduation have passed and I hope everyone enjoyed themselves. I know Bob must have. Yesterday I kept trying to figure out what everyone was doing at home and I was going to call but I didn't know where everyone would be so I'll have to wait until the letters arrive giving me a blow by blow account of the festivities.

When I was making the return trip from Korea I'd sit up on deck at night and think about you. No evening can be as beautiful as an evening at sea and Lake Michigan is close enough to being an ocean to suit me. A moon light cruise in September. That will give me something to think about for the next 92 days.

I just checked the afternoon mail. No luck. I guess I'm getting spoiled but whenever my mail box is empty I take it out on the mail clerk. I think he's just as happy to see me receive a letter as I am to get it.

I'm going to close now and write a few lines to Bob. I haven't written him in quite a while and I'm curious about his plans. Pretty big kid isn't he?

Only 24 hours to the next mail delivery. As I said—I'm getting spoiled. I love you,

Mick

El and Dor are Dad's sisters Eleanor, born in 1921, and Dorothy, born in 1922. Michael is Eleanor's son. Barb is Eleanor's daughter, who would later marry Carol's older brother, Bob.

Though we don't have her "blow by blow," Carol's May 30 diary entry suggests Dad's family was almost as happy as he was about his new—or newly public—love: "Went to Bob Royko's graduation. Was Treated Royally. Even got a kiss on the noggin from Mick's Mom. I'm afraid they consider me part of the family already. El told me Mick's favorite dish, and Helen said, 'She'll have to know everything pretty soon.'"

Wednesday

Dear Carol,

It's a little after midnight. I just returned from Seattle where the drill team put on an exhibition. We left early this morning so the first thing I did when we returned was wake up the mail clerk and check my mail box. When I saw three letters waiting for me I nearly did a flip. I can't go to sleep without writing so my roomy will just have to endure the light.

The last letter I wrote has been bothering me since I mailed it. The best thing for me to do when I feel low is to squirt all the ink out of my pen and lock up my stationery. When I wrote that letter my morale was pretty low. I had just been notified that I wasn't going into the radio section, the engine of my car started making funny noises, so funny in fact that it will cost me most of the money I won in golf bets this month to have it repaired, and an application for transfer that I had written was turned down. I had applied for the transfer a few weeks ago and hadn't mentioned it because if it came through I wanted it to be a surprise. I requested a transfer to any base east of the Mississippi. I'd consider anything within 1000 miles of Chicago as being nearly home but as I said, it was vetoed so I'll just have to tolerate these red necked clam diggers for the next 21 months.

My Dad has always had an eye for a pretty girl (I think he's the pinching type) so it doesn't surprise me that he remembered you from the pictures. When I showed him the pictures he asked me if you were a girlfriend and I said "No, married." He just said "too bad." I guess I've been guilty of neglect as far as he's concerned so the first chance I get I'll write him a letter. I think he's taken my being in the service harder than anyone else in the family. When I left for overseas everyone was at the airport and to avoid making me feel any worse no one shed any tears. I was very proud and very appreciative of the self control exhibited by El, Dor and my mother. When my plane taxied in for passengers and I grabbed my bag everyone kept a stiff upper lip and I thought I'd be spared the sight of tears. Then my Dad, of all people, started crying. As far back as I can remember he's always had a rough type personality and he was the last one I'd expect to break down.

I'll have to send my mother a bunch of roses. She usually shunts the dishes off on someone else and leaves the refilling up to the individual.

Those poker games you mentioned, rather the poker game at my Mom's house is inevitable when my Dad and Aunt Pauline are there. No one else plays well except those two but they usually don't win. My mother sits there, plays terribly and wins all the money. If I had her luck at cards I'd never work for a living.

Michael must be growing like a weed. When I was home all he did was lay in his crib and drink milk so I didn't pay much attention to him. I really miss those kids when I'm away. When I get discharged Bob will be halfway through college, Barb will be 17 and none of the small ones will remember me. When I walked into Dor's house in December her kids both started crying and hid in the bedroom. I was home two weeks before they had anything to do with me.

I mentioned earlier that I wasn't going into the radio section. The captain who is presently my boss tried to talk me out of going by promising me a three day pass, a promotion and more authority. I gleefully declined. Then he took off his kid gloves and told me I wasn't transferring. It seems I make the mistake of being too efficient. Now he's afraid to trust some one else with the work that I've been doing. No three day pass, no promotion and I'm still here. I'll never learn.

While I was in Seattle today I was walking around town killing a few hours and I happened to walk down to the train station. There I stood, dressed in civilian clothes, enough money for the ticket and I couldn't work up the nerve. I've never considered going AWOL as seriously as I did today. I felt like I did when I was a kid and was thinking of cutting school. The only trouble was that I'd have to face more than an irate teacher when I'd return.

It just started raining and thundering and my roomy woke up. Now he claims he can't get to sleep because of the light so I'll have mercy on his worthless soul.

Maybe when I stop thinking of you long enough to fall asleep I'll dream about moonlight cruises and all my other hopes for the future. I hope so.

Love

Mick

Glenn Miller recorded "At Last" in 1942.

Friday

Dear Carol,

How could you write anything wrong? If I reread all your letters a hundred times, and I'm coming close to doing it, I doubt if I could find anything that wasn't perfect. No, the lapse in letters is my fault and I should be kicked for letting it happen.

About an hour ago I finished the best meal I've had in two years. A few days ago I ran into a guy on the golf course who was having a terrible time trying to master the game. I gave him a few pointers and they helped a little. After we finished playing we stopped at the club for a drink and I discovered that he is chief chef at a resort near here. While we were drinking Chris and a couple of other fellows from the base walked in and the conversation centered around food. He invited us to his apartment for a meal and tonight was the night. He went completely overboard. We had spaghetti and meatballs, pizza, some Syrian dishes for Joe who is Syrian, Shish Kabob for Chris who is a Greek and when he brought out a tray of pierogi I couldn't believe my eyes. All this because I simply showed him how to hit a golf ball straight. I guess that the time I spend on golf hasn't been wasted.

OK, we've both written a gloomy, depressed letter and neither of us feel any better for it. I've taken a personal vow to hold all letters that sound wrong for a few hours, then when I feel better I can tear them up and write something much better. I've discovered a darn good system for snapping out of any fits of rage I fly into while I'm working. This afternoon, just as I was swamped with work, a youthful looking airman asked me if he could have a leave and if he could have money to travel on. After questioning him I discovered that he has been in the service 3½ months. He's been in for 14 weeks and he wants 30 days leave. After I lectured him he fled from the office, probably to write his mother and tell her what a mean bunch of soldiers he's stationed with. Things like that happen all day. When can I get a leave? Can I get a different job? Stupid questions. When I reach the saturation point I go to my room, look at your pictures, read your latest letters and come to the conclusion that these people and their problems are part of an unimportant, unpleasant interlude that must be endured. Then I return to work feeling a lot better.

I just checked the calendar and I was pleased to see that we've left the 90 class and are now in the 80 bracket—88 to be exact. Time is starting to pass quickly. Whenever I think about my first day home I actually get nervous and my stomach starts fluttering. I'll probably be in a daze when I arrive and if I'm speechless and glassy eyed I hope you'll understand. Chris told me that he'd give me odds that I'd fall flat on my face when I get to your door. I wouldn't be surprised. So far my arrivals have been unusual if undramatic. The last time I was home I arrived in Chicago without a red cent. I was in Seattle Christmas Eve and had a very expensive celebration and my ticket broke me. I took a cab to Dor's house and was greeted with shouts, kisses and tears. Very dramatically I said "give me a couple bucks for the cab." Next time I should be prepared to say something more appropriate. Time after time I picture the way you'll look when I see you for the first time in twenty one months. That's a long time. The last time I saw you, I never anticipated returning under such improved conditions. When I left your house I sat on the bus and added up everything in my mind. Things can look so bad that after a while they get funny. I actually sat and laughed. Any type of humor is based strictly or indirectly on someone else's troubles and I guess I was laughing at my own. Things can look just so bad then after a while they become ridiculous. That's how I felt. I was going to Korea, you were married and the future was hopeless. I guess when things get to a certain point they can't get any worse and have to improve. I should have realized that. It's kind of foolish to be twenty and think that your whole life is ruined but at the time it looked that way. That's the past and it's better forgotten. I've got too much of the future to think about to be worrying about what's already happened.

The radio is playing some Glenn Miller music and I'm thinking abut the quiet little place you mentioned. That's the kind of music I want to be dancing to in 90 days. In fact the song they are playing is "At Last." Very appropriate. Have you ever been on a large ship? The sea is wonderful at night and I know that the evening we go on that midnight cruise is going to be calm and warm. My luck is going too good to change.

The clock says one and I anticipate a busy day tomorrow so I'll close. I wish I was lyrical and poetic but every time I try to close a letter the same words come to my mind.

I love you,
Mick

Hydramatic was an early type of automatic transmission.

"Hernando's Hideway" is from the musical The Pajama Game. Mike mentions that he heard it done by a female vocalist, which would have almost certainly been the 1954 original Broadway cast recording by Carol Haney. Carol apparently mentioned this song in a letter to Mike.

"Marie," by Irving Berlin, was a hit for Tommy Dorsey in 1937, and again by the Four Tunes in 1953, which was most likely the "souped up" version Mike mentions.

POSTMARK: JUNE 9, 1954
Monday

Dear Carol:

I just hobbled into my room after a fast trip to the hospital at one of the larger bases. I bruised my instep this evening and though it's nothing serious, I won't be playing golf for a few weeks. Just five minutes before I usually stop work I was helping move some large boxes of equipment into the radar room. The box slipped and I did an original dance. I guess it could be called the one foot quick step or something accompanied with a loud vocal background. We don't have x-ray facilities on this base so we went to one of the nearer bases. No broken bones but a lot of bruises. The x-rays were taken by a nurse and not only was she fat and homely but she gave me a verbal lashing for letting the box drop. In my hour of grief when she should have been noble and sympathetic she acted like a shrew. Luckily it was my left foot and since my car is hydramatic it won't stop my driving. I'll probably go nuts if the weather is good for the next couple of weeks and I have to miss my regular golf games. Chris, being a true friend, laughs loudly at me and calls me "gimpy." I've a very attractive wooden cane that I'll use until my foot can support my weight. Now when I enter the local bars I'll have a new dignity. People might even give me dimes if I carry a cup. I tried to talk my way out of work but was unsuccessful. All I got was sympathy but no three day pass.

The days are getting longer out here and it doesn't get dark 'til nine. This makes the time pass a little slower which is something I don't appreciate.

I finally heard "Hernando's Hide Away." It was done by a female vocalist and if nothing else it's novel. Believe it or not, the big hit on the juke boxes around here is still that souped up version of "Marie." When I got here it was the most popular and it's still going strong. The people out here are pretty unaffected by what I consider the outside world. I was in a bar that had an organist and drummer which is practically a concert band for these clam diggers, and when they played a tango one couple tangoed and the rest did their strange native dances. To use one of my brothers' sayings, these people are not only squares, they are 3D squares—cubes.

I promise. Never again. If ever I stop writing for that long again it will be because I'm dead or at least have a broken arm. I must be crazy. I'm the person who should be writing daily. To rearrange the old saying— I've got everything to gain and everything to lose. No, I'll never let that much time pass between letters again. I might even send you notes while I'm home. It occurred to me that while I'm home I'll be able to take you out on a Saturday, be with you for hours and first thing Sunday go over and see you again. That seems so wonderful it hardly seems possible.

How could anything that great happen to me! When some of the guys I know start talking to me about their girls I often wonder if they could possibly feel the way I do. I don't think they can. They aren't that lucky. There's only one you.

Love,

Mick

The "stationery" is lined notebook paper.

POSTMARK: JUNE 11, 1954

Thursday

Dear Carol:

Pretty sharp stationery isn't it? I've been so swamped with work the last two days I haven't had a chance to get to town to replenish my paper supply.

I wish it had been my hand that I banged up instead of my leg. I've spent the last two days banging away at a type writer and doing my little bit to make the AF more confused than it was. Yesterday, I was approached by a captain laden with papers that had what appeared to be chicken scratches all over them. This, I was informed, was a financial report that he had been compiling for the last three months and was finally ready to be typed and sent to bored, uninterested colonels and generals all over the AF. I made the mistake of typing up my monthly job activity report too neatly and this guy happened to see it so he thought I was a hot shot typist, which I'm not. I combine the two traits of typing slowly and making an abundance of errors and I tried to tell him this but he wouldn't be swayed. Yesterday I sat and made marks on paper for 14 hours and today I topped that by two. After about a ton of paper I finally completed it and was rewarded with a pat on the back and Monday off—big deal.

This foot has created quite a problem. I can't play golf, and if I go to town people all stare at the slipper on my foot and cluck sympathetically. The drill team is out and I don't collect stamps so the coming weekend looks to be very dull.

I no longer have the problem of Chris bouncing in and out of my room. We decided to bunk together but I doubt if it will last. We've already had two battles on who will sweep the floor first under the new arrangement. So far it's unswept and since he won't agree to flip a coin it will probably remain that way.

I've figured out the time between now and Sept. and as close as I can get is 80 days and about 12 hours. I'll probably arrive during the day and on a week day. First I'll call your house and if you're home I'll run every red light and stop sign getting there. If you're at work I'll walk in and demand that you be given the day off. After your boss cordially complies we'll go to some place that's quiet and secluded and I'll say all the things that I can't say on paper. This may take two or three days but since I'll have three weeks that's okay.

One little word you used in your last letter has had me floating all over Washington. One word and I'm completely "shook up." You called me "Hon." Maybe you didn't realize what an effect it would have when I read it. I was reading your letter as calm as usual. That means I was chain smoking and my heart was going at twice its normal pace, when suddenly that word hit me in the eyes. Believe me, it was as if you had been right here and kissed me. I wasn't the same for the rest of the day and I'm afraid to read the letter again because of the unnerving effect that one word has on me. If a one syllable, 3 letter written word can effect me that much I can imaging how being with you will be. Who says I have to die to go to heaven!

I agree. Eventually you'll have to stop turning down dates but I can't say that your recent refusals lower my spirits. When you do go out I just request one little favor. A lock of your date's hair. Then I can make a little doll of clay and hair and spend my evening sticking pins in it.

I found the most beautiful spot in the world for a picnic and as my luck would have it, we can't be together. It's only 5 miles from here but it is like being in another world. I'm not a nature lover but this place is so perfect it'd be impossible not to appreciate it. It's on the bay and is almost impossible to describe. I happened to find it a couple of weeks ago while I was taking a drive. It's a beach that is bordered by high pine trees and calm blue water. There is a small clearing on the edge of the trees and situated in the clearing are three large rocks that make a perfect fire place. The clearing is only about 20 feet across but the wall like effect of the trees and the noises made by the water make it an escapist's or a picnicker's paradise. I hope I can find something similar near Chicago. A warm, sunny afternoon, you near me in some quiet, peaceful spot and I'd be as content as could be. At times it seems hard to believe that these things will come about. Whenever I have any doubts I tell myself "it will happen." Then I feel as if I've had too much to drink. Only 80 more days and all these dreams will come as true as I can make them. Is it true? It can't be. No one could possibly have anything that wonderful to look forward to.

They say that a sincere love increases with time, so until tomorrow when I'll love you more than I do today,

Mick

POSTMARK: JUNE 16, 1954
Tuesday

Dear Carol,

It's nearly one AM and I'm trying to pull myself out of the doldrums I've been in for the last five days. I'm not meeting with much success. Did I say five days? It's been longer than that but lately I've been at a lower ebb than ever before. What's the trouble? I wish I knew. Over the weekend and for the last couple of days I've been feeling half crazy. Saturday, when I should have stayed in my room and stayed off my banged up foot, I felt like I was in jail. I got out of here and stayed out except when I had to sleep. I've been in town most of the time sitting over coffee or beer trying to get my mind straightened out. No matter what ideas I get, it all adds up to the same thing. I want to be with you and right now it's getting to be nearly an overpowering fanatical urge. This morning when I finally went back to work, I made the commanders office my first stop. I argued, pleaded and nearly begged for an immediate leave. He turned me down cold. I guess he realizes how badly I want to leave, despite my not telling him why, because he warned me that going AWOL would result in severe punishment. I'm at the point of complete disregard. As far as I'm concerned, the two stripes I've got and the one I'll probably get this month aren't worth 5 minutes of being with you. The only thing that's stopping me from leaving this place fast, and believe me, it's the only thing, is that it's not the way we've been planning it and you probably wouldn't be pleased. One word from you, just one word of assent and I'll be on my way. You probably wonder how I can feel the way I do and still write so infrequently. I've got so much love for you bottled up inside me, feelings I've had to suppress for a long time, that I can't put them on paper and I can't say them over a phone. I've got to be near you or everything I feel will be unsaid. The 11 weeks separating us may not seem like much but each day contains the same things. Worries, doubts, fear for the future and worst of all, a slow dragging of time. I've never been so completely miserable. The only time I have any resemblance of happiness is when I read your letters. As soon as I finish your letter, the feeling that I'm with you leaves me and I feel the way I do now. It's funny the effect your letters have. When I'm reading them I feel as though you were right here saying everything that's written. In fact, as I read them, the words seem to be spoken by you. I actually hear them in your voice. Maybe I've got a few screws loose. It wouldn't surprise me a bit. I'm afraid to re-read this letter because it probably sounds like the wanderings of a demented mind.

I agree. It's a completely accurate description of the type of place I've got in mind. I'm talking about what's his name's Hideaway. Actually, I don't give a hoot where we go, what we do when we get there, or what any place is like. If you're there, it'll be perfect. If you're not, it's worthless. It's as simple as that. Few things can be that cut and dried but that's exactly how I feel. Naturally I want to go to places that you'll enjoy but as far as my enjoyment goes, you're the only essential factor.

Chris just came in and interrupted me for a half hour. The little guy has got great troubles and I sympathize with him. He's been planning on going home in July and possibly marrying his girl but a wrench was just tossed into the works. He refuses to change religions and so does she. He's Greek Orthodox and she's Catholic. I've tried every argument to change his mind but he's so stubborn I feel like booting him one. They're both being foolish. Maybe I feel that way because I've never been overly exposed to religion but it doesn't seem fair for them both to be so unhappy because of something that is created essentially as a provider of peace of mind. I'm going to keep arguing. Maybe he'll see the light.

Sure, I know that you don't feel the way I do and I've never expected you to and maybe you never will. That's one of the facets of the future that frightens me. But if ever you say you do, I'll probably be so exultant I'll probably bust. That's my dream for the future. Let some other sap dream about making a million or becoming president. I've got more to hope for than any of them. Despite its being one sided I'll always feel the same way—I love you.

Mick

Mac was apparently one of the many young men who failed to beat out Mike for Carol's affection.

K.V. party = Korean vets party.

POSTMARK: JUNE 19, 1954

Friday

Dear Carol,

I just finished work, the sun is shining, it's a warm, calm day and because of my own stupidity I can't go near the golf course. Instead of taking it easy on my foot I've been running around and its improvement has been nil. Last night we had another little K.V. party and as usual it was a near riot. We toured all the local snake pits and topped the evening off with an invasion of the base. We tested its security by coming in under the fences, crawling on our stomachs and establishing the mess hall as our headquarters. Then we frightened the night cook into preparing us scrambled eggs. Today I was told by the commander that such conduct will cease.

When I opened my eyes this morning I was sure I'd never live the day out. I was rudely awakened by Chris who brought the news that I was to meet a promotions board at 7:30. I had overslept and it was 7:15. By the time I entered the meeting room I was sure that I was in the process of dying and most of the questions that they asked I answered in my subconscious only. It was all like a dream and a bad one at that. This afternoon Chris came over to my desk and sorrowfully told me that I had finished 4th out of 20 men. Since there was a promotion quota of three, that left me out in the cold. This peeved me because promotions come out every second month and I didn't want to wait 'til August for another try. After Chris left, the officer in charge of my section came over and congratulated me. I thought he was being wise so I nearly bit his head off. He gave me the facts. I finished first and I'll never know how. I guess I should get drunk before I take tests or meet boards. It might be the key to success. After patting me on the back and lecturing me on my new responsibilities he came up with the grand prize. After I return from my leave he wants me to start school at Western Washington, a college about 30 miles from here. I'll go in the morning and work six hours during the afternoon and the government will pay two thirds of my tuition. I was so stunned I couldn't answer for a moment but when I did I didn't give him a chance to change his mind. I'll carry 10 hours and that means I can get over a year's credit before my discharge. I guess this is my day. A promotion and a chance to get some book larnin. If I could play golf I'd probably get a hole in one. All I need to make it perfect is a plane ticket and some leave orders or have the dream I had a few nights ago come true. It was a crazy dream but at the same time it was so wonderful I hated to wake up. I dreamed that while I was working I received a phone call saying that I had a visitor at the gates. When I got there, you were the visitor and the crazy part was that we started dancing. I don't remember the song but it was probably Hernando's Hideaway.

The calendar says 74 days and though I can't say time is flying at least it doesn't have the awful sound that 130 and 140 days had.

Chris and I finally got the floor swept but it took a lot of arguing to do it. We settled on two brooms and we each swept exactly one half.

The only thing I can say to Mac is a very half hearted and insincere "too bad." I can understand how he felt. In fact I don't see how anyone who knows you could avoid feeling the same way. Maybe it's your destiny to leave a chain of broken hearts in your wake.

It just started raining so I don't feel bad about not playing golf. The weather lately has been terrible. According to the local rustics, the weather has been unusually bad but from what I've heard, the clam crop has been good this year—Hooray.

If I have to wait 'til 8:30 then that's what I'll do. I'll sit there and wait 'til 8:30 and while I'm at it I'll tell all the other people waiting that I'm from the health department and Doc Marks has been using rusty instruments. Finally I'll drive all the patients away and you'll have the day off. Where there's a will, there's a way.

Rather than post this at the base mail drop, I'm going to drive to town and mail it. That way it might make a train tonight, a plane tomorrow and your house on Monday. If I mail it on the base, it's likely that it will take longer. If you ever run across a map of Washington and can find Blaine, you'll understand why the mail delivery is slow. This is the last frontier and we are the last outpost. One of these days I expect to see Indians come galloping in through the gates.

It's pretty late in Chicago right now and most likely you're retiring so I'll pick this moment to say Goodnight.

Love,

Mick

POSTMARK: JUNE 23, 1954

Monday

Dear Carol,

I just dealt the last hand of a long profitable poker game and though I won, I managed to think of you often enough to sit through complete hands with worthless cards. I gave up poker when I arrived here but this was an emergency. My gas bill on my car was high this month so I had to supplement my pay. We started playing at 4:30 and it's 12:30 now.

The game was going strong when I decided to quit and I know that all the losers aren't too happy about my quitting with their money but enough is enough. I spent the entire weekend at my boss's house, the officer who wants me to go to school, and I didn't get a chance to do any writing. One of the boys just came in with the request that I play tomorrow night. I'm tempted. A few more games like this and I'll have a new set of golf clubs.

The past weekend was one of the best I've had out here. After work Saturday I stopped in at the café in town and ran into Narns, the officer and his wife. He invited me out to his house for dinner and as the evening progressed it developed into an impromptu celebration with my promotion as the excuse. It was pretty late when the party ended so I stayed there. Sunday I was talked into a golf lesson and that I didn't enjoy. Neither of them has played very much and she is not the athletic type. I gave him a few pointers that helped and he was bubbling over with gratitude. Funny thing about golfers. Improve their game just a little and they're friends for life. After watching them chop up the golf course I was happy to return to their house for dinner. She can't golf but she can cook. We decided another party was needed so we called the base and before long the place was crawling with people. That broke up late and I had the pleasure of oversleeping two hours this morning without fearing a reprimand. I had planned on asking for the day off but some unexpected work developed and my plans for spending the afternoon writing were foiled.

When I received your second letter this afternoon I felt like a cad. How do you do it? I'm amazed. Amazed at your ability to write so wonderfully and amazed at my good fortune to be the recipient of the letters. I've made a habit of taking an extra half hour for lunch so I can reread your letters and mentally leave this place for a while. I know that I sound erratic and gloomy in some of my letters but mark that up to impatience. Sure 11 weeks is a short time but I'll be dissatisfied until I'm banging on your door. And it's not 11 weeks. It's only 10 weeks and one day. One of these days I'll be counting hours and then minutes. Unbelievable but true.

I hadn't planned on wearing my uniform, but for you, and only you, I'll do it. I actually feel silly when I wear the thing in public. People always expect the unusual from a G.I. especially if there's more than one. When I docked in Seattle I joined some of the guys I had been stationed with for a tour of the town. Every place we went to had the same reaction. People expected us to consume drinks by the gallon (we tried to oblige), play dice, start a riot and everything to that effect. To make matters worse we were all sporting handlebar mustaches, a diversion we utilized to break up the monotony of looking at the same faces for a year, and that plus our emaciated appearance made us look more like desperados than airmen. That was the last time I wore my uniform willingly. I was going to wear the mustache home but a little girl got hysterical when she saw it so I didn't want to take the chance of frightening my nieces and nephews into idiocy. I'll wear the uniform. I'll even put some ribbons on it if you'd like. I'll wrap a bandage around my forehead, sing and play a fife. Anything to please.

The only preference I have in anywhere we go is that the place has a minimum of people and noise. I won't be able to pay any attention to my surroundings anyway so it doesn't make much difference to me whether we're on your porch or in a dimly lit bar. You'll be there—that's all that matters to me.

Tomorrow looks to be a bad day. We, that is most of the base, are all going out to fire rifles at the local gunnery range. I can think of better things to do but since they insist, I'll go out and fill the air with noise and gunpowder fumes too.

Chris just came in. I hate to be a prophet if I can't prophesize the better side of the future but I think he and his girl won't be he and his girl much longer. Hope I'm wrong. I can't write with him crying on my shoulder so I'll have to stay up half the night trying to console him. That's not much to ask for because if my troubles are ever as weighty as his I'll have him to moan to.

Love,
Mick

Riverview was a well-known amusement park on the north side of Chicago from 1904 until 1967.

Carol held several jobs at the time, including dental assistant.

POSTMARK: JUNE 24, 1954

Wednesday

Dear Carol,

I just finished an answer to a letter I received from El this morning. It was the first letter I've had from the family in quite some time so an immediate reply was in order. I got a big kick out of what Barb said after returning home from Riverview. All the fellows stared at Carol but she didn't even notice them. Look at that young airman's spirits soar!

Yesterday was a bad day. Chasing around the countryside firing rifles, then getting swamped with work. I had just finished work and was preparing to write, then get some needed sleep when those infernal sirens started blowing. An alert. By the time the all clear blew and we were done with our little game of mock warfare I was in a poor frame of mind. The sirens blew too often while I was overseas so I'm not impressed with this business of playing soldier. Ever again I was stuck with a bunch of slap happy youths as my compatriots. For 6 hours I told them blood curdling stories and assured them that within the year they would all be in Guatemala or Indo-China fighting for their country and their lives. One kid who I'm sure is still spending his 17th birthday money asked me in a small voice "Sarge, is it rough?" I told him that where he's going, it will be rougher than is imaginable. For the rest of the evening he clutched his rifle and tried to look brave. He'll probably get sent to Paris but it'll make him more appreciative if he has to worry awhile.

I quit the drill team this morning for a multitude of reasons. I'll be going to school in the fall so I won't have time for it and my foot still bothers me a little but the main reason was the punk lieutenant who runs the team. Chris and I were coming into our room this morning just as he was inspecting it. He noticed your picture taped above my pillow and he asked me, that wet eared ROTC graduate asked me, "Who's the babe?" If Chris hadn't shoved me out the door and down the hall I would have been saying goodbye to the stripes that adorn my sleeve. As it was, I only had time to tell him that his mouth was much too big and I'd like to remedy the situation. Thanks to Chris I didn't get the chance to enjoy this expensive pastime. After I cooled down I realized that in his blundering way he was being complimentary but his selection of terms didn't appeal to me.

Look at those days drop off the calendar. Sixty nine to go. I don't know what our first moment together will be like other than the fact that I'll be deliriously happy. Maybe you'll be waiting at your door, maybe I'll come busting into the dentist's office and shock all the patients or you might be out somewhere and I'll sit around pulling my hair. I'll worry about all that when the moment arrives because the setting and background are all secondary to the fact that you'll be there.

At times I start thinking of how easy it would be to buy a plane or train ticket and just take off. Why if I left tomorrow, and I could, I'd be with you in less than two days. Of course when I returned there would be the unhappy process of starting out as a private again. Maybe this waiting is the best way. It will just make being there all the more wonderful.

I don't remember what I was doing at 3:30 Sunday but next Sunday at the same time I'm going to go to some peaceful spot, clear my mind of all thoughts except those of you, over and over and over. Maybe you'll be able to hear me.

Right now you're asleep. Maybe you're dreaming of us. Thinking of you sleeping reminds me of a poem I once read, in which the poet plans on stealing into the chamber of his love and stealing a kiss while she's asleep. He explains that if she should awaken and object, he will offer to return the stolen kiss and a thousand more as interest. The poor poet died penniless and has been forgotten but at least I appreciate his genius.

It's getting late and if I fall asleep right after a letter I might dream of you. If I don't dream of you at least I'll have the pleasure of starting the day off by saying "good morning" to your picture. If only it could answer.

Love,
Mick

A/1C refers to airman first class, the third enlisted rank in the air force.

POSTMARK: JULY 2, 1954

Dear Carol,

By now you probably think I'm dead or most likely crazy. If it's the latter then we're of the same mind. The last few days I've been suspecting myself of having more that a few loose screws somewhere. This morning brought to an end a week that could aptly be called the "lost week." I'm not sure where to start because I'm still wondering where this wild week began. Last weekend the bottle boys of the KVs took off on one of their usual weekend parties, leaving chaos and confusion in their wake. This time we forgot where to draw the line because we stretched the weekend an extra three days and brought it to a fitting climax last night with three of the 4 lads making a tour of the local jail and bringing the wrath of the local citizenry down on the commander's head. Yesterday, after pay call, we all gathered at the town hall park to cheer for the base team as they did battle with the town team. Spirits run pretty high at these games and yesterday was no exception. By spirits I also mean the distilled type. By the fifth inning one little group was the recipient of some very baleful glances and when the game ended vociferous heckling of the opponents had stimulated the entire town. After the game we returned to the main pub and continued our commentary on the physical and moral attributes of the town athletes. The inevitable happened and when the battle ceased the police had corralled the most enthusiastic of the fighters and given the rest of us a very short time to return to the base. We complied and the party was over. Somehow I get tabbed as the leader in affairs of these kinds and the commander decided that I've been living it up too much lately so I've been restricted to the base until Sunday morning. That was unnecessary because I hadn't planned on going anywhere for quite a while. The fellows who were pulled in received $25 fines and what can be considered the last warning. Next time, the judge said, the book will be thrown.

If nothing else, we've all taken oaths. I'm not sure how sincere the others are but I'm all finished. The last time something like this happened I stopped drinking for three months. I've vowed, and at times I'm pretty strong willed, not to drink anything stronger than a milk shake until September.

You're probably wondering what it is with this guy who writes letters to you. Look, I'm no lush. Usually I'm a pretty sociable, moderate drinker of good scotch but I just got carried away this time. The main regret I have is the lapse that was created in my writing. I'm sorry. Sorry isn't a good word. I hate myself. If ever I should be on good behavior it's now. Five months ago it didn't matter what I did and the last week would have been strictly routine but now there's no reason for it. I've got more to look forward to than ever before. Maybe that's what caused this last time. The days did pass rapidly.

Next week sometime the summer maneuvers start. One week of guard duty in a dress rehearsal for when the Russians arrive. This playing soldier gets tiresome.

To be truthful I do prefer long hair. Of course styles have to be conformed to and when it's not carried to an extreme the short haircut looks pretty good. That "tiger girl" photo you sent wouldn't have been quite as appealing if your hair wasn't long. Tell that self styled reformist and beauty expert to kindly look to his own smoking habits and haircut and why bother to stop at Wisconsin. There's a lot of room farther up.

You can address my letters A/1C any time now. The medal was a nice touch. When I heard it rattle in the envelope I couldn't figure out what it could possibly be. Garsh I was thrilled.

Sixty one more days. Less than nine weeks. This is the time of night I like to think about September. It's nearly 2:00 and this time of the night I'm able to picture you and be sure I'm right in knowing where you are. It bothers me to think that you won't get a letter tomorrow. I can't promise to write every day but I can say that there will never be another lapse like this again. This restriction accomplished one thing. I'll be sure to write three nights in succession.

Your new stationery is like its user. Sweet and perfect.

I can't be late again tomorrow. Starting to like this new stripe and I'd prefer not to lose it.

Tell your cynical girlfriend that I'd gladly debate her theory of the nonexistence of love but she wouldn't stand a chance. I know I'm right.

Love,

Mick

I don't know what to say. I finished your letter fifteen minutes ago and since then I've been sitting here performing a self analysis in an effort to figure out if I'm half crazy or all the way gone. I don't know what causes these lapses. It's not because I feel any differently about you. If anything, I love you more now than ever before. I know that lately I haven't been acting it but don't ever have any doubt. One word, just one little word of assent and I'd be legging it towards the nearest airport.

Something is wrong though, and I can't put my finger on it. The closer I get toward September, the more the tension increases. I'm a bundle of nerves. I should be happy with the time getting as short as it is but I'm not. If someone tried to prevent me from taking a leave it would be fatal, but yet when I think about September I actually feel a dread about going. I think I know what's been causing that. Self confidence is an absolute necessity in any endeavor. If a person doesn't have it, he's sunk. In anything I've done—golf, gambling, school, any job I've had, I've always been confident. But now I lack it completely and that brings to the surface the thing I fear most in life. In fact it's the only thing I'm afraid of. That's failure. I've never really failed at anything. Now, when I find something in life that completely over shadows everything else, the possibility of failure looms before me. Sometimes I wonder if it would have been better if I had never exposed my feelings. One way to avoid failing at something is not to make an initial effort. If I hadn't written I'd probably be in some far off place again still living in my dreams. Future events might show that to have been the best thing to have done.

The effect that all this could have on you is another continual source of worry. You've had it rough enough. I don't ever want to be a source of trouble or unhappiness. I've had a thought in the back of my mind for a long time and it's not a pleasant one to have but I know it's true. I'm not good enough for you. It's not a very reassuring idea to have but that's the way I feel. Sometimes, after reading one of your letters, I tell myself to break everything off, get on a boat and out of your life. Your happiness comes before everything else and unless I can add something to your life, that would be the best thing for me to do. I'm not kidding myself in any way. I'm no world beater and you deserve the best which I'm not. If I did end this completely you wouldn't have lost anything. The sense of loss would be mine and if it was for the best it would be a justified move. You've had more tough breaks than anyone should have in an entire lifetime and by rights the future should hold nothing but happiness. If your being happy means being happy with some one else, then that's the way I want it. You deserve nothing but the finest and I leave a heck of a lot to be desired. Remember, if ever there is someone and the problem arises of how to tell me, just tell me. I'll wish you the best.

I'm on my lunch hour and I'm already working on an extra one so I'd better close before they send out the blood hounds.

Love,

Mick

Dear Carol,

I've got your letter in front of me after reading it a dozen times. My lunch hour begins in about twenty minutes but unless I get an answer on its way I'll be more useless than usual.

You said certain things that are justifiable but I've got to answer them in some way. You said that you're probably making something big out of something that isn't really. I'm not sure what you meant by that. If you're talking about the way I feel then let's get something straight immediately. You are all that matters. There is no one or anything that is worth one word from you and it'll never change. Don't ever doubt that. When I look to the future and try to visualize it without you, life looks to be very empty. Hopeless would be a better word. Maybe there are people who can turn their emotions on and off. Fall in and out of love but I'm not capable of it. I've been in love once. That's the one and only time. I'll stay that way no matter what happens. I don't even want to be near another woman. I'm not trying to convince you of my faithfulness or anything like that. I want to illustrate my feelings. I just don't want to be around any other women. My family always seemed to wonder why I had so little to do with the fair sex but I never told them that I continually made comparisons and the girl of the moment was always woefully lacking. As I said, I'm not sure what you meant by that statement but if anything, I don't think you realize how much I love you. Maybe in about 56 days I'll be able to begin proving it. Just remember, never doubt it or underestimate the way I feel.

I quote, "I guess it's time I stopped to realize that I'm not the only thing in the world that you've got to think about." You're right. Once in a while I think about my job. Sometimes I spend as much as five minutes thinking about something else. And when I'm not on a golf course I do think about my game often enough to play about half as well as I used to. How can I prove myself? I don't know, to tell the truth. Any suggestions would be appreciated.

Considering the distance between us, Blaine might just as well be in China. The one catch is that if it were, on September first I couldn't start out for Chicago. I spend a lot of time thinking about that first day home. Where you'll be the first moment I see you. What you'll say. I just hope that there isn't anyone else present then because I don't want to be considered rude but I'm afraid I'll be forced to ignore them completely. Maybe you'll be at home. I hope so. If you are at work it will cause a nerve wracking wait because propriety will prevent me from bursting in to your place of employment. Hang propriety! If you're at work I'll come right down.

What will we do the first evening? Maybe dinner at some place that's a replica of Hernando's Hideaway? How about a stroll through the park or a long drive? Nope, a drive is out because I'd have to look at the road instead of at you. I think the nicest date I ever had was with you. You probably don't remember it. We went bike riding one summer day. I remember I rode up all the way to your house and anticipated a much needed rest. When I arrived you wanted to ride around the countryside so I gentlemanly complied. Even then I didn't care what we were doing. I guess I didn't realize why.

The frame of mind you were in when you wrote Tuesday is bothering me. You sounded very depressed and let down. If it appears that I was out having a great time, with all thoughts of you completely disregarded, try to realize my position. I've been in the service 30 months. Just being in creates a lot of tension that has to be relieved now and then. The fact that I'm on the precarious side of a one sided romance doesn't help my state of mind either. When I was out on that tear, it was mainly because my mind was beginning to get so snarled that I needed to do something before I went psycho. If you can partially realize the effect you have and how much more you could have on my life then maybe you'll understand some of the things that have been running through my mind. For one thing, if ever it should look like I'm out of the running I could never make Chicago my home. It would be too painful. I'd probably get an officer's commission and stay in the service. It wouldn't make much difference what I did because I'd just be going through the motions of living. With you I think I could not only set the world on fire—I'd melt it. Most people never realize their full potential because they lack a sufficient incentive. If a person has that motivation, then he's unlimited. You'd be the incentive. I could do anything. That may sound a little over confident but I know the extent of my own capabilities and I also know the limitations of my own personal ambition. For myself I don't want anything. I could probably go through life hitting a golf ball and wishing I had you. Every person has unused, dormant reservoirs of ability that never come into use because they lack the spark that can only be provided by some strong emotion. Love, hate, fear—In my case loving you isn't enough. I can love you and still have no necessity for success because the love is one sided, but if ever the situation changed, there's nothing I couldn't do within reason.

I hope that I never again cause you to write a letter filled with so much doubt. I'd never do anything intentionally that would hurt you. If you were hurt by what appeared to be indifference on my part—forgive me. When you answer this letter, say I'm forgiven. I won't have any piece of mind 'til then.

I love you,

Mick

Many of the envelopes from Mike have jottings by Carol, usually spelling variations of a word or two that Carol wanted to see before using the words in a letter—this was long before word processing and automatic spelling checkers, and if a dictionary wasn't handy, you were on your own. But this envelope, for the letter above, contains what appears to be a draft of a full paragraph of Carol's, one of the few examples we have of what Carol wrote to Mike: "You'll never cause me to write another letter so filled with doubt because I'll never be doubtful again. If ever the time comes when I don't hear from you for what seems like a lifetime I'll just read your letters over again and feel confident that within a couple days time, I'll receive a letter and everything will be alright."

POSTMARK: JULY 11, 1954

Saturday

Dear Carol,

It has been said that each person is three different people. The person that other people see—The one that they themselves think they are, and the person that they actually are. Apparently we see you in a different light. I see you as the most wonderful person in the world. I'm dogmatically correct. Your self analysis contains many flaws. You're prettier than Monroe, smarter than Margaret, and much more regal than Elizabeth. If my views were brought before everyone else that knows you I'm sure I'd receive agreement from all. There remains one other person. The person you actually are. El has always accused me of being very frugal with praise and of undervaluing things so if that's true you must be more wonderful than even I can see.

The yearly maneuvers have got off to a rousing start. Yesterday, just as I was leaving for the golf course, the sirens went off. I spent the entire night riding around in a jeep checking on guards and assuring the young airmen that no harm would come to their cherubic souls. When dawn finally came, I caught a few hours of much needed sleep and then was rudely awakened at 10:30 with the request that I come to work. It's about noon now and I'm on a two hour break. I'm hoping that I can get out of tonight's guard because it's raining and a jeep doesn't offer much shelter. This is going to continue for at least five days. I hate to think of the condition the local bars will be in when the restriction is lifted. Hundreds of very thirsty airmen swooping down on these unsuspecting clam diggers. The men who were here last year tell me that the local jails had more airmen than the bars did.

I've got a calendar in front of me and I see that the time has dwindled down to seven weeks and five days.

Just as I finished that last line I was summoned again. It looks like I'll have to start resorting to nefarious tactics to get a little free time. Whenever I've got to get away I resort to my favorite trick. I scoop up a bunch of papers, put them into a folder and in a deliberate manner stroll importantly from the office. Then I dash over here. When I return to the office I slam the folder on my desk and condemn the AF for having so many idiots. Everyone gets the impression I'm in the midst of an important project of some kind and doesn't question my absence.

It is now five o'clock in Chicago. What are you doing?

Chris just bounced in here so excited he could barely get out his good news. He's due for discharge in December but a regulation has come out permitting men to be discharged 90 days early if it will permit them to start a full term in college. That means he'll be getting discharged while I'm home. September seems to be a fine month for everyone.

Funny you mentioning yourself as a pigtailed kid. I just can't remember you that way. As I look at your pictures I try to remember if you ever looked any differently. You must have, but it's beyond my memory.

I'll never have any peace. They just let out a yell for me over the P.A. system. Everything we do during an alert has to be reported to higher commands and one of my jobs is compiling the data for these reports.

It's just as well that I close. I want this to get to you by Monday.

I just remembered a nightmare I had last night. Put me in a terrible mood 'til mail call. All during the dream I kept chasing you and talking to you but you ignored me completely. I'd rather not sleep than have dreams like that. I guess having dreams come true might contain some bad points.

Love,

Mick

The above letter's envelope had the following written on it by Carol: "Don't let that nightmare bother you—"

The following letter, postmarked July 14, was written on Monday, July 12. Baseball's 1954 All-Star Game took place in Cleveland on Tuesday, July 13, and was broadcast nationally on television, for only the third year.

Dad's love of Dixieland jazz continued throughout his life. His "indoctrination" took place in Biloxi, Mississippi, 90 miles east of New Orleans, where he received his radio technician training.

POSTMARK: JULY 14, 1954

Monday

Dear Carol,

The alert has ended and I just woke up after sleeping for fourteen uninterrupted hours. I'm glad that we won't have any more of this 'til next summer. Playing soldier just doesn't agree with me.

As a reward for my tireless duties as a keeper of the peace, I've been given tomorrow off. That'll come in handy since the all star baseball game is being played and will be on T.V.

The alert ended this morning at about 6:30. I heard the sirens go off just as I was falling asleep. The last thought I had before going into my trance was that I'd better call work and ask for the day off. It's 10:30 PM right now so they apparently got by without me. And here I thought I was indispensable.

As I expected the base went slightly berserk when they were turned loose on civilization once more. A few of them over did it and as a result the base club will probably be closed permanently. It seems that two of the lads, their courage and tempers sharpened with red eyes got into a brawl at the club. It came to a resounding climax when the guy who was taking the beating used a small boulder to massage the scalp of his adversary. According to what I was told a few minutes ago, he will live, but just make it. Good clean fun.

I've been on the phone trying to get in touch with the mail clerk. It bothers me to think that there is probably a letter waiting in my mail box and I'll have to wait 'til morning to get it.

Sixty two more days to "C" day. "C" stands for Carol, naturally. I expect the time to pass quickly between now and the middle of August but the last couple of weeks will probably crawl by. I remember how time dragged during my last couple of weeks overseas and I wasn't looking forward to coming home then as much as I am now. Occasionally I experience that funny feeling of telling myself that it's going to really happen—that I'll be in Chicago with you—that you'll be there. That's when I get so nervous my knees nearly knock.

Do you like Dixieland music? I'm somewhat of a fanatic for it myself, having been completely indoctrinated when I was stationed near New Orleans. There is a place in Chicago that I used to frequent quite often before my death and resurrection as airman. If you like that type of music we'll drop in there some evening. If not, you can just sit and talk while I look and listen. Hmm, my ideas are getting better all the time.

Chris just came in and insisted that I drive him to town for a drink. He's loaded so I'd better comply to keep the peace.

Love,
Mick

POSTMARK: JULY 21, 1954
Tuesday night

Dear Carol,

I just finished the worst week I have ever spent in the A.F. I have been up to my ears in trouble because I picked the wrong place to stop for a beer. Last Wednesday, after playing golf, I stopped at the golf course bar, ordered a beer, minded my own business and had the misfortune to be there when an A/2C and a 1st lieutenant got into a fight. Both of them were drunk and were fighting over some silly insult. The A/2C won the fight but it's a costly victory. Probably a couple years at hard labor. The officer is being thrown out of the AF. (That's bad!) Where do I come in? I was a witness and I also worked with the investigating officer in getting statements from everyone who was there. Friday I was ordered down to McChord Field near Seattle. I was grilled and regrilled by a couple of Majors 'til we were both blue in the face. They thought I was lying and making my story favor the enlisted man in an attempt to make things look bad for the officer. It's a pretty good idea but it's not true. The trial should be coming up any time now and I'll be going back to McChord to appear as a witness. What a mess. The lieutenant has a long record of "goofing" and the A/2C is quite an 8 ball too, but I really feel sorry for the guy. He's a cinch for two or maybe longer because there is an iron rule in the service. You don't hit an officer under any circumstances. Even if he throws the first punch he isn't to be hit. As I expected, the brass hats are trying to put all the blame on the airman and get the officer, who was really at fault, off as lightly as possible. Some of us have started a little movement that has been gaining quite a bit of backing. We're collecting money to hire a good civilian lawyer to defend our boy. It's a cinch that if the AF assigns a lawyer he won't have a chance but there is a local lawyer who spent a lot of time in the service and after getting all the facts, feels that he can get him off with a light sentence, and with luck and some good officers on the court martial board, possibly with a suspended sentence. Everyone I've talked to has thrown in five dollars or more so I think we'll have enough to hire this guy. If this doesn't help and the officer gets slight punishment and the airman gets racked, then we are going to start a wave of letter writing and some of the master sergeants are prepared to resign from the service in protest. This business of officers being treated as gods and getting away with murder has got to come to a screeching halt and this could be just the thing to start it.

It does seem a little amazing that all we have left is six weeks but even that is too long. At the usual bull sessions in the mess hall there are always some jokers who pipe up with "two more months to discharge" and then they gloat. Chris usually asks me how many more days and I give him the latest count. Everyone knows that I'm far from my discharge date so they can't figure out what I'm counting days for. Poor fools.

Chris came up with a suggestion a few days ago and got a shoe thrown at his head for it. Since he's getting discharged in September he thought we should leave here together, take a train to Las Vegas, win a fortune at poker and continue on. He was serious. When I declined he decided to try his luck anyway so he'll probably be stopping in Chicago to mooch a free meal after he loses his shirt. I'm trying to talk him out of it but he's the most obstinate little runt I've ever seen. He's saved enough to get a marriage started but now that he and his girl are through he wants to have a fling. Since he's made up his mind I'm trying to teach him a little about blackjack. He's such a wild player and that type usually goes broke fast but if he listens to me he won't go broke quite as fast.

Of course your going on dates doesn't bother me. Every time I read about one of your dates I get so happy I run to the nearest bar and drink a toast. "May he soon see Indo China."

Love,
Mick

Carol's "dates" seemed as enthusiastic as Mike to win her newly available hand. According to her diary, on July 10 Carol received a marriage proposal from "Johnny," on July 15, another one from "Ron," and "J.T." popped the question on the 16. Carol wrote in her diary that night: "That makes proposal #3 in the same week. Must be the full moon." Mike might have beaten them to it in his mid-April letter, but he had plenty of competitors, and they had the advantage of being in Chicago.

In the next letter, Bob is Mom's brother, and "the country" is very possibly Bohner's Lake, Wisconsin, the location described twenty-five years later in Dad's "November Farewell" column.

POSTMARK: JULY 22, 1954
Wednesday

Dear Carol,
About twenty minutes ago I walked into my room, after spending the day in Vancouver, and as I had hoped there was a letter on my desk. I had told the mail clerk to drop my mail in my room in case I didn't return early enough to get it myself.

Early this morning Chris and I talked our way into the day off using plain laziness as an excuse. Since we can play golf any time, we decided to do something different so we went to Vancouver, went sightseeing, didn't even have one beer, rented a motor boat and made like sailors all afternoon. We happened to find a place called Deep Cove. It's an ocean inlet surrounded by high wall like cliffs which in turn are surrounded by mountains. There are a few islands sticking up here and there but we found no treasures. We spent the afternoon putting from island to island 'til I felt like Tom Sawyer, then I knew it was time to quit.

After reading your letter I was struck by the similarity of our day's activities. While I was out in the boat you were probably still in the country with Bob. Along the cove there were a few cottages. What seclusion! The cliffs and mountains make roads impossible so they have to go by boat to reach their summer homes. One of them had some kind of party going on along the shore and naturally I could see us in that setting. Chris even started throwing some digs with his usual ability to read my mind but the threat of a dunking quieted him.

Always said Bob was a genius but his suggestion is too good to come true. Nothing that wonderful could materialize. You must have been kidding when you asked me what I thought of the idea. I reiterate: The more time I spend with you the happier I'll be. Anything that makes spending just a few extra hours with you possible is a wonderful idea.

I've checked the transportation schedule, so I know exactly when I'll arrive in Chicago—to the minute. Now when I figure up the remaining time I can get it right down to hours and minutes.

I'm having a hard time writing this. I keep reading your letter, dreaming about Bob's idea and the time is flying by. More investigation headaches tomorrow.

Love,

Mick

KP refers to kitchen patrol, which, as Mike says, was universally despised by servicemen. These days, the tasks of KP are largely handled by outside contractors. C.O. refers to Mike's commanding officer.

Sunday

Dear Carol,

Never have I spent a more miserable week as this last one. It has really stopped raining and started pouring. My troubles are as follows. Four days of K.P. A car accident. A new C.O. who is a disciplinary maniac. And the crowning blow—I stand a good chance of getting transferred to a station atop a desolate mountain in Oregon.

I went on K.P. Wednesday, worked 16 hours a day each of the four days, was restricted to the base today because my room wasn't ready for inspection yesterday. This new C.O. we've got is strictly a soldier of the old school. Spit and polish and all that stuff.

Thursday night I had my car parked outside a bar in Blaine, a drunk nearly tore off one of my fenders, dented the side and the idiot doesn't have any insurance. I'll have a fine time collecting the repair costs from him.

Yesterday I received a phone call informing me that a new radar site in Oregon was direly in need of experienced radio operators and I was being considered for a transfer. I don't object to the transfer but if it happens to come through about the time my leave comes due, the leave will be cancelled. That I couldn't take. I haven't decided what I'll do about it but I'll do something. When I first came in the AF they told me that my obligation to the service comes before anything else. We disagree. Right now my leave comes before anything else. Especially the AF. I've got your pictures propped up on my desk, I've just reread your last letter. They aren't preventing me from going to Chicago in September. If I transfer it will be another 3 or 4 months before I can take a leave. I can't wait that long. If I go AWOL for three weeks the most they can do is take one of my stripes. It will be well worth it. I'm going to explain the necessity of a leave to some of the people here and if they don't cooperate I'll just depart when the time comes. I don't want any arguments out of you. We have been planning those three weeks far too long to let the Air Force ruin everything now. All I've thought of for months is getting to Chicago and being with you. Now with less then six weeks left I'm not letting a transfer interfere. For once the AF is going to have to take a back seat. You come first despite anything to the contrary these idiots say. No matter what happens I'll be in Chi. In the magic month of September.

The only good thing that's happened lately is the progress being made in the defense of our officer-punching airman. It looks like he's getting off light. The court martial hasn't started yet but the lawyer has promised him that he'd get him a light sentence. He can't possibly get off scot free but he'll get a pretty soft deal. Considering what we're paying the lawyer he should get a short sentence.

It's been over a week since I've written but things have been so confused I haven't been able to get my thoughts unwound enough to write. While I was on KP I just barely made it to my room after I finished. KP is probably the most hated job in the service and I share the sentiment completely. Sixteen hours of washing dishes, pots, pans, floors, windows, and walls is definitely not my idea of fun. Just a few short weeks and I'll be able to forget all this for a while.

How about checking on the schedule of the boat that makes the Chicago-Milwaukee cruise? I must have spent 4 hours dancing with you on that boat while I had my hands full of greasy pots. If I didn't have you to think about, the AF would be too much for me. Whenever I really get peeved I just look at your pictures, read a few of your letters and remind myself that I'm luckier than about a billion other guys. You're wonderful and I'm the luckiest guy in the world because I love you.

Mick

"MYMTICS" is written twice on the August 2 envelope, and apparently appeared in the letter Mike received several days later.

POSTMARK: AUGUST 6, 1954
Wednesday

Dear Carol,

I was just confronted with an empty mail box for the third successive day. What can I say? Naturally there has to be a reason for your not writing. I've tried to determine what could be the cause and though

I've got a few general theories, it's the deeper possibilities that have been disturbing me. I've eliminated the possibilities of your being sick, because unless you were mortally ill I think you would have written. That leaves a few more items for thought. 1. You're mad; 2. Your feelings are hurt; 3. Indifference.

The first two would go hand in hand. If your feelings are hurt because of the latest lapse in my letters then undoubtedly you would also become angry and the natural reaction when hurt is to return the hurt and not writing would be a form of punishment that would be an automatic success. If you think that not receiving one of your letters for three days can make me unhappy, can make the days drag, keep me awake half the night, create a feeling of worry and sometimes even panic, then you are absolutely right. If I thought that a lack of letters on my part could make anyone feel as I have for the last few days, it would frighten me. I don't want to have the power to hurt anyone that badly. My feelings aren't hurt. I'm not angry. It's closer to a feeling of emptiness. I think I know how a person feels when they are stuck on a deserted island. If you're angry, I would have much preferred being told off. You probably realize that. The fact that you don't feel the way I do and probably never will is a very old, old story. It's happened thousands of times. I'm prepared for that—nearly expect it. If fate had it that you not only didn't feel love but that you should hate me, I could even bear that. Indifference is the most frightening possibility of all. I could bear anything but that. If I thought that you hadn't been writing because you were unconcerned, didn't care if you ever wrote again or received a letter again, if I thought that and was sure it was the reason, then I could be marked off as an empty life. Suicide would be too easy. It would be a great deal more miserable to go through life exposed to your indifference.

Why can't people foresee the future? It would make life a lot simpler. Then again it would be a lot duller. If I could look ahead one day I'd be happy. Then I'd know if I were going to receive a letter. I guess it took something like this to make me realize how big a part of my life your letters have become. I've never had three days drag by so slowly—and so unhappily. The power, a definite concrete power that you could exert on me if you wanted to is unfair. No human should have that influence on another. But it's there and I've got to live with it.

If this was meant as a punishment, then write. If you've discovered that my letters, the way I feel, mean nothing, then silence will be the best indication.

Love,

Mick

In 1954, the US military was constructing the Mt. Hebo radar station, part of the cold war–era air defense system. Located ten miles from the Pacific coast in Oregon, the 3,100-foot summit of Mt. Hebo was known for cold, nasty weather. It was deactivated in 1980.

POSTMARK: AUGUST 13, 1954

Thursday

Dear Carol,

What is meant by "MYMTICS"? Rather than tear this up and start over, I may as well say that as I wrote that first sentence, it hit me. For days I've been going over those letters when just like that they fell into place. I must be right because they work out perfectly. I just had the great pleasure of marking a couple more days off the calendar. Three weeks, just three short weeks. I hope no one is around the first second we're together. All these letters—all these words—all these months, and for me, years, of dreaming. When that moment arrives there will be no writing, talking, or dreaming. It seems a bit unreal. It was just a dream for so long, then a far off hope, but now, now when I tell myself, "You lucky sap—it's for real," I feel like I'm sitting right smack on top of the world and I want to laugh at everyone and everything. I can't describe how happy, absolutely happy I feel. No one, nothing, could make me mad. The whole world is wonderful. When Columbus saw land, the Wrights flew, they couldn't have felt any better—better! What kind of word is that! They couldn't have felt as enraptured, as blissful as I do. If I sound like I'm drunk it's because I feel like I've been drinking, but I haven't had a drink.

Everything has been working out perfectly. I'm not being transferred.

The officer I work for got a bit rough when I started the ball rolling to collect money for a good lawyer for the kid who had the fight with the stupid lieutenant, but when it looked like I might get transferred, he changed his attitude completely and intervened. The chances of a transfer have died. I would have gone to Mt. Hebo in Oregon and from what I heard, it is no picnic. In my desk I have a set of orders authorizing me 21 days leave. They were given to me today. I keep taking them out and looking at them. Then I look at your picture. Then I read one of your letters. Then I want to jump in the air and click my heels. It's just too great! These lads you've been dating had better heed your words and stay away for three weeks. I could be dangerous.

How can I be reassuring about the time that's going to follow my leave? I've tried to put it out of my thoughts and I didn't think you were worrying about it. The only solace I can offer is that those 21 days will be so fine, I'm sure they will, that we'll have enough memories to last us 'til my next leave. I can say that, but I know I'll be completely miserable. I'm trying to forget that the three weeks will end. Nothing can ruin my thoughts as completely as the thought of waiting months and months again. If I could be with you always—but this will just lead to another proposal and I guess you've had enough of those lately.

I don't mind all your dates proposing. It just reaffirms my belief that you are the most perfect girl that ever lived. But, I don't want to see their miserable faces while I'm home. Just keep turning them down with an emphatic no and I'll be satisfied.

I'll try to write more often. I should, and I'm being selfish in receiving so many letters and writing so few. Oh, three weeks of being able to say things to you rather than wrestle with a pen and feel that I'm not putting what I feel into words.

Miss you more than I can say. Is that what it meant? Can you possibly imagine what you saying that means to me? I'm not a person easily swayed by words and for a long time, out of disappointment, I developed an emotional veneer against anything that had any traces of sentimentality. Now, one little word from you can melt me. The writers of the dictionary are foolish enough to try to define love. It can't be done.

The way I feel defies all definition and explanation. When I say I love you, what I feel is, without you, there is nothing. Everything would be a meaningless void.

I wish I knew a pretty poem or quotation to close with but I'm at a loss.
Yours forever,
Mick

POSTMARK: AUGUST 16, 1954

Dear Carol,
Let's get a few things straight right now. I'm coming home. Nothing could stop me. Right now it looks like nothing will arise to prevent a leave but if it did I'd be home anyway.

You wrote something that hurt. It hurt me very much. My "undying love and affection." The way you said it made it sound very trite and very doubtful. Right now I'm willing to give up anything, anyone, do anything, all because I'm foolish enough to think I stand a chance. I'm in a wonderful situation. I'm crazy about a person who is thousands of miles away, I'll see you twice in the next year and a half, I haven't got one iota of assurance to base any future hopes on, but you doubt the way I feel. Let's face it, there is no reason to believe you'll ever feel any differently than you do now. I'm a kid you grew up with. It's nice to know that I feel the way I do—everyone likes to be loved. I exposed my feelings at a critical time in your life, a time when such a feeling as mine could serve as a balm. But the rub is there—all the love is one sided. When you wrote that letter you must have forgot that. My whole future hinges on you. I'm 22, have yet to establish any place in life, and I'm chasing a rainbow. If I go right out of your life it won't be more than a momentary feeling of loss, if that much. You are my life. Do you think that when I don't write I'm out having a big party, my mind free? I've never been so emotionally messed up. When you were married it wasn't quite as turbulent. I accepted defeat because I had never made an effort, never experienced a rebuff, never made my hopes known. Now, do you think it's easy to face the possibility of failure? It doesn't make sense, your doubting me.

I've told you time after time how I feel. I love you. Shall I say it again? I love you. That letter, it's right in front of me, has knocked me for a loop. For the first time in months I was feeling great for more than a short period. That's over. I feel let down. Only seventeen more days and now more confusion. It just doesn't make sense. I'm the one with the genuine, concrete reasons to worry. Right now, in the eyes of society and the law, you're married. When you get your divorce I'll still be out here. In the meantime, you go on dates, meet other guys, my chances fall. I can't build up my own hopes. Even if I was home, out of the service, I might not be able to compete. You write about your dates. Sure, you think of me when you're out with someone else, but that doesn't lessen the possibility of someone else coming along. I've never mentioned your dates. I have no right to, but I'll tell you now, every time I read about one of them, it tears me apart. I've got a lot to look forward to. You could meet someone, I'm in the cold. Good old Mick, he'll get over it. That's the big trouble—I won't. After you there's nothing.

I hope the dinner and stage play wasn't a complete failure. That was Saturday night wasn't it? I stayed in Saturday night. Around here there are three things to do on a Saturday night. Go on a date, see a movie, or get drunk. I haven't been dating, I've knocked off drinking, and the movies bore me. I decided to stay in my room and read. I started out with Emerson and ended up with all the letters I've received from you. It was one of the nicest Saturdays I've spent in the service. If I had realized that my "undying love and affection" was on trial, being doubted, I would have probably written a letter instead of reading yours.

Look baby, why do we have to make each other so miserable with such a short time to go? Right now I want to hold you so badly I could drive my fist through a wall.

I don't know when I'll write again. The letter I received has got me confused. I'm still trying to figure out what's happening. Tell Mable to keep her dark thoughts to herself. Damn, people I don't even know are making things tough.

I hope you didn't write Saturday or Sunday. If you did, the letters will sound like they did today. My own doubts are so great that when you start wondering if I'm sincere or not—I don't know. What do you think I am? That just occurred to me. If you doubt that I really love you, then what kind of person do I appear to be in your mind? If I try to conjure a picture of a person who would say all I've said and not mean it I wind up with something bearing a striking resemblance to a snake. Carol, don't ever doubt me. I've asked you that so often, I've told you that I love you repeatedly, and now doubt appears.

I don't know what to say. I'm not lyrical or poetic—Sometimes I must sound pretty stupid. I think I'll go get drunk.

Love,
Mick

Sunday

Dear Carol,

If I didn't know you I wouldn't believe that anyone could be so perfect. Some people go through life with a hazy picture of their "dream girl" in their mind, never seeing her, never believing that they'll find her. I'm unique. My dream girl, the girl who is my personal consolation of all the fine things I've seen in people is real and I'll be with her in days, just a few days.

How can I forgive you for anything? You were right. My not writing isn't a display of the way I feel. It was just that your saying it hurt. I'll never tear up that letter though. I couldn't destroy anything you've written.

I've had your letter with me for the last two days. I've read it a hundred times. I mean it. It must have been at least a hundred times. It's sort of dazed me. You know how I feel so you can imagine how your letter affected me. Carol, to me the future without you is no future at all. Life wouldn't have any meaning. Anything I accomplished would be worthless, I'd have no incentive. I can understand why so many men have joined the Foreign Legion because of a woman. That probably sounds silly but believe me, I don't know what I would do without you. I wouldn't join the Foreign Legion of course but I doubt if I'd ever return to Chicago.

So much misunderstanding, so many misinterpretations can result from letters. I want to be with you. I want to be able to say what I think and I want to hold you in my arms. That day I walked down Central Ave. I felt that I was leaving my whole life behind me. All the time we sat and talked that day and especially when you saw me to the door I had to keep reminding myself that you were married and that I was seeing you for the last time. I never expected to see you again and if your marriage had worked out, I would have lived up to what amounted to a personal vow. Never to see you again—that seems too awful to try to imagine.

I'll be home on the 2nd. I'm not sure if I'll be there in time to pick you up at work but if I'm not, don't leave your house for a split second. I'm stopping at home just long enough to get the car. In eleven days I'll see you. I'll be with you. I can hardly believe it. I won't believe it 'til it happens.

The wonderful picture of coming home, having you waiting for me—It's too much. I can't let myself have such dreams. Carol, someday when all the present complications are surmounted, I'm going to propose again. I won't ask you to marry me until I'm sure that any answer I'd receive would be definite. If you say yes, then I'll devote my life to making you happy. How can I describe the thought of having you for my wife? Happiness isn't an adequate word. It would be more than being happy. It would be like having light after complete darkness. I know we'd be happy. I love you so very much.

In eleven days I'm going to take you in my arms and tell you I love you. I'm going to say it the first time I'm with you, be it on your front porch or in Doc Marks's office. I'm going to say it over and over again for twenty one days. I'm going to say it so often you'll never forget it. And all the while I'll be hoping that some day you'll feel the same. I've got to not only hope that you will but also believe that you will. It's like having faith in something. Without having faith and belief in something you want badly, you'll never have it.

It's getting late. The days are starting to pass so slowly but I know that in just a few more days—

I love you,

Mick

In 1952, the Mills Brothers had a hit with "Be My Life's Companion," which included the lyric "Be my life's companion and you'll never grow old." Mike also quotes "September Song" and Irving Berlin's song "Always," which, by 1954, had already been recorded by many artists.

POSTMARK: AUGUST 24, 1954
Monday

Dear Carol,

It's 11:30 and I've just given the "heave ho" to tonight's discussion panel. Near the end of the month when everyone is broke they usually converge on my room for an evening of hot air. After hashing out the problems of the world, the subject of the pictures on my wall came up for discussion. As usual, my stony silence was met with theories of assorted types as to who you are. One lad in an infrequent burst of intellectual brilliance mentioned the very truthful adage that opposites attract and therefore I'd have to have a beautiful girl. Sitting there listening to all this talk made me feel that it was all a waste of time so I threw them out. Now I feel that I'm talking to you. The radio is on and the Mills Brothers are suggesting that someone become their life's companion so that they can all have ever lasting youth. Great idea.

This evening, just as I left the mess hall, the loud speaker boomed out my name and said that I had a long distance phone call at the switchboard. Long distance calls and telegrams—they both scare me to blazes. As I dashed to the nearest phone I had all sorts of wild thoughts. Someone died—some emergency—It was my Aunt Pauline. She and my cousin Gloria are in Seattle. My cousin Glo is taking a plane to Alaska to join her husband who is in the navy. They wanted me to drive down for the evening but unfortunately my car has been acting up and wouldn't make the trip so I had to be satisfied with three minutes of one sided conversation. If you noticed, my Aunt has a way of talking endlessly, occasionally asking a question and immediately answering it for you. I seem to be her favorite nephew and that surprised me since she hasn't given me a chance to say more than a few words in years. Maybe that's why she likes me. As a matter of fact she's my favorite aunt but only because she's the best poker player in the family.

Did you say that you can't tango? Eleanor once accused me of worrying about minor details too often. She might be right. This evening for some reason I began worrying about the possibility arising of a tango playing and my inability to do that dance coming to light. That's crazy, I know, and if it was some other girl I wouldn't care if I mutilated her instep, but when it's you—I worry.

Ah, these long days and evenings. Isn't that part of the lyrics? And the days grow long as we reach September? I hope the time passes this slowly when I'm with you but I'm afraid it won't. I remember that time always passed very quickly—too quickly—when I was with you. It doesn't seem fair. Right now, when I'm unhappy because I'm here and you're there the minutes tick by at a creep, but when the most important three weeks of my life become a reality it will pass like the snap of my fingers.

My good old reliable radio. I can always count on it to play the most fitting music. Right now I'm hearing the song that's always been my favorite and has become more so of late. I'll be loving you, always.

It's after midnight so it's less than ten full days to go. How long ago did you send me that little picture story? It doesn't seem like more that a few weeks ago. I'll keep that set of pictures as long as I live. It was great.

New song—My Wonderful Girl. I think that's the perfect song to say goodnight to.

Goodnight, Wonderful

Mick

Carol's diary, September 2: "My baby came home at last. We're in each other's arms. I love him very very much. Ecstasy!"

"My darling, as soon as possible be with me again."

Carol's diary, September 21: "Mick left today. Pa R. [Mike's father] took us to the station in a cab. We kissed good bye and held back the tears. One of worst days in my life."

On leave in September, Mike proposed and Carol accepted, but her agreement to become his wife did little to calm his insecurities. If anything, to have his dream within reach yet not yet assured seemed to make him, if anything, more terrified of losing her—and this phase begins with four letters written in one day.

Thursday Sept. 23

10:00

Hi Sweetheart,

I'm sitting in the station in Seattle waiting for the train to take me on the last lap of this unhappy trip. My blues have subsided enough so that I'm able to think of you without having to choke back a very unmanly fit of tears. Oh my babe, I miss you. When you turned and waved at the station I couldn't move. If I had raised my arm it would have been enough to make me pick up my bag and call this trip off. I watched you walk away 'til I couldn't see you, then I wiped the few tears that couldn't be suppressed and boarded the train. I sat and stared out the window and tried to follow your progress home in my mind. I felt more lost and alone then ever before in my life. My baby, these separations are too painful. While sitting there I realized that we have lost our individuality. I'm no longer one person. When I'm away from you I'm only half complete. Being "me" no longer is enough. It's got to be "us" or nothing at all. As long as I'm away from you I'll be as unhappy as a person can be. I fell asleep on the train and had a dream in which I was kissing you. My family was there and seemed quite happy about it. I awoke and felt so empty and alone that I nearly cried. Honey I feel so lonely. This station is full of people but I'm completely alone. I swear that after I'm out of the service I'll never be away from you again. It's too painful. Did you cry when you left me? The mail room will be closed when I return to the base tonight so I won't be able to get your letter. Instead I'll sit and write. My darling, I'm not going to let a day pass without talking to you, without telling you how much I love you. I think of you constantly. I went to the dining car and the fellow across from me started a conversation. For a brief moment my thoughts were diverted, then the waiter brought me my black coffee and I couldn't talk, I became so choked with longing for you. I must have been a pathetic sight because the guy didn't say another word.

Baby, will you think I'm unmanly if I tell you that right now there are tears in my eyes? In my hand there is a handkerchief smudged with your lipstick and some of my tears. I'm going to carry that handkerchief with me until you're here in Seattle. You told me how painful it is to hold back the desire to cry. Now I know. Oh I love you so, honey. God, there is such misery.

There is a long row of phone booths about 50 feet from me. If I had a few more dollars I'd be on the phone talking to you. It is 1:25 in Chicago. To be with you, to hold you and kiss you.

All during the ride I thought of everything we did together. Running out of gas, sitting on El's back porch, sleeping with you in my arms my last night home. What sweet memories. My darling, as soon as possible be with me again. Nothing has any meaning, the world is empty without you. Life is too short to spend away from you. Write often. Tell me you love me. I can't hear that often enough. I love you so much that if I lost you all that would remain is death. Leaving you made me realize that I couldn't live without you. Death would be more meaningful than life.

Goodbye for a little while baby. Once more I'm 2000 miles away with my love for you as my only companion. I love you, I love you, I love you.

Mick

Carol was Lutheran. Before and after this period, Mike was an atheist, but for a brief moment, he seemed to be a believer.

POSTMARK: SEPTEMBER 23, 1954

Thursday

Sept. 23

A little later

Hi Honey,

Forty minutes ago I mailed a letter and if this arrived with it I hope you read that one first. After I mailed it I noticed that I had two hours to wait for my train, telephones handy, and some change so I called up the marriage bureau and checked with them. Baby, we can be married as soon as you get off the plane. No blood test required. I can get the marriage license, mail it to you, you fill out your part in the presence of a notary public, mail it back to me and that's it. As soon as you arrive, we're off to a Lutheran church for the ceremonies. When I get to Blaine I'll check with some Seattle boys and find a nice place for a honeymoon. I feel better now that I've started making plans and got something accomplished. There must be a quiet lake nearby, with a cozy cabin and a lot of solitude that doesn't cost lots of money. This isn't the vacation season so that shouldn't be difficult to find. Oh my sweet, how I'm longing for you and the day you'll arrive. I'm going to have everything prepared so that everything is as perfect as can be. My darling it will be the most perfect week two people ever had together. Honey, you caused me to have more ambition and determination than I thought possible. I've got a rough draft of my request for transfer prepared and when I return to the base I'll complete it. I'll make it so eloquent that it will melt their hearts. If they don't transfer me it won't be because I didn't try. I'll try to keep as busy during the next six weeks as possible in order to keep time passing rapidly. I'll clean my room top to bottom, work my head off on KP, write every day, and even more than once a day, tell you I love you over and over again and reassure myself that you'll soon be here. Oh my honey I love you, miss you, and long to be with you so badly that I feel like I'm going to bust. I won't be happy for one second of the days that separate us but I'll be able to face them because I know that you'll soon be with me. Just think hon, the next time we're together will be as man and wife. Baby, how I long for that moment. Within two months we'll be married. My darling, the dream I've been dreaming will be true. I love you so. When you step off that plane I'll be the happiest guy in the world. Right now despite the many miles separating us, I'm the luckiest guy in the world. I'm loved by the sweetest, most beautiful, gentle, kindest, perfect person there is and my flippant attitude towards religion is gone. I feel like getting down on my knees and thanking God for giving you to me. I'll thank him anyway without being on my knees and I'll thank you for being so perfect. And I'll thank you for giving me a chance at happiness. Oh how brave we were at the station, both of us smiling and talking about the six little weeks. If you felt as sad as I did then we were sad enough to be in tears.

Honey, my train is leaving pretty soon and I want to get something to eat so I'll close now. Write and love me. I love you with all my heart.

Mick

Gus was Eleanor's first husband.

If it is not clear what the sources are for the money Mike was gathering, it is clear that he was scrimping for every cent he could find.

In 1954, the Illinois US senators were (Democrat) Paul H. Douglas and (Republican) Everett M. Dirksen.

POSTMARK: SEPTEMBER 23, 1954

Thursday

September 23rd

My Darling,

I walked into my room ten minutes ago, sat down to write and all the grief and misery I have felt for the last two days came pouring out in the form of tears. For the second time since my childhood I have cried. I'm not ashamed to admit it. I've been sitting here and crying and I'm still at it. Oh to hold you in my arms. This room is so empty and I feel alone. I've never felt so completely disattached from the world. I should be telling you what my trip was like, what I've been doing but all I can think of is how I miss you. I love you so my honey, it actually hurts. I feel a pain inside that won't end 'til I'm with you. Baby I want to get up and walk out of here and take the first plane out for Chicago. My God, I don't know if I'll be able to stand a long separation from you. I'm nearly out of my mind with longing for you. To hold you in my arms, kiss you, just to have you near. My baby I'm trembling so I can barely write. It's raining very hard, the wind is blowing and I feel as though the world has ended. Nothing matters to me now that we're apart. I'd do anything, give anything to have you with me. Why won't these tears stop. I feel as tho I'm going to crack up. I'm shaking and crying—I just can't stop. I've been walking around the room. I don't know if I'll mail this. I must sound crazy but I feel a little crazy. I can't stand being away from you. I'll be in the hospital if I don't get over this. Write me every day honey, tell me you love me over and over. Fly to me and marry me. I've got to be with you. Oh honey honey honey I'll never take a long separation.

It's been a half hour since I wrote that last line. I've been lying on my bunk trying to get calmed down. I don't remember ever feeling like that before. I thought I was going out of my mind. All I could think of was that I'm away from you and I can't stand it. I've got to stand it. We want that house. Oh babe, it is going to cost more than money, that house. It's going to cost me much more than money. It's going to cost me grief and tears and the endless pain of being away from you. No one has ever loved anyone more than I love you. I'll do anything—everything; to make you happy. You're all there is for me in life. I love you so. I found my ID bracelet. It was among the clothes I packed. I found it a minute ago when I yanked everything from my bag. I felt so relieved when I saw it. I'll kiss the picture inside it goodnight every night.

I figured out why my bond hasn't arrived. It will come next month. It will be worth $75 and I'll also send $40 of my pay. I don't think anyone can cash the bond so send it to me—I'll cash it and send you the money. That plus the 40 plus the 50 plus the 30 should cover transportation. I'll have my November pay and whatever I'll have to borrow from Gus to take care of the wedding and our honeymoon. I found out what your allotment will be each month. $137.10. I'm going to let the bond continue in effect. That will mean $400 by the time I get discharged. Of course if I take a leave part of it will go for transportation but it will still help. Baby, pray every night that I'll be transferred. I pray too. For the first time since I was very small. I'll pray and I'll mean every word of it. God, I miss you. My sweetheart, how I love you.

As soon as Dr. Marks' statement arrives I'll complete mine and submit the entire request. If the AF has any kindness, I hope they display it for me. I'll try as hard as possible. If they turn me down, I'm going to write to Senator Douglas and Senator Dickson. I have nothing to lose and everything to gain. I may become unpopular with the officers but I don't give a damn. I want to be near you. I've got a better idea. If I get turned down I'll have Eleanor and Dorothy write the two Senators. It's a long shot but it might work.

When I stepped off the train today I felt as if I was condemned to a living death. I took a cab to the base, went to the mess hall, ate, walked into the drab emptiness of this room and broke down. For a moment it was more than I could take. The thought of spending most of the next 18 months in this room became terrifying. Oh my sweet, you can't realize the loneliness I'll endure. There is no one here I can talk to, no one I can sit and tell my problems to. A person needs an outlet. You have your family. I'm wrong. I have my pen and paper. How foolish of me. I have you. You, my own personal goddess.

I'm going to get my room straightened up and try to sleep. I probably won't be able to but I'll try because I want to be fresh when I start the transfer campaign rolling. Goodnight my darling. I just close my eyes and see you in our bed, the pillow hugged to you, Otsie protecting you, and I feel a little better. I miss you so my babe. It's 38 days 'til November first. I'll miss you more each day.

Sweet dreams

I love you honey

Mick

Though Mike never specifies, it is likely the song he refers to is Johnny Mercer's "Dream," which had been a hit in 1945 for both the Pied Pipers and Frank Sinatra.

POSTMARK: SEPTEMBER [POSTMARK SMUDGED]

Hi Wonderful,

It's still Thursday but it's getting late. After finishing my last letter, putting it in the envelope, addressing, stamping, I cleaned up my room, took a shower and now I'm all set for bed. I'm going to try something new. I'll start my letter before I turn in at night, say good morning when I awake and write a little each time I come in my room. At night I'll finish it and start a new one before I turn in. Sound OK? Baby, I love you. I'm going to turn out the light in a minute and pray that our dreams will become our reality. I'll smoke a cigarette, open my bracelet, kiss you good night and pray that you'll always love me. That's my hope for life. Goodnight my sweet. The radio just started Hernando's Hideaway. Until morning when I'll kiss you and say good morning. Goodnight Honey.—

I can't sleep Baby. They're playing the "Dream" song. I've got to talk to you, be it only with a pen. Oh baby, I miss you so badly. Don't ever stop loving me honey. Just like in the song, I've opened my eyes and you aren't here. Oh honey, be with me soon. Goodnight this time. I love you my wife. Sweet dreams—

It's 6:15 AM—First thing I did when I woke was say good morning to your picture. Seems funny not having Chris stomping around. Slept a little late so I'll have to run to make breakfast. Good morning my baby. I'll be on pins and needles 'til that mail room opens. See you in a little while.

Hi babe, it's 8:15 and I'm on my coffee break. I picked up my mail a little while ago and I was happy to hear that it's a cold winter. I'll be getting another letter today since the one I just read arrived here yesterday. Oh babe I am very very glad the winter will be cold. Everyone seemed happy to see me back. The C.O. said "welcome home." I saluted and said "home hell! I just left home." He thought I was joking. Back to work now. They allowed everything to pile up—'til lunch Hon.

Hi Babe. This system of writing is great. Every time I walk into the room I jot down a few lines and that way I feel that I'm talking to you throughout the whole day. I'm on my lunch hour now and I don't have to go back to work this afternoon. Chris left the room in a shambles and it will take a whole afternoon to get it cleaned up so I was given the afternoon off for that purpose. In fact I don't have to return to work 'til Monday morning. That doesn't mean much to me because there isn't anything to do. I may take in a movie but that will be all. Honey, being away from you is like being dead. It's just an empty existence while waiting for the only thing that creates happiness for me—being with you. The weather has cleared up and the sun is shining brightly. Golf weather. Speaking of golf, the big Air Force tournament has started, rather the selection and submitting of players has started and I was picked as one of the three members from the base to participate. That was OK 'til they told me the tournament will take place in November—early November. Despite the rage of the officer who organized our team I decided there is no time for that sort of thing! I checked my mail before I started writing and there was no letter so I'll have to wait 'til this afternoon.

That's OK. The letter you wrote Tuesday was there this morning so I can wait a few hours. The mess hall will be open for 15 more minutes so I'd better run if I'm going to get something to eat. After I eat I'll come back here, clean up my room and write a bit more. For a few hours then, I love you hon, with all my heart.

Hi Hon, I've finished the cleaning up project and I've got two hours between now and the next mail call. Near me are your pictures, the radio is playing. The song is new but the lyrics are OK. "I just love you, so there can never be anyone else for me." How true that is. We have so many years of happiness ahead of us. For two people to be as much in love as we are is a rare and wonderful thing. In a few weeks we'll be together again. Payday I'll buy the license and send it to you. As soon as your divorce is final, fill it out, have it notarized and return it. Then when you get off the plane we can take our vows. Honey that will be a wonderful moment. I'm going to Seattle before November and get a honeymoon cottage reserved somewhere. I want to spend every minute of our five days with you. When we are asleep I want to be able to touch you every minute of the time. After we are married I'll wait 'til May or June before I take my leave. That is absolutely the limit. That's seven months apart and I can't be away from you any longer than that. During the day it doesn't hurt as much. There are people around. Letters arriving from you. But at night, especially at twilight, is when I get that blue, empty loneliness. It hurts to be away from you darling. The phone rang and they want me to return to work for little while. I'll be back in a little while hon, don't go away— I'll love you always baby.

I'm sitting here in a sort of daze. I've been telling myself to go get something to eat. To calm down—but I can't. Mail call is over and there was no letter. If I had missed a letter later on—but today, my first day back on the base. That hurts, baby. Something must have happened in the postal department. We've got a new mail clerk. Maybe he put it in the wrong box. If he did, I'll break his neck. Please Hon, don't miss writing. I'm trying to get my mind organized. Wednesday was when the letter would have been written if it would arrive today. I'm going to walk

Carol's first wedding day on her eighteenth
birthday, when she became Carol Wozny
and broke Mike's heart, November 21, 1952

above: Mike, with unknown friend, Korea, ca. 1953, before his transfer to Blaine

left: Mike on the day trip to Mt. Baker, Easter 1954. Photo by Don "Chris" Karaiskos.

opposite page: Carol in the early 1950s

Circa 1954:
"Good girl" though
she was, Carol
knew what she had.

right: He coulda
been a cartoonist—
Mike's sketch about
the toils of letter
writing

TUES. MAR 23
YOUR Letter
RED EYE
WED MAR 24
THU MAR 25
BLANK
FRI MAR 26
TWICE AS BLANK
DONT MISS THE CONCLUSION TO THIS EXCITING STORY—TURN THIS PAPER OVER!
SAT APRIL NOW
SUCCESS

A pensive Mike, outside 5408 N. Central on the leave when he proposed

A very happy Mike with Carol, ca. 1954

Living his dream—Mike and Carol, in the Duckman house on Central Avenue, 1954

Newlyweds, ca. 1956—Carol, Mike, Carol's brother Bob, and his new wife (and Mike's niece), Barb, Riverview Park

The tale of the envelopes—
from nightmare to dream come true

over to the mail room, take another look, eat supper, then return to the room and finish this letter. I hope the mail clerk goofed.

He didn't. I just finished supper and I put on a fine exhibition. When I sat down in the mess hall the look on my face told everyone to let me alone. One jerk didn't. He started riding me about how nice it must be to be back in Blaine. By the time I finished with him he had a hot pair of ears. I must have talked for 10 minutes without pausing once. I let him have it with both verbal barrels and when I finished I gagged I was so disgusted with myself. I didn't get a letter so I took it out on that poor farmer. If a letter had arrived I'd be sitting here, happy as could be. Instead I want to crawl into my bunk and sleep 'til mail call tomorrow. That's no good. Sleep was meant to be a rest when a person is tired. When it starts becoming an escape from reality it starts resembling a desire for death. It's amazing isn't it? I'm sitting here in a space 20×10, not a human being in sight, and what another person, over 2000 miles away does or doesn't do can twist me up inside my brain and inside my body so badly that I want to crawl inside a little hole and stay there. Napoleon once said that love was living hell and that a person was blessed if he was free of it. He said that when he received no word from Josephine while he was in Italy and she in France. I just stopped writing for a while. I sat on my bunk, smoked a couple of cigarettes and tried to get my mind and my emotions organized. Honey, answer this question when you write. Do you love me as much now as you did when I was home? That sounds crazy but I've got to know. What about Johnny Hon? I shouldn't admit this but he bothered me while I was home and the thought of him still bothers me. He was the only one of all your dates that didn't have any major flaws. God knows, I've got more that my share of flaws. Honey, being away from you like this has made me realize something quite vividly. I couldn't live without you. Not receiving a letter today clinched it. If I lost you I wouldn't have the courage to go on. I'm not telling you that as a threat the way Larry did and I'm not mentally disbalanced. It's just something I've realized and accepted. If I lost you again then life would be just a continuous feeling of pain and complete unhappiness. To live through something like that would be pointless. I'd kill myself first. Not having a letter today made me want to sleep for the next 20 hours. Losing you for good would bring a desire for eternal sleep. I didn't think anyone could make me feel that way but now I've discovered that it's possible. You're everything. You're my whole world. I love you so much I can't think clearly, my outlook on everything has changed.

I just finished killing an hour watching a fight on television. Just as I was finishing that last paragraph September Song came on the radio. I ran out of the room. I would have got the shakes again if I hadn't got out. When I came back in I did something strictly to kill time. I took all your letters, wrapped them into a bundle and put them into my bottom drawer. Now I'll start a file on all the letters received while we're engaged. After we're married I'll start another file. I'll always keep those letters—as long as I live. You said in your last letter that we are perfect for each other. I think you're right Hon, and that makes us a rare, lucky couple. I love you. I seem to be writing that often. I love you. I love you so much that I can't hold it inside. I've got to keep telling you that. You are my life, baby. If I could hold you in my arms right now, kiss your neck, your cheeks, your eyes, your lips and tell you that I love you. Thirty seven more days and I'll be able to. My darling, if I sound erratic and half crazy in my letters, please, don't worry. As soon as we're together again, I'll be back to normal. When I think of you and look at your pictures I get a pain inside my chest that isn't my imagination. It's possible to love someone so much that it hurts. It's 9:00 PM, Friday night. I pray to God that I'll have a letter tomorrow. If there isn't, I'll call on the phone. For a little while,

Good night my darling, my sweet.

Mick

Mike mentions singing with Carol, which they continued to do together throughout their life together—I happened to tape-record a family Christmas gathering in 1978, the last before Mom's unexpected death, and there they were, singing songs in harmony, with Dad's guitar in accompaniment.

"This Ole House" (Rosemary Clooney, with a prominent bass vocal by Thurl Ravenscroft), "In the Chapel in the Moonlight" (Kitty Kallen), "The Little Shoemaker" (The Gaylords), "Skokiaan"(no fewer than three versions: Ralph Marterie, the Four Lads, and the Bulawayo Sweet Rhythms Band), "I Need You Now" (Eddie Fisher), and "If I Give My Heart to You" (Doris Day) were all in the Billboard Top 20 Best Sellers chart the week of September 25, 1954. The meaning of "DP songs" is unknown to me.

Barb is Mike's niece, Eleanor's daughter.

Si is Simon Babin, a friend.

MYMNTE = Missing You More Now Than Ever.

POSTMARK: SEPTEMBER 26, 1954

Hi Sweetheart,

It's Saturday morning, I just finished breakfast, I'm going to mail the letter that I finished last night and see what the morning mail call holds for me. Last night, after finishing your letter, I crawled into my bunk, not intending to sleep and the next thing I knew, it was morning. I feel good today. I'll be around the base most of the day so I'll write this as the day progresses. There is a football game on TV so that will kill the afternoon. I'll drop Si a line if I have time, but I'll finish up the day by writing to you. I love you babe. When the mail clerk goes in for the mail I'll ride in with him and get it that much earlier. The letter I finished sounded depressed at times but I think you will understand. I miss you so, and not receiving a letter upset me terribly. When you receive this it will be Tuesday, and we will only have 33 days separating us. I'm Mr. lucky himself. Baby I love you so. I'm going to drop the letter off and ride to town on the mail run. I'll see you in a little while Hon.

Hi Doll, I just picked up 2 letters in the mail room. While bolting down my lunch I read the one you wrote Wednesday. Honey, have those two guys you work for get rid of your aches and pains. That bothers me. I've saved the big letter to read while I'm in my room. I'm going to light a cigarette, sit back, and lose myself in your letter.

My sweet, wonderful Gal. How I love you. Baby, remember what I told you. When we're together and something makes you sad or unhappy enough to cause tears, I want you to cry, not locked in another room, but locked in my arms. In all the years we have ahead of us, we can't hide the happy or unhappy emotions from each other.

Your letters have made me feel so much better. This was a very long morning and the only thing that made me feel halfway decent was the knowledge that you will receive some letters today. It's another fine, sunshiny day but all the rain that's fallen in the time I was gone has turned the golf course into a bog. My car is suffering from some mechanical ailments that render it useless, everyone is broke so no one is going anywhere so it looks like I'll have a safe and sane weekend right here on the base. After this weekend, we'll only be separated for five more, then those five wonderful days as man and wife, then————. Well, we won't think about that now. I like this type of letter writing. Instead of trying to describe the way I feel about something hours after experiencing it, I just sit down and write about it then. The pictures are a welcome treat. As usual, you look like a wonderful dream and I completed the "beauty and the beast" motif. I'm going to catch part of a football game on T.V. Ah, in my old frivolous days I would have placed many a wager on the game, but them days is gone forever. (And I couldn't be happier).

Hi Honey. Does it sound kind of goofy for me to keep saying hello so many times in one letter? When I start to write again, it's as if I've been away and suddenly I'm with you again, so bear along with my odd system of letter writing.

I watched most of the football game then I had supper. Had a good time after the meal. I took some wind out of a windbag. While I was gone a new man arrived on the base. It seems that he's a pool shark and a fair golfer. He had beaten one of the fellows I had played golf with out of about $15 in a pool game. He was riding him about it and using his 220 pounds as a bit of insurance while dishing out verbal abuse. He kept asking him to play pool for money and when Welch wouldn't agree he started in on golf. "Let's play for five or haven't you got guts." He kept it up knowing that Welch isn't much of a golfer. He didn't know me from Adam but I had been told what he shot in golf. I'm better. He kept it up 'til finally he got on my nerves so I waited 'til he quieted down for a minute, then I let him have it. I quietly suggested that tomorrow morning we go to the golf course and play for twenty five dollars. Did he choke up. He laughed and tried to make it all a joke but I kept a straight face and asked him if noon was alright for him. Then he started hemming and hawing and making weak excuses, so all the guys at the tables snickered and left, including me. He had a very red face and I felt very good. Now I know what you might be thinking. I shouldn't be betting money like that. Baby, if there was one chance of my losing, I wouldn't have offered the bet. I knew he wouldn't accept. That kind never does. But if he had, it would have meant $25 in our pocket.

I'm going to read your letter again. I can't stop reading it. You're wonderful Honey. Well Babe, I've read it for the umpteenth time and it sounds as sweet and wonderful as if you were standing here talking to me Neuralgia can be unbearable. I can't stand the thought of you experiencing such pain.

I like the way you wrote that—Mr. and Mrs. Michael Royko—that looks good but knowing that you are going to be the Mrs. is what makes it great.

I've been trying to read but all that's available are recently written fiction novels and they have the same types of plots. Romance. I'm the last person who would be against romance, but baby they all sound so shallow and weak. I'd like to write our story. I wonder if it would sell. It's got the ingredients. First we take a boy, a very mixed up boy who has a crush on a girl. The girl has already shown indications of someday being a beautiful woman. Then we take the conflicts. The boy feels inferior and never voices his love. Time passes and someone else appears. The boy accepts this because he is young and the young heal very easily and in the young there is hope. Then one day there is no longer any hope and the new wounds hurt and they don't heal. Then the boy goes to war and he carries with him pictures. Pictures in his bag and pictures in his mind. The pictures in his bag are pretty but the pictures in his mind aren't. Now we have a boy become a man. A broken heart and war can make great changes. He comes back and he hides. He hides from the thing he loves more than anything else. Then one day there is hope again and the hope becomes promise and the promise becomes love and love like theirs can only have one consummation—they lived happily ever after.

So I could write a wonderful love story—if—I were a writer but since I'm not, the world will have to suffer along its way without knowing about us.

I just ran out of GI stationery so I'll have to resort to this. The hit parade is on the radio and the first song played is "Goodnight Sweetheart Goodnight" Memories! Us driving along—you singing and me providing the bass. It was on one of the boulevards that lead out of Logan Square. We make sweet music together honey and I'm not being funny.

Now they are playing "this old house." We were driving somewhere and I thought that your quartet could do this song well. I think you could. I thought that you, Barb and I could make a pretty good arrangement of it. Memories—Nothing can happen without connecting us to it.

Now it's the Chapel in the Moonlight. We may not be married in a chapel honey but it will be in the evening and there will be moonlight and I'll love you always.

Now something to make me laugh. One of the D P songs. The Shoemaker. Oh baby, there is nothing about you that isn't perfect. If they play Skokian? I'll probably laugh out loud. How you disliked those two songs. Baby, I'll learn to hate them.

The song that's playing now doesn't bring back any memories but it does sum up the way I've felt most of the last two days. If I've ever needed you—I need you now. If you get a chance listen to the lyrics. It hits the nail on the head.

Yes honey, if you give your heart to me I'll handle it with care, I'll be true to you, I'll always love you. I'll never forget that song—I'll never forget any of them. Honey, no one ever spent a more perfect three weeks than I did. You and your love made it perfect. Nothing happened that was regretful and I don't think we could have jammed any more happiness into it than we did. Even when we were half asleep that last night we were in each other's arms. Our last night together was so sweet and wonderful it was the high point of my life. Waking, turning, and having you there, in my arms, answering my kiss. My darling, that is a memory that I'll treasure always. I love you honey.

It's getting late, I want to shower and do some laundry so 'til tomorrow, when I'll talk to you again.

Goodnight my sweet

I love you

Mick

p.s. I can't figure out MYMNTE

What?

"September in the Rain" was a popular song that had been recorded many times by 1954.

The quote Mike uses is from Beethoven, written to his "Immortal Beloved": "Ever mine Ever thine Ever ours." Mike's version—probably unintentionally—replaces "ours" with "together."

POSTMARK: SUNDAY, SEPTEMBER 26

Hello Sweetheart,

It's still Saturday night and about two hours ago I finished a letter to you but I feel a lot better if I write a few lines before I turn in. When I awaken, it will be Sunday and another day will have elapsed and we'll have that much less time to wait. The radio is playing September in the Rain. I miss you Hon. I'm going to turn out the lights in a minute and if I dream I hope I dream about you. Goodnight Honey—I love you always—

Hi Babe, it's Sunday afternoon, the sun is shining brightly, the weather is warm and I wish you were here. If you were here we could drive to one of the points of the bay, walk down the path to my private beach, and be a million miles from everyone. But, since you aren't here I'll stay on the base, watch T.V., (sigh), go to the mess hall for coffee whenever I get tired of where I am and dream of November.

As I expected, I've become somewhat of a puzzle to many of the men. I've been asked by at least a dozen of them to go to the club but I've declined and that they can't understand. I was invited into a poker game and again I politely refused. They can't figure it out and I'm not going to help them. I'm going to keep our marriage a secret 'til after it happens, then I'll casually let the word get out. I'll have to tell my boss so I can get the three days pass but I'll swear him to secrecy. I've made up my mind to something since I've been gone. We'll never, and I mean <u>NEVER</u>! be separated after I'm released from this penal institution. When I'm a civilian there will be none of this business that other couples allow to happen. Separate vacations, husbands on trips. Without you I'm incomplete and I never want to spend more than a few hours away from you. I love you so much that the shortest separation would be painful.

I was watching TV a little while ago and the movie I was half noticing suddenly caught my attention. It was filmed in California and upon the screen were a long row of pretty ranch style homes. Not as pretty as ours of course, but enough to set me off on a long day dream. It made me realize once again how much I have to live for. You'll look so wonderful standing in the doorway of our home, the most beautiful, sweet, wonderful, perfectly understanding wife a man ever had. I've got to pinch myself. A man can want something so badly all his life that when finally it's within reach it's still hard to believe. You, the girl of my dreams, the most important person in my life, you are going to be my wife. When we're celebrating our 30th anniversary I'll still be a bit amazed and I'll still be the luckiest guy to ever walk the earth.

I was just looking through the pictures you sent and I'm becoming fonder and fonder of the one that you took with Barb and Bob. You look beautiful in that one. There is a look on your face that's hard to describe. It's one of the most beautiful expressions I've ever seen. My babe's a doll.

Next weekend I'm going to Seattle to look around and find a nice place for our honeymoon. I'm not going to be satisfied with just anything. It's got to be as near perfect as can be. It's going to be secluded, clean, nice, comfortable and homey. Just you and me honey, for five days, just the two of us away from the world. I love you.

I'm going to pause long enough for supper. I'll think of you every second of the time, honey.

Hi Doll, it is now 10PM, I've had supper, drove to Blaine to get some cigarettes, watched the Sunday night shows on TV and feel pretty good. Another day has passed. You should receive this Wednesday. That means from the time you read this to Nov. will be only 32 days. In a little more than a month, we'll be together. Too bad there aren't songs written about November.

I've calmed down a bit this last day or so and I'm glad I did. The two days on the train and my first two days back were pretty rugged. Being so sublimely happy for three weeks and then being thrown back into this life after being with you was quite an emotional strain. There were moments when I had to tell myself to calm down. If ever I was close to cracking up, it was Thursday night. My mind was whirling, everything that had happened seemed unreal and I thought it was impossible to be away from you and still go on. It will be hard honey, but we both know it's the best way. I've given a lot of thought to the possibilities of having you out here with me. We'd be happy, because being in love would make it impossible for us to be unhappy when we're together, but we would both realize what we'd be throwing away in the future. I've got one great consolation in your folks. Knowing that you are near them, with their understanding and affection, lifts a burden from my mind. If I had to think of you alone, with no one to share your problems, you'd be out here in very short order. It's going to be very very difficult to take at times and there will be times when I'll sound so low down and disconsolate in my letters that I'll give the impression of hopelessness. I dread the thought of holidays in particular, but we have the very consoling thought that some day this will all be over and we'll be able to look back at it and appreciate all the more our happiness.

I'm going to take a shower now, turn the radio down and turn in. I've got a new room mate and I don't like him but the lad does need his sleep.

I miss you honey. I just remembered something I read once
Ever mine
Ever thine
Ever together
I love you,
Mick

The song "You Were Meant for Me" was published in 1929, and though Mike doesn't mention which version he was hearing on the radio, it did appear in one of his favorite movies, 1952's "Singin' in the Rain."

POSTMARK: SEPTEMBER 28, 1954

Monday

Sept 27

Hello Honey,

It's evening, quiet, the radio is playing something very appropriate. "You were meant for me, I was meant for you," and my daily period of happiness has begun. Out of the 24 hours in a day, the only times I feel good are when I read your letters or when I sit here and write.

It has been a rough day. At 4 AM the sirens blew and in the cool, cool, cool of the morning I was toting a carbine while still half asleep. The playing war ended just in time for me to eat breakfast and go to work. No one has done anything since I've been gone so it was a fast moving day. I only took a half hour for lunch, long enough to bolt down my food, hurry to my room, and relax with your letter. Honey, without your letters, I'd be in a padded cell. I broke my own work record in the afternoon and even worked overtime. But now the day is over, I've reread your letter, looked through my pictures and relaxed for a few minutes of reminiscing and hopeful planning.

Baby, every time you told me that you loved me while I was home, it was such a wonderful feeling that I can't even try to describe it, but when you told me that again, in your letters, I felt the same way. Honey, I love you and I'll love you always, and I'll love you more and more as the years pass because, like a wonderful work of art, a wonderful thought, or a wonderful talent, a wonderful person becomes more wonderful with the passing of time. I'm the guy who found the gold at the end of the rainbow honey.

It's Monday night so by now Doc Marks has finished with your ears and I hope that your pain has been alleviated. I hate to think of my honey going through anything uncomfortable. I wish I could be with you.

It's a funny evening. The base is so quiet that if I didn't know better I'd think that it was deserted but this time of the month no one has earned enough money to go anywhere. Even the club is dead. I went there for cigarettes a little while ago and there was no one there but the bartender. Well, Thursday is pay day, so it must be the calm before the storm.

Baby I miss you so. I've realized how unimportant everything is without you. Nothing holds any pleasure, nothing can be fully enjoyed unless you're here to share it with me. I can't go one minute without thinking of you. Even when I was working my head off today, you weren't out of my thoughts for more than a few seconds and it will be like that always I know.

Some men find the main theme of their lives in some art, science, or in the service or in a job. You're my main reason for being alive. Anything I ever accomplish, any achievements I experience, they'll all be because of you and for you.

Your leopard skin picture is in front of me. God, when you came walking out with that on honey, you took my breath away.

My eyes are getting very heavy honey. It's been a long day but it's another day of separation that's no longer standing between us. Goodnight honey.

I love you. I'll always love you. 'til tomorrow my darling.

Micky

p.s.
I love you

The 1954 World Series, carried by the Mutual Broadcasting System on the radio and televised by NBC, was between the New York Giants and the Cleveland Indians, September 29 through October 2. The Giants swept.

POSTMARK: SEPTEMBER 29, 1954
Tuesday, Sept 28, '54

Hello Sweetheart,

It's late, 11:30 to be exact and I've finished what I hope will be the last day of all the work that was left for me while I was home.

Your letters arrived in the afternoon mail but this is the first chance I've had to answer them.

I guess we both felt the same way a week ago today. Boarding that train was a lot harder to do than walking after you would have been. One of these days, one wonderful day, we'll be all through with this unpleasant business of saying goodbye.

I don't know if I mentioned it before but Chris called me from Seattle before he flew home and was very pleased to hear about us. When I told him that we were going to be married in Nov. he nearly flipped.

I hope having your ears fixed will take care of some of that pain. By all means get something for Doc Marks. Hon, I'm going to use his statement as the guide for mine.

All you have to say in yours is that my mother's condition appeared to be better while I was home and took a reversal while I was gone.

I'm going to say goodnight now and finish this tomorrow. 'Til then, I'll love you always—Goodnight Honey.

It's lunch time, Wednesday and I'm going to finish this so it will get to you Friday. I'd be miserable all day if I thought that you hadn't received a letter.

I have a letter in my mail box but I'm going to wait 'til this is mailed before I answer it.

The World Series is on and they have it broadcasted over the base P.A. system. Does our bet still hold? I doubt if it will be necessary. We think so much alike that when the next election rolls around we'll probably see eye to eye on that. I'm glad the World Series came up at this time. God, I needed something to keep my mind occupied. I got my job all caught up and just might take the day off to watch the ballgame on T.V. The faster these days go by, the better. I don't think I could miss you any more then I do. I woke up at 2 o'clock last night, started thinking about you, smoked a few cigarettes, and dozed off again feeling perfectly miserable. This morning my roommate told me that I was talking in my sleep most of the night but he didn't hear the gist of my one sided conversation. I don't remember what the dream I had was about but I do remember that it was about you and it was unpleasant because I woke up feeling terrible this morning.

They've been after me for that golf tournament in November and I had to give them a reason for not wanting to be interred so the cat is out of the bag. Your pictures have been a subject of much admiration and speculation in the squadron and when word got around that we had set the date I was looked at with a great deal of admiration. See hon, I can't miss with success. Everyone thinks that a guy who can have such a wonderful wife must be on the ball. I've said it before and I'll say it a million times more in the years to come—anything I accomplish, any success I have, it will be because of you and for you. I love you more than life itself and life in the future represents a continued effort to make you happy. If I can accomplish that, I'll be a success. I miss you my darling,

Mick

POSTMARK: SEPTEMBER 30, 1954

Thursday

Sept 30

Hi Baby,

I told you before I left that there would be days when all I'd have time to write is a few lines and today, payday, is one of them. I couldn't get anything written last night because of the big inspection we had this morning. I was cleaning up the barracks 'til the wee hours this morning and today, report day means a short lunch hour and no chance to write 'til tonight. I'll be darned if I'll let a day pass without getting a few words to you. The longer I'm away, the more I love you. Everything I see or hear brings to mind something concerning us. When I woke up this morning the "Dream" song was playing and it caused me no end of remorse at being here. Remember the first time we heard that song together? We were sitting in the kitchen in the morning. When it started playing, you came into my arms. It was one of the sweetest moments I've ever experienced.

I'm not sure about that 60 day deal on the bond. Here's the $40 and that should take care of the plane fare once I get that bill of sale mailed to El and get the bond cashed.

I love you honey and in less than 35 days we'll be together again and I'll be able to hold you close and tell you how I love you.

I hate to make this so brief baby but I'll do better next time.

I love you, always

Mick

p.s. I love you

POSTMARK: OCTOBER 2, 1954

Friday

Oct 1

Hello my darling,

I'm having a hard time trying to keep up with you in the letter writing. I may not always come up with a long letter, but honey, you can expect one every day.

I just finished work and today will be the last of the overtime. I'm all caught up and from here on in, it will be soft.

After I got off work this evening, I stopped in at the mess hall for a cup of coffee. While I was sitting there thinking of so many things I started to think about something I hadn't actually given much thought to. The moment when we will both be standing before the fella who is lucky enough to marry the two happiest people in the world. Honey, it's when I start thinking of moments like that, I really am amazed at how lucky I am. One year ago I was in Korea, Mr. Misery himself. Eight months ago I had hopes that I really didn't believe in, four months ago my life was (and still is) in your hands, and ten days ago, that wonderful, perfect, indescribable Monday night, I had become as completely happy as is humanly possible. All because of you. I love you. Someday honey, someday, when I'm a success in other people's eyes, I'll be asked how success is achieved. I'll have an answer all ready. By wanting it for someone else's sake more than for your own. All these things we want, I'd never give a thought to without you.

I've got all your pictures in front of me. I'd give anything to be able to hold you in my arms, tell you how much I love you, kiss you again and again and again. So many little things keep popping into my mind. The way you'd tell me I look good when I'd pick you up from work, the sweet softness of your voice, when you talked over the phone, when you sang in the car, when you told me you loved me the first time. I love everything about you. Do you remember that silly movie we saw at the drive in? Things like that are the thoughts that occupy my mind hour after hour. The picnic that we had planned for so long, that resulted in a long walk while the car sat at the side of the road in need of gas. That seems a long time ago. The moment that you said you loved me. What a wonderful, glorious, life giving moment that was. Years and years of hopes, disappointments, tears and finally, new hopes, were all in anticipation of that moment. When you said those three words, I started to live again. Oh my darling, I love you so much. Sitting here, alone, yet with you because I know that at this moment you are thinking of me, I feel a certain amount of contentment. I love you.

Hey Hon, if I ever get another sure thing like the Giants to bet on, I'll be sure to bet it. I couldn't resist betting all of $2.00 on them. Forgive me? I bet another dollar on a fight that was finished a few minutes ago. I won. I'm trying to get a newspaper that contains the final baseball batting averages. As soon as I do, and if my calculations are correct, I'll be $44 richer. I don't think we'll have to borrow $200 from Gus. I think that $100 will do the trick. With my next pay plus the $44 that I'm nearly positive I've won, we should be able to get more than $200 together and I think that we can make it on $200. If we just borrow $100 from Gus, the first allotment will take care of that and eventually the bonds will make up for it.

When you receive this, it will be Monday, October 4th, leaving only 27 days to November. November—it's a magic word now. September,

November, yes, they do rhyme. We rhyme too—You and I. Maybe not in name, but in heart.

I love you my darling. I live only for the future when I'll be able to hold you in my arms and tell you I love you.

For now I can only write what I feel. I love you, I love you, I love you. 'Til tomorrow my sweet,

I love you,

Mick

p.s. I'm your baby

POSTMARK: OCTOBER 2, 1954

Hello Sweetheart,

It's still Friday night and it's been two and one half hours since I finished the last letter I wrote. After I sealed the envelope, I took a shower, shaved, and heard music coming in through my window. I dressed and walked down to the source of the music—the club. When I walked in the door, a sudden and very surprising cheer went up. It took a few seconds for me to realize that the cheers were for me. Someone handed me a drink and the ribbing started. The news that I'm getting married spread around the base like wild fire and everyone was getting their two cents in. One of the guys was making long speeches against marriage. Someone yelled "show him her picture." It was one of the guys from this barracks and one of your sincerest admirers. I showed him your picture. He could say no more. It was a pleasant two hours. I had three free drinks, sang in a make shift quartet and to top it off, won two dollars in my favorite bet. A new lad thought he was quite a bass and was low noting all over the place. A two dollar bet was made and I left him somewhere up among the baritones—easy money.

Going down to the club was actually a smart thing for me to do. Since I've been back I've started to think of the club as a representation of the evils that should be avoided. That isn't so. I can go in the club and drink a couple of beers and stay out of trouble and the club is the only place to go for a few laughs. I'm better off going there than staying around my room and driving myself into fits of melancholy. And don't worry about the farmers' daughters hon, I couldn't see them to begin with and they are looking for husbands so an old married man like I'm going to be couldn't get to first base.

In a few minutes I'm going to turn out the lights and sleep. I'll go to sleep with the vision of you in my mind. You, sleeping in the big double bed, alone, when we should be together, hugging your pillow when we should be in each other's arms. In 30 more days a man is going to pronounce us husband and wife. I'll be the happiest and luckiest groom ever. I love you babe—Goodnight my darling. I love you.

Good morning honey, I just woke up and I'm smoking my first cigarette. This looks to be a well occupied Saturday. At 10 the World Series comes on and if the Giants win I'll collect my two dollars. In the afternoon Illinois plays one of the west coast colleges and I'll have some fun ribbing some of the locals. The weather is dry and fairly warm so I may try the golf course today. I just thought of that and it seems like a pretty good idea. It's 9:30 here so that makes it 11:30 in Chicago. You're at work, dressed in white, thinking of me I hope and feeling as happy as I am I also hope because we are in the twenties as far as November goes. Just a few more weeks and we'll be together again.

Tomorrow I'm going to write out the receipt for the car and send it to El after I see a notary. I'll wait a week or so before I write to Gus because I want to make sure of the exact amount we'll need.

I'll have an orchid waiting when you step off the plane. That will be a wonderful sight, you walking down the ramp from the plane. I'll have an orchid, a license, and a marriage ceremony all waiting.

I love you baby and I'm living for that first week in November when we can be together again.

'Til tomorrow my darling
I love you
Mick

p.s. I love you

The party was for Mike's twenty-second birthday, September 19. Carol's diary entry for September 19 describes the same moment: "Mick blushed when he made his birthday cake wish—our eyes met." They had twenty-five years left.

POSTMARK: OCTOBER 3, 1954

Hi Honey,

It is 6:30 Saturday night, a cool clear evening. It's a nice evening for a lot of things. It would be a nice evening for a young couple to go somewhere quiet, stay fairly late, then drive home, a little tired, neither saying much 'til the girl says "What?" Then the boy could tell her how much he loves her. It would be a nice evening to stay at home, eat dinner and just sit and watch T.V. while the poor unhappy people frantically rush around trying to find what this couple has found. It would be a nice evening for a lot of things but unfortunately none of them are possible right now due to the fact that we are over 2000 miles apart. Someday honey, but not right now—damn it!

Two weeks ago at this time we were driving past Joker Joe's and deciding not to go in. From there we went to that place on Central Avenue, then to the restaurant where I very stupidly dropped my hamburger, twice as stupidly got mad and then I pulled the world's crowning achievement of dumb outright idiotic conduct. You asked if we were going to park somewhere—you, the most wonderful girl in the world, the center of my life asked me, a guy who at that moment should have been sitting there thanking God for just letting me be with you, you asked me if we were going to park. Instead of doing what so many other guys would have given their right arms to do, parked, I said that we were going to get to bed early and get some sleep. The minute those words left my lips I knew I'd regret them the rest of my life. I stopped the car and told you I was sorry for acting like a spoiled kid and honey, my actions that evening have bothered me ever since. Having you ask me to park and then to say no. After that we drove to the house, went up and that night, as far as I'm concerned, we were married. Sitting here, so far from you, wanting to be near you so badly, my darling I miss you so much. I love you my darling. I wonder what you are doing right now. It's 9:10 P.M. in Chicago. I've collected the five dollars I won on the World Series, and I could go to town and call you up. I'd like so much to talk to you, even for a couple of minutes. I could make it person to person so if you weren't there I could call later. I could and I'm beginning to give it more serious thought—I'm going to do it! I'm off to town.

I made it as far as the gate but I turned around and came back. The last time we talked to each other was when we were with each other. I want that to be the next time too. To talk to you over the phone would eventually make me feel worse because I'd want to reach out and take you in my arms and not being able to would make it kind of rough. I love you honey, and I want everything to be perfect.

The story you read sounds like us alright except for this Seattle woman I'm supposed to be running around with. I'm afraid I can't cooperate in that respect. I'm going to save that clipping—we can show it to the kids someday.

I'm going into town for a movie. It is Saturday night you know. Bye for now Hon.

Hi Hon, it's Sunday, the movie was awful, and I'm rushed right now because I overslept and the time is drawing near for the mail pickup in town. The mail isn't brought in from the base on Sundays so I'll have to rush this into town myself.

It's a nice day. God, I wish you were here with me. I can't put into words how badly I miss you. It's a feeling of such complete emptiness. Two weeks ago today was my party. It was the day we blushed when I cut the cake—We'll never forget that Hon.

I've got to get this to town. I love you baby—I love you, I love you. For a little while babe.

Mick

p.s. I love you

Unfortunately, we kids never saw "the clipping" Dad mentions.

H.F. likely refers to Household Finance Corporation, which was eventually absorbed by HSBC Finance Corporation.

POSTMARK: OCTOBER 4, 1954

Monday

Oct 4

Hi Honey,

At this moment I feel a tremendous sense of appreciation for what we have. I spent most of the evening at the club and a wilder night I have never seen. I saw airmen drink themselves into complete oblivion. I saw lonely, confused girls chasing after these airmen. I sat and listened to a girl tell me a sad story then saw her slash her wrists in a suicide attempt. All in the space of four hours. The club had the usual dangerous Sunday night crowd, a mixture of civilians, service men, women and drinks. I picked out the quietest corner of the bar and watched everyone go berserk. While sitting there minding my own business, a girl came up to me, started a conversation, told me of her divorce, her sterility, her loneliness, her confused mental condition and her great love for one of the airmen. While talking to her I discovered that she is tremendously lonely, has a terrible feeling of guilt because of her promiscuousness, and is in need of psychiatric care. All my conclusions were proved correct when she broke a glass and went to work on her wrists. Fortunately this was done after she rejoined her companions. I would have been embarrassed if she had started her self punishment while talking to me. This whole wild evening just adds to my already great appreciation of the love and happiness we give to each other. We have something that so many people are looking for—most of them in vain. People seeking happiness in material things, alcohol, sex, and finding instead, frustration and unhappiness. Honey, we have been blessed. I mean that literally. We have received a gift that could almost be considered sacred. To love someone completely, unselfishly, and with no bonds of restraint is in itself something wonderful. But to have that love returned, equally, is something so precious that its value is greater than anything else that exists. In complete seriousness honey, I repeat what I've said many times before. I'm the luckiest man alive. I'm going to turn in now. I love you baby. Goodnight my sweet.

Hi Hon, it's 11:45, I just finished reading your letter, looking, I should say gazing, at your newest picture and I'm all set to spend a pleasant half hour writing.

I'm afraid that we were due to have a disagreement and I see that we have. What do you mean "the picture isn't very good"? You happen to look beautiful. I've got it right in front of me. If only it could come to life. It seems impossible that I can read your letter, look at your picture, and still be so far away. I'm getting kind of shook. Looking at your picture, wanting to reach out and take you in my arms, put my face in your hair and just stay like that. Baby I miss you. In 32 days, just one month from tomorrow, we'll be together and if all our plans work out right, we'll be married. God, the time is dragging. Honey, how will we endure a separation of 18 months, broken only by a few short weeks together. It's rough to be practical. I love you so much that being away from you just kills any enjoyment that I could have. Everything seems like such a waste of time. My work, going anywhere, the least little deviation from my daily routine—all a waste of time. I've only got one thing to live for and having to be apart from you makes it pretty tough.

From what you've written, it seems that the best thing to do is pay off H.F. Take the money from the allotments when they arrive. We can replace it with the money going into the bonds. See if you can stall them off or arrange to have them wait a month or so before the payments begin. Then when the allotment begins we can clear that up. Don't worry about it, because the loan companies will usually be fairly patient in cases like that. Assure them that they'll get paid. They'd much rather have the money than start preferring felony charges.

As soon as I get a few more arrangements made we can start making more definite plans for Nov. Today I'm going to see the chief about that 3 day pass. I'd like to have you arrive on the 5th because that's payday in Nov. and also, because it's a Friday and the weekend will be starting. Mmmm, my wife—that sounds good.

I've got to run honey, the mess hall is closing in a few minutes.

I love you honey. I love you.
Mick

p.s. I love you

Tuesday
Oct 5th

It's still Monday, 5:40 to be exact, and I'm done with work, I've eaten, thrown a load of laundry into the machine, lit a cigarette, stared unhappily at your new picture and I'm lonesome as can be. Just looking at your picture prevents me from saying anything else but I love you. It seems sort of empty having to write it. I love you. Yes, it would be lots nicer to hold you close, and whisper it to you. I love you.

It's been about a half hour since I wrote the first paragraph of this letter. I've been lying on my bunk, smoking, listening to the radio, and trying to break this mood. I haven't felt so low since I stepped off the train. Looking at your picture, remembering that when it was taken I stood just a few feet away from you. The radio is playing "it's a lonesome old moon." That helps. All afternoon it's been like this. I was talking to Pete, the electronics engineer who takes care of the equipment. He has a girl in Seattle that he drives down to see every weekend. She's in college and he seems to be in love with her. I've been talking to him about standing up for our wedding and he was very pleased. He asked me where we were going to live in November. When I told him that you were returning to Chicago, in his very mild mannered way he gave me hell. I explained to him in terms of money and being practical why we were doing it that way but he continued to argue. Finally, at 3:35 he said "the money you save can never replace the time you'll be apart." With that I put on my hat and went for a walk. I walked to the club, drank a coke, didn't bother to go back to work, and sank deeper and deeper into the mood I'm in now. Six months ago, uncertainty, doubt, lack of hope, and other things caused moods like this but then I had a sure cure. Now I just have to weather them and hope I feel better in the morning. Honey, you said you felt lonely in a big city, a place where you have your family, your friends, people who understand your feelings and try to help. You experienced loneliness under those circumstances, I guess you can understand how I feel here. I spend most of my time working or sitting in this room. Except for a rare trip to town or to the club that's how I spend my time. It can get a person honey. Looking at your picture right now just tears me up. That's the worst part of it. If I could lose myself in something for a while, a book, my job, some kind of distraction, but it's impossible. All I think of, every minute, every single minute of the day, is you. Baby, you must know how much I'm looking forward to the day you step off the plane. That's all I live for. But I've never mentioned the dread that I also feel when I think of November. Dread because of the little time we'll have together and because of the long time we'll be apart after you leave. We both realize how lucky we are to be so much in love, to have found each other, to have so much to look forward to. Still, fate hasn't been giving us all the breaks. The years that preceded all this were filled with such unhappiness that I hate to look back on them. And now, when we found each other, when we finally become husband and wife, we're still faced with a year and a half of separation. I'm not a discontent honey, a day doesn't pass that I don't count my blessings and appreciate them, appreciate having you, but you must admit that people have labored under fewer obstacles than we have. I guess I should try to train myself to keep this kind of thinking out of my mind but sitting here with these four walls as my only scenery isn't too conducive to cheerfulness. I'm in such a dark mood I think I'll turn in and finish this tomorrow. Goodnight Hon. I love you.

Hi, I'm on my lunch hour. No better this morning, but I've got high hopes for this afternoon. This morning has been one big headache. I received a call from the orderly room telling me that four of our men are being transferred to another base in Washington. They are maintenance men so that means that anytime now I'll be starting to do radar maintenance work, and that means I'll be a very necessary man around here, and that all adds up to one thing. It'll be tougher to get that transfer.

Had a bad dream. We were in a car and I was leaving to catch a train. Just when you started to cry, I woke up. It was six o'clock so I went to the mess hall for some coffee. Just can't take such dreams.

Time to go Hon, parting in letters is even hard. Gee I love you. I love you, I love you.

Mick

p.s. I love you.

POSTMARK: OCTOBER 6, 1954

Hi Honey,

It's one o'clock in the morning. Today, when I discovered that it was a no letter day, I sat myself down in front of the TV set in the day room, fell asleep and woke at 11:30. I've taken a shower, shaved and I'm all set for bed, but first a letter.

The post office must have goofed because I know that you won't miss a day without writing. I'm not being complacently confident when I say that. You said you wouldn't let a day pass without writing so I know you won't.

I was happy to see the mobile library arrive today because I've been running low on reading material. I took a huge volume, the complete short stories of Maugham and in the first story I read I received confirmation on one of my pet theories. Maugham stated that in his opinion some people can fall in and out of love, while some fortunate or unfortunate people, as the case may be, can fall in love only once. When I read that, I gave it quite a bit of thought and found certain conclusions on this emotion called love. I've decided that people who fall in and out of love are not really in love with the object of their affections at all. They love the person they have created in their own mind but when they discover the person to be what he or she was, the love ceases to exist because the person they loved actually didn't exist. When love exists for the person, the real person and not the mental image, and the love creates a feeling of oneness that is so intense that it prevents a person from existing as an individual any longer, then it is love. The ability to love the faults as well as the good points is necessary. I remember reading somewhere that a man who can only tolerate the good in his friends, has no friends. Honey, all this leads me to arrive at a remarkable earth shaking conclusion—We're in love! By the way, I've found it impossible to love your faults since I haven't found any. I hope that you can mine. I hope that you can tolerate my temper which only flares when I myself do something stupid, as with the hamburger—My dark moods which occur when I'm away from you mostly, and the fact that all other young ladies are shallow, foolish, and not half as beautiful as you. Actually, in that respect I'm not prejudiced—I'm right.

Look babe, I hate to think of you walking to that mail box in the dark. In fact I'll be truthful and say that it bothers me a great deal. Why not write the letters before you go to sleep, or in the morning before work and then mail them during the day. How about it honey, work something out that will eliminate those trips to the corner. Will you? Honest—to—God? I love you honey.

Something cute happened today. We have an officer who is about two years older than me, fresh out of college, eager to please, and very confused with the AF. He was sitting around the office and he overheard someone mention something about me getting married. He was politely interested and asked to see your picture. I showed him your leopard skin cheese cake and he gasped and said "Gosh she's prettier than Marilyn Monroe." The he looked at me, looked at your picture, at me again, so I said, "I can't understand it either." This embarrassed him so much that he stammered and said, "Oh, you're nice looking too." When he said that and realized how silly that sounded he got red and couldn't say anything else. Gosh hon, you sure get these guys shook up.

Looking at that empty mail box twice today was sort of depressing but I know that the letter will be here in the morning so I'll keep myself in check. I'm having a hard time writing because you insist on staring at me (your picture) and I keep staring back. This of course has a very distracting effect because I start feeling awake and wanting to reach out and hold you. Your picture always seems on the verge of coming alive, always on the verge, but it never does. Baby, Sweet, I miss you so. Missing someone as badly as I miss you isn't only in the mind. When I look at your letters, reminisce, look to the future, or try to think of what you're doing at a certain moment, I get butterflies inside. Right now, you're in bed, sleeping, maybe dreaming of me. I remember how we held each other, loved each other, were happy beyond any dreams I ever had. I remember how wonderful it was to waken to your kisses in the morning. Baby, I miss you with all my heart. Honey, it was heaven, heaven couldn't be any better, to be with you so much. For the first time in my life I was content, alive, complete. To think that it will be like that forever makes me want to tell the world how lucky I am. I love you, my sweet, my perfect, my wonderful. I love you.

Goodnight,

Mick

P.S. I adore you.

POSTMARK: OCTOBER 7, 1954

Wednesday

Sept 6 [Mike made a mistake; he meant October 6.]

30 more days

Hello Wonderful,

My sweet, surprising baby. The picture arrived this morning and I had to tear myself away from it in order to spend some time at work. I must admit that I was a bit disappointed when there was no letter in my box this morning. What's wrong hon? I live for those letters and my day is a complete blank when I don't receive one. Probably it got delayed on the way out to this god forsaken country and I'll bet my life on receiving one this evening. I love the picture. It makes me feel pretty good when I look at it and think of the many times we were in each other's arms as we are in the picture. I love you honey.

I've been working like mad today. Every time I get caught up, and look forward to loafing they come up with something new. I'm only taking a half hour for lunch so I'll have to run now. It is exactly 4 hours and 22 minutes 'til the next mail delivery. It's going to be a long four hours but when I read the letter I hope will be there, everything will seem fine.

Hi Honey, I just finished work, dinner, mail call, read your letter and collected that baseball bet. 44 brand new crisp dollar bills. It's a shame I didn't play my hunch on the Giants. I was pretty sure they'd win but four straight—Wow. Now I've got dollar signs flitting through my mind. After figuring out what I'll have coming in, going out and other expenses I see that I'll have about $100 to $110 when I leave for Seattle. That will never do so I guess we'll have to borrow $100 from Gus. Since we've already got plane fare taken care of, or will as soon as I get that note sent to El and get that bond cashed, we aren't doing too badly. The first allotment check will take care of Gus and the bonds will eventually replace that. When I left Chi I thought we'd have to borrow $200 from Gus and I'm glad we cut it down. I don't think that we'll ever have money problems and it just occurred to me. I've talked a lot about gambling and you may have got the idea that I've got the gambling fever. Uh Uh Hon. I only gamble when it's not a gamble as with this baseball bet. I knew when I made the bet that the worst I could do would be to break even. I've given up cards and I've never believed in taking a chance on losing what's needed. We'll never have money worries honey. Ever since I was fifteen I've been working and supporting myself. Despite the fact that I lived more lavishly than an airman can afford to live I saved a little and now that I'm a man of responsibilities (that sounds pretty good) I'm going to set all kinds of saving records. So you think I could tell you a little dream I've been nurturing during the last month without being laughed at? OK, here goes. Someday I want you to have a mink coat. According to movies and books I should rebel at the idea but it works just the opposite. That stole of yours looks wonderful on you so I imagine a mink coat would look great. For a $120 a month GI I guess I'm thinking along pretty expensive lines but since we'll have a dream house, I'll have a dream wife, I don't see why you shouldn't some day have a dream coat. Babe, I love you. Since I'll have the best wife, my wife should have the best.

Honey, sometimes I look at your pictures, tell myself, "she loves me" and I'm so happy I could sing. It's amazing. The girl I've always loved, the girl of my dreams, the one and only girl in the world for me, and she loves me. Talk about having the Gods smile at me. I'm Mr. End-of-the-rainbow himself. Baby, in less than a month, a month from yesterday, we'll be married. It's nearly unbelievable. I'm in a continuous state of being thrilled. Nothing this wonderful has ever happened to anyone. I miss you honey and I'm terribly lonely but it's loneliness I can bear because I know you love me. I know that at this moment you're thinking of me. I know that someday all the dreams we have, the plans we've made will be fulfilled. That fulfillment will result in happiness that could not be exceeded ever. When I say that we'll be the two happiest people in the world, I mean it.

When I try to think of life without you, it's frightening. It's impossible. I couldn't live without you. You are my life. Darling, you're the most important person in the world. There's nothing I wouldn't do, very little I couldn't do and nothing I wouldn't attempt, for you. Anything you ever want, no matter what, I'll do everything that could be done to make it possible. To me you're the beginning and the end of everything. I love you. I love you with my entire being. Nothing is important without you. You give my life meaning. Other things can make me sad, but nothing can make me happy, really happy, unless you give it meaning. I've discovered what is meant by that song Prisoner of Love. I'm a slave, actually a slave. I'm not a person any longer. I'm half of that divinely happy unit that's formed by two people—you and I. Us. I'll love you more every day, every month, every year. My love will become greater as time passes. I'll dedicate my life to one goal. Making you happy.

I love you my darling. I love you more than life itself. I can't do anything and give it my complete concentration. You're always in my thoughts whether I be thinking about the past, present, or future, you're on my mind. I told you that my favorite song has always been "Always." When I was younger the words seemed to represent what I thought love should be. As I grew older and realized that I loved you the words began to contain more meaning than before. To me they are beautiful in their simplicity.

Not for just an hour
Not for just a day
Not for just a year
But
Always
I love you my sweet, my wife
Goodnight,
Your Baby

p.s. I love you

POSTMARK: OCTOBER 8, 1954
Thursday night
7 Oct

Hi Sweetheart,

I just finished a very pleasant task. I've got the picture you sent located right over my desk so that while I'm writing all I have to do is lift my eyes and it's there and when I walk into the room it's the first thing I see. I look very happy on that picture. The fact that you're in my arms might have something to do with it.

It's early afternoon and the day is mine. This morning I had a splitting headache and it must have shown because I was at work 5 minutes and I was told to take the day off. I took a couple of pills and went to bed. I awoke at 12:30 and went to the mailroom but my luck wasn't good so I'll have to wait 'til later this afternoon for my daily bit of happiness. When I receive a letter in the morning I know that there won't be any in the afternoon but I still feel bad when I check and don't find any. That's why I dread Sundays. No mail call. That sort of wasted the day. I expected one this morning because the letter I received yesterday was written Sunday. That means Tuesday's and Monday's letters are floating around somewhere. The mail delivery must be slowed up somewhere because normally I'd receive the letter written Tuesday, today.

Last night I was sitting in the mess hall, drinking coffee with a bunch of the guys when the "Dream" came over the radio. I was sitting back, listening to it and looking at the picture in my ID bracelet. I didn't think I was creating any interest 'til I looked around and all the guys were smiling. When they saw me look up they all bust out laughing and informed me that I really had it bad. As if I didn't know. Baby, I have it bad. The love I feel for you can't be described in words.

I interrupted this letter for 8 hours. I've been a busy bee since I wrote the last paragraph. I checked my mail and I'm happy to have a letter.

Honey, I'm not "mad" about your going to a tavern with Joyce and Freddie but your Dad was right. I'm not happy about it either. Here's why. I've met them both only passingly so I haven't had the opportunity to make any first hand impressions but according to everything that I heard, the reports on their midnight brawl, and especially your family's opinion of them they fail to impress me. Bob dislikes both of them and that's good enough for me. What can I say now. Just saying what I said puts me in the position of criticizing you for going with them. That's something I've never wanted to do and that's not what I'm doing when I write this. Let's put it this way. If I had to, I'd associate with them but I'd rather not. Am I a snob? I don't mean to be. Here's another point. Joyce liked Ron, Freddy knows him, therefore I imagine they were, and still are rooting for him. That doesn't bother me. You love me and that's all I have to know, but it strikes me as being an odd coincidence that he should walk into the bar while the three of you were there. Is it inconceivable to consider the possibility that their asking you to join them and his arrival may have been prearranged? It wouldn't have taken a great deal of imagination on their part to figure something like that out. It's too obvious for me to consider myself as being unduly suspicious. Now I feel rotten. I felt lousy when I read your letter. The fact that you were with Ronny doesn't bother me, it's the fact that I'm up here and that, I'm trying to think of a good name, that kid can be near you. After writing that 99% of the female sex would say that I'm jealous. Sure I'm jealous. I'm jealous of anyone who's near you, I'm envious of everyone who sees you, talks to you, has anything to do with you. I'm jealous because it's not me. As I'm writing I keep glancing at your picture and out of the corner of my eye I just read the last page of your letter. Reading the words that you wrote, you love me, chokes me up so much I couldn't talk if I had to. Oh baby, I didn't realize how much I love you 'til I had to be away from you again. We've agreed to be truthful with each other, always. OK, I'll be truthful. Do you know how I was affected by your letter, by thinking of you being with Ron? I wanted to go out and get blind drunk. I didn't but I felt like it. All I've been able to think about for the last two weeks is us. I already think about us as being married. I look at the ceremony as a ceremony. Suddenly I have to picture you sitting with him and it hurts. Sure, I'm being unreasonable, but my love for you, the feelings it creates in me, the state of mind it has me in, it defies reason. Shall I continue to be truthful? I hate Ronny. I don't think I could hate a person more. I hate him because he's held you in his arms, he's kissed you, because Sunday, when I was here, miserable because I couldn't be with you, he was with you. I'm a fool—a stupid fool. Every logical facet in my mind tells me to tear this up. Jealousy is detested by women. I'm hurting myself. All these things I know. But I've got to be myself or I'd hate myself because anything I wrote would be a deception. I warned you one night honey, that I'm not perfect. I tried to point out my bad points, I know them well. Baby, I swear I'll do everything I can to make you happy but it's only fair to warn you in advance. I've got many flaws. The state of mind I'm in right now is frightening. Frightening because I have to look forward to months and months of feeling like this. Being away from you is hell. I love you so much that if I ever lost you, life would end. Honey, maybe I can make you see how I felt when I read your letter. If I wrote you and told you that I ran into Joan Huntington, that girl I told you about, in a bar and we spent an evening sitting and talking with each other, and while I was with her you knew that you had been thinking about me, how would you feel?

I'm a fool to send this. I can't write anymore. My mind's whirling.

I miss you, I miss you so terribly that I can hardly bear it

I love you,

Mick

Hello Baby,

It's 9 AM, I'm on my coffee break, and I feel like a beat out old rag. Last night, after I went to bed, I couldn't sleep. I must have smoked a half pack of cigarettes while I was laying there awake. I heard something through the wall of my room so I went next door and there was a dime limit poker game going. I played two hours, won ten and quit. These lads play all month and are fish. Baby, I'm going to see if I can't supplement our honeymoon fund. I can't lose with them and I might be able to make quite a bit. I know I swore off poker but this is too much to resist. Such easy money is not to be bypassed.

Baby, that letter I wrote last night must have sounded crazy. Did I sound wildly jealous? I'm not hon, a person who is jealous must have doubts to create jealousy. I don't have any doubts. It's just that I've always detested that kid and thinking about you being with him got me kind of upset. I yearn for you so much, miss you terribly, and love you more than anyone could, that it hurts to think of him being able to see you, talk to you, and be with you when I can't. God baby, being away from you is no picnic.

Coffee time is just about over so I'm going to run. 'Til this afternoon, I love you my darling.

Hi hon, I just made arrangements to drive down to Seattle this afternoon. I'm going to stay over 'til tomorrow and get the wedding license, check on the place we're going to stay, and see about a church. I just checked my mail and there was no letter. I was hoping that there would be one because I won't be back 'til tomorrow night and two days is much too long to go without a letter. Your letters mean so much to me honey. If I didn't have a letter to look forward to each day I don't know what I'd do. I'm kind of proud of myself because I haven't missed a letter a day since I've been back. I didn't think that I'd be able to do it but I feel better knowing that a day doesn't pass when I don't write. Baby, I love you. I can't write a paragraph when I don't feel like telling you that. I love you. While I'm writing I keep pausing to look at the large picture of us and when I do my mind wanders. I remember how wonderful it was to hold you in my arms, to turn while driving and see you sitting there, next to me, to open my eyes in the morning and see you, to be near you. Oh baby, you can't realize how important you are to me. Without you I'd be the loneliest person in the world. When I think of you stepping off the plane in Seattle, coming into my arms, becoming my wife, together always, I can't describe the way I feel. That will be the fulfillment of my great hope in life. How many people can say that they are happy, truly happy. Very few. That's why I'm so thankful. You are bringing me more happiness than I ever thought possible. I'll do my best always to return that happiness.

Baby, being away from you is pain. As long as I live I'll never be away from you again. Someday, this will all be over. Someday we'll be together and nothing will ever tear us apart.

Baby, make reservations for the 4th. You'll arrive the 5th. I'll get off work at noon on the fifth, get paid and take off for Seattle. I'll be there when your plane arrives. If you think of it, check the airline schedule and find out the time that you'll arrive, Seattle time, then I'll have everything arranged. The wedding license will arrive in a few days and you can get it filled out, notarized and returned after the divorce. I'll get all the arrangements made for our five days. Honey, would you bring the light colored knit suit along? It looks wonderful on you. As a matter of fact, everything does.

My lunch hour is nearly over so I'll have to close. I'll write from Seattle hon and again tomorrow.

I love you honey, with all my heart I love you. I'll never stop loving you. You're my life, my whole life.

I love you,
Your Baby

Sunday

Oct 10th

Hi Baby,

I just woke up and I'm still a little groggy. I got back from Seattle last night at three and fell right into bed. It was a swell trip. I went down there with Bill Varns, the officer in my section. I had planned on staying at the "Y" but after having supper at his folks' house they insisted that I spend the night there. Bill, his older sister, her date and I went out and saw some of Seattle that night and I had a fine time. Saturday morning I accomplished what I had really come down to do. I went to the University Lutheran Church and set the date for the wedding. You'll love the church Hon. It's small, very pretty and the people there are nice. It's on the University of Washington campus and is very modern. When I saw it I made up my mind that we would be married there. When you arrive, I'll be waiting at the air field and from there we will go to the Varns' home. I couldn't get the church for the night you arrive so I took it for 11:00 Saturday the 6th of November. Varns' folks want you to spend the night at their home and I accepted the invitation. You'll like them hon and you'll love their house. It's a $35,000 ranch style with furnishings that are great. After the wedding Saturday we'll go to Lake Wilderness, a resort about twenty miles outside of Seattle and there we will stay for five wonderful days.

When I woke up this morning I had the mail clerk called over the PA. He called me on the phone and said that I received two letters Friday afternoon and he had put them in one of my drawers. I just finished reading them. One was the "short" one and the other the long one. When I read the first one I'll admit that it sort of bothered me to think of you quitting Linell and Marks, but I'm glad you came to your final decision. You're wonderful and I love you. You must be able to read my mind. I repeat—I love you.

Honey, I can't change my three day pass for more than one reason. We could make it 'til payday but then I'd have to come back on Friday and get paid and that would waste a whole day. We wouldn't be able to have anyone stand up for us because the people who are coming to our wedding work during the week and couldn't make it if it wasn't on a weekend and I've already made the arrangements at the church. How 'bout it hon, will you still marry me? Varns is also creating a problem as I discovered on the way back last night. I hadn't realized how highly he regarded and valued me 'til we had a talk last night. He is going to try to get me promoted to Staff Sergeant without my waiting the required year as an A/1C and eventually he wants me to be chief of the section. Right now the radar maintenance section is set up in this way. He, as the officer, is in charge of everything. A master sergeant is in charge of the maintenance and I take care of all the personnel work and all the paper work. He wants me to train in the maintenance end of it, get one more stripe and take over the M/Sgts job when he leaves. That's a tall order because the M/Sgt has been in for 8 years and I'd be taking on the responsibility of supervising the men who maintain 2½ million dollars worth of highly complex electronic equipment. I was dumbfounded when he told me this. The days that you suggested I get my pass are the busiest days of the month for me and I'd be loading him with all my work if I left them. Honey, even if it isn't as safe, we'll have to take the risk, OK?

Turning down that modeling job with my wishes as your main reason makes me realize all the more how wonderful you are. I'm the luckiest guy in the world and I know it.

Time is starting to slip by a little faster but I have never seen a month go this slowly. Only 21 more days 'til November and then we'll only have 5 days to go, five days 'til we take the step that has been the "impossible dream" for so many years. It still seems slightly unreal when I think of us being married but I know it's going to happen and as I write this my stomach is full of butterflies.

The mail deliveries are getting erratic. I received the picture the early part of this week and some of your letters are taking four days. Well, as long as they keep arriving I won't argue about a day or so.

I love you honey and I miss you terribly.

Your Baby

p.s. I love you

Captain William Varns was "an officer that all the enlisted men liked," recalls Don Karaiskos. In 1958, Varns was killed when his US Air Force Beaver airplane crashed on Nose Mountain in Alberta, Canada.

POSTMARK: OCTOBER 11, 1954

Monday

Oct 11th

Hi Honey,

It's the end of another Sunday and as usual it was quite lively. I went to Blaine, mailed a letter, had a cup of coffee, bought stamps, came back to the base, watched a football game on T.V., ate supper, shot a couple of games of pool, read a letter and here I am. This wild social whirl will be the death of me.

It's raining and the wind is blowing and wailing. It's a perfect night for sitting in front of a fire place with the person I love. As usual the word "why" comes into my mind. Why can't we be together as we are in the pictures before me? Why are we faced with an eternity of being parted? Why, Why, Why. Emerson once wrote an Essay on "Compensations" and that's probably the answer. For every good there's an evil. For every gain there's a loss and so on. I guess that's the answer. We have so many years of happiness before us that we have to be unhappy for a little while. Sweetheart, when I look at your picture, at the sweet smile on your face, at the way your arms are around me, I still have a hard time believing that we are going to be married. It's too wonderful to be true. I love you so much honey and I've got so much more to be thankful for than most people. I'm thankful for our three weeks in September. I don't think anyone has ever spent a more wonderful 20 days. To be able to look forward to a whole lifetime of such happiness makes me realize that I'm blessed with something that millions of people are looking for and will probably never find. The person I love more than life itself loves me. That's a Godsend and I know it. Honey, every time you say you love me, every time I read those wonderful words, I'm as thrilled as when you first said them. That memorable moment when we were sitting in our Clover Club. When you said it my knees actually got weak. Baby, can you realize what that meant to me, what it means to me now? Can you understand the feelings

I experienced when, after years and years of loving you, hoping and yet hoping without hope, seeing dreams shattered, dreams that I'd had since I was a small boy become sources of pain rather than pleasure, when after all this you said you loved me? Honey, it was like being brought to life. You're wonderful. I love you. In twenty six days you're going to step off a plane. You're going to be 2200 miles away from your family, your friends, and everyone you know but Baby, you're going to be home because we'll be together. No matter where we are, if we're together, that's home. I'm going to be waiting when that plane lands, I'm going to squeeze you as hard as I can, I'm going to kiss you, over and over. I'm going to tell you I love you and I'm going to hold you in my arms for those five days and let go only when you leave and then I'll be crying, if not on the outside, inside where it's much more painful. People can joke all they want about marriage, they can be cynical, sarcastic, and try to be discouraging. I love you and I want you to be my wife. I want to be your husband. I want to dedicate my life to making you happy. That's my happiness. It's the greatest thing that's ever happened to anyone. Oh honey, I love you so much.

The heat has gone on the fritz and it's darn cold in here. Since it's getting late anyway I'm going to turn in. You're probably asleep by now so I know that we'll be doing the same thing. Goodnight sweetheart.

Hi Baby, it's noon Monday and I've just finished reading the three letters that came this morning. They were dated the 7th, 8th, and 9th. After reading them I see that I'd better write some of the family tonight and let them know that this transfer is a sliver outside chance. People are always hearing about someone who got a good deal, a transfer, an early discharge or something like that. They don't know about the hundreds that are turned down. I've kept myself from putting any hope on the transfer and I'm glad you did the same. It's tough to get a transfer in the AF and now, with the shortage of men in my section and the increased responsibility that I've been stuck with it's really a problem.

I've arranged to take the afternoon off tomorrow so I can get some things done that I didn't have time for over the weekend. I'm going to get that transfer of ownership on the car, buy the wedding license, and a few other things I've been neglecting.

I hate to see you get stuck with all these problems right now but honey, all this is just temporary. Someday, when I'm a civilian (what a wonderful word) and wallowing in money, all that's going to be something we can laugh at.

I know the family would like to see me get transferred so we could have our wedding at home but Bob's right. It's such a slim chance that we'd better go ahead with our plans. Make your reservations well in advance and send me the arrival time so I can get things arranged out here. It's got to be the 5th hon as I already explained. This damn AF.

I'm really starting to rate. The inspecting office asked me if I wanted a roommate and I told him that I'd prefer to live alone so now I have this big room all to myself. Just me, with all your pictures and our hopes. Gosh I love you.

This is one of those rush rush days and I'm swamped with work—promotions, transfers, and trying to cram my head full of electronics so I can switch to maintenance. I've got to run so I can get into the mess hall.

I'll write after work. I love you my babe, I love you, love you, love you. Your husband in 26 days

Mick

p.s. I'm your baby

According to the October 1954 edition of the official Monthly Weather Review, the 6.72 inches of rain that fell in Chicago during a forty-eight-hour period of October 9–11, 1954, set a new record, and caused "what was undoubtedly Chicago's greatest flood in history."

POSTMARK: OCTOBER 12, 1954

Tuesday
Oct 12th

Hi Sweetheart,

It's noon, I'm taking the afternoon off and in a few days the wedding license I'll be buying this afternoon will be in your hands. Only 19 days left in this month baby, only 24 days and we'll be together, and only 25 days and we'll be married. I can hardly believe it. I love you.

Last night I went to town and took in a movie. After I left the show I stopped at the restaurant for a cup of coffee. I was sitting there feeling pretty low when someone played the juke box. First I sat through Skokiaan and then, it never fails, they played our Dream song. That song just tore me up. While it was playing I relived one of the most beautiful moments of my life, the morning it played while we were sitting in your mom's kitchen. I don't remember ever feeling quite like I did during those few minutes you were in my arms. It's at moments when those kind of memories become very vivid that being away from you becomes nearly unbearable.

According to the radio Chicago had a small flood. I hope it didn't affect you baby. Lots of rain would be fun if I were inside a house, holding you in my arms, listening to it fall on the roof. I guess that anything is OK as long as I'm with you. Only a few more weeks baby, just a few more weeks and I'll have you in my arms. Then for a little while all the problems that seem big right now will be forgotten. For a little while we'll be complete again. Honey, honey, I miss you so. The longer I have to be away from you, the more I'll detest the Air Force.

Last night when I returned from town it was quite late and I felt 100% blue so instead of writing in such a mood I went right to bed. I didn't drop off for two hours. I just smoked and dreamed about the future. Actually, they weren't really dreams. Plans would be more accurate. Thinking about our house, our kids, our wonderful, perfect life together, and all the happiness we'll have. Right now as I look at our picture I have a great sense of well being because I know that as we are standing together in the picture, we'll be standing together the rest of our lives. I love you my darling. I love you and I'll love you always.

After I get the license this afternoon and get that title sent to El this evening, all that will remain is the bond and the letter to Gus and I'll take care of that in short order. I'll be glad when we have everything set, cause then it will be just about November. Baby, baby I miss you.

Honey, for five days I'm not going to let you out of my sight. We'll have no rest time. We'll be away from people and I'll kiss you a million times a day. It'll be the most wonderful honeymoon two people ever had, and the most wonderful thing about it is that our whole life will be that way. We'll never reach that casual, bored taken for granted type of marriage. We're too much in love for that. Our life together will always be happy, sublimely happy, and exciting because love created a calmness and yet an excitement in marriage. I'm so lucky, so lucky.

I've got to run now baby. I didn't get a letter this morning so I'll be keeping my fingers crossed for tonight.

I miss you honey, miss you, love you, long for you, and I guess that in my own way I worship you too.

Your baby,
Mick

p.s. I love you

The medical statements likely refer to Mike's mother's recent diagnosis of the cancer that eventually took her life in 1959.

Wednesday
Oct. 13

My Sweet Baby,

Gee it's lonely here. As usual I'm in my room. It's late, about 11 PM, my radio doesn't work, the clock is ticking loudly and the base is so quiet if I didn't know better I'd think it was deserted. I just came back from town and I didn't get as much done as I had planned. I forgot that today is Columbus Day and City Hall was closed so I'll have to put off buying the wedding license 'til next Saturday. I went to a movie and it was awful. If fact I fell asleep after the first twenty minutes. I feel like I'm waiting between trains in a strange town and trying to kill time. That's how I've felt ever since I came back and I'll feel that way until we're together again. Just looking for diversions. Anything to kill time. I guess the change that's come over me is apparent to everyone here. I don't go to the club very often, don't go to the bars in town and avoid the gatherings of GI's that occur anywhere and everywhere. I just don't care to be around people. All I live for are your letters. I wish, how I wish, that your picture would come to life. That I could hold you, kiss you, tell you how I love you, and sit with my head on your lap. I love you my darling. Everyone may not agree when I say that you are the most beautiful girl in the world but that's because most people don't know what beauty is. To be beautiful is more that having fine features. To be truly beautiful emanates from within a person and only when that person is as wonderful in every way as you are.

Being away from you is misery. I can't kid myself into feeling any other way. I know that someday this will all be over and we'll be glad that we're doing things this way but baby, right now I feel so empty and alone that it almost seems as if I'm the only person in the world. I'm going to bed hon. When I sleep at least I don't feel this pain. Goodnight my sweet. I love you.

Once again it's lunchtime and I just finished reading the medical statements I received in this morning's mail. I also read the letter you wrote and if I had to choose between the two I'd rather read your letter.

Today has been a bad day. I overslept, got to work a half hour late, got hit with a bunch of stupid AF paperwork, felt disgusted because all this mess is such a waste of time and tonight is cleanup night in the barracks. Baby, the next guy who asks me to re-enlist is going to wind up on the ground.

As I told you before hon, don't count on the transfer. In fact, try not to even think about it. It's such a long shot that I'd hate to think of the odds against it and the air force is holding all the aces. Why, with all the bases near Chicago, didn't they send me to one when I returned from overseas? It would have simplified things so much. Oh well, just 17 more months and I'll be free from all this and just 21 days from when you read this we'll be together. That's a much more pleasant thought.

It's a beautiful day. Sun shining, fairly warm, no wind, and here we sit, thousands of miles apart. Every minute we're apart is just wasted time. I don't think anyone would like to be out of the service as much as I would. All that money I could be earning, the house we could be saving for, and most important, in fact all important, we would be together.

That's all that really matters.

Oh sweetheart, nothing has ever mattered to me as much as you do. I didn't think I could love you as much as I do.

I'm going to prepare my statement and submit all of them in the morning.

I love you baby.

Your baby

p.s. I love you

POSTMARK: OCTOBER 14, 1954

Thursday

Oct 14

Hi Sweetheart,

I miss you baby. I love you. I can't start this letter any other way because that's all I can think of. This morning I had the oddest experience. I had a long dream about us last night hon. I rarely dream and when it's about us, that's really something. It was so vivid and realistic that when I woke, for an hour or so reality seemed unreal and I was in a daze. When I arrived at work I couldn't keep my mind on anything I was doing so I leaned back and concentrated on us. All this seems to make me very unhappy to be here but it also makes me look forward all the more to next month.

Last night after I finished helping clean up the barracks, I decided to relax for a couple minutes before I started writing. I was stretched out on my bunk, relaxed completely, listening to a radio I borrowed and missing you, missing you so, when suddenly it was 2 AM and I was just where I was at nine. I decided to wait 'til now to start a letter. I'm on the tail end of my coffee break, time is running out and I hate to return to work. Baby, instead of feeling better as time passes, I feel worse. I try to snap out of it but honey, baby, when I'm away from you, all I can be is miserable. Darling I miss you. I'll be back in a little while sweet—I love you, I love you.

Hi honey. I just bolted my lunch, picked up the letter you wrote

Tuesday and I'm going to try to get as much written as I can before I have to get back to the mad house. When I finished my coffee break this morning and returned to work I was surprised to see two captains waiting for me. They are the training inspectors for the West Coast and I had to spend all morning showing them how we train the idiots in this outfit. I was introduced to them as the "administrative supervisor" and I nearly laughed out loud. Such a big title for such little money. When I go back this afternoon I have to take a test to determine how much I know about electronics and tomorrow we are being visited by a one star general. If he happens to come into our section I'll be stuck with the job of giving him a two dollar tour of our little snake pit. Very unwelcome job. Baby, all this is such a waste of time. I'm sure that there must be thousands of people who would get a kick out of this kind of stuff. Why me?

Baby, I ask you again. Please don't count on a transfer. I'd give anything if I could get one but honey, the service is a pretty cold, heartless organization and they have a frightening disregard for the feelings of the individual. Try not to think about it hon. I want it as much as you do, you know that, but I can see how slim the chances are. Whenever I think about it I also think about not being with you for 16 months. Baby, time drags by so slowly now and all we were worried about was six weeks. I hate to think of how it will be when it's sixteen months. That's approximately 480 days of walking around like a lost dog, 480 nights of coming into this room and looking at our picture, 480 days of missing you the way I do now, and 480 nights of lying in my bed in a dark empty room and feeling like I'm living for the sake of occupying space. It seems impossible. It's so awful that I tell myself very often that it can't happen but then I stop kidding myself and try to accept it.

My God, I hope Larry doesn't pop us at the last second and throw a wrench into the works. He can't—we've got more problems than is fair as it is. I don't think he will. I hope I'm right.

Baby, no matter what I have on my mind when I start to write, all that I can think about when I'm sitting here, is how much I miss you and how much you mean to me. You're all there is honey. Nothing, no one, means anything more. You're my whole existence. Everything I do is just going through the motions. There are times when I want to be with you so badly that I'm not really in my right mind. Sometimes I wake up in the middle of the night and I feel so lonely, so absolutely lonely, that it's frightening. Never stop loving me honey. My life is in your hands, such beautiful hands. I love you my sweet. Oh to be able to hold you now, for just a second. I love you honey.

Your baby

p.s. I love you

World War II had been over for less than a decade, hence the "social blights" regarding a Japanese/American marriage.

POSTMARK: OCTOBER 16, 1954

Friday

Oct 15

Hi Baby,

The noon whistle just blew and that means I have a half hour to spend writing. I wonder what you are doing right now. It's a beautiful day here. It must be 75 without a cloud in the sky. I've got my windows opened completely, my radio is playing, your picture is smiling at me and I just checked another day off the calendar. We'll be together in three weeks, but when you read this, it will only be eighteen days. I happened to remember something that happened a few months ago. When you sent me that first bunch of pictures one of the officers saw them in my room and told me that I'd better get home and marry you. At the time it was something that I considered quite impossible. In fact I was trying to condition myself and prepare for the day when you'd fall in love with someone and I'd be out in the cold. Today he heard that I was getting married and he said that I was pretty smart to take his advice. I couldn't resist the chance to squelch him so I said, "Oh yes sir, your advice was the deciding factor."

Today is the day that the general is on the base and I've been told to stay in the office 'til he leaves. He's sure to drop in and I'll have to give him the three dollar tour of the section. I've got on my blue uniform, shoes shined and I've been ordered to wear my one row of ribbons. I'll always be a civilian at heart so this is definitely not to my liking. He's liable to be one of the congenial kind that asks people how they like the service and the officers in my section are going to hold their breath if he asks me. I'm the number 1 AF hater at this base and I don't keep it a secret. The AF keeps us apart and as far as I'm concerned, that's enough reason to hate it. Of course, they are going to help pay for our house but I'm sure we'd have the house without their help.

Gee honey, I didn't notice the fact that you needed a manicure. I guess I'd better take the picture down.

Darn it, they just called for me over the speaker. That means that the wheel will be appearing any minute. I've got to go hon. I'll finish this after work. I hate to leave. See you later hon. I love you.

Hi baby. It is one o'clock in the morning and I have just returned from the club and a few other assorted places. When I went back to work this afternoon I got here 2 minutes before the General did, everything went fine, I came down with a splitting headache so after work I hit the sack. About ten, someone got me out of bed for a phone call. It was the T/sgt from my section. He was down at the club and wanted me to come down for a beer. I wasn't tired so I did as he asked. He's got five stripes and has been in six years. He's going to stay in the service for good and normally I have nothing but contempt for people like that but he's a rare exception. According to the book I'm supposed to be under him but we've got a good arrangement at work and I handle my job without any interference or supervision from anyone. He's being forced by circumstances to stay in the service. He's married to a Japanese girl and the service is the only place that offers him the chance to go to Japan where they'll be free from social blights that arise out of such a marriage. When I got to the club, he was loaded and told me the full story. He doesn't like the AF any more than I do but as I said, he has no choice. He gave me all sorts of advice on marriage and made me promise to be a good husband and not to get drunk as he'd done. Then I drove him home, brought his car back here and here I am. I just took a shower so I'd be wide awake but it's working just the opposite and I'm feeling drowsy. It's when I'm sitting here like this, all alone, late at night, that I feel the worst. Baby, I don't know how I'll take being away from you for so long. It's rough hon. You know how much I love you. No one could love anyone more. It's only been 25 days since we parted and it seems like ages. Every day has been terrible. Those two days on the train and the first day or two that I was back were the most unhappy experiences I've ever lived through. Being with you so much and then being parted is hell—literal hell. When I feel like this, when it gets unbearable, the best thing for me to do is try to sleep and right now I miss you so badly that I can hardly stand it. My sweet, I love you so. I guess that everything that is really worthwhile takes some sacrifices but I doubt if anyone ever went through anything this painful. I'm going to bed now hon, goodnight, love me always. I love you.

Hi baby, I just woke up and in a few minutes I'm heading for town to get the marriage license and I'll have it in the mail tomorrow. I feel better than I did last night. Sometimes this place gets so depressing that I'm a bundle of nerves. I usually feel better in the morning but those long, lonely evenings. Baby, I love you. I'm going to run now hon. I love you always.

Your baby

p.s. I love you

POSTMARK: OCTOBER 17, 1954

Sunday
Oct 17

Hi Baby,
I just finished a letter to El, included the notarized note for the car so pretty soon she'll be giving you the balance of the money.

It's exactly 7:22 in Blaine, 9:22 in Chicago. Baby, what are you doing right now? It's Saturday night, all the workin' folk are out cavorting. All but me. I'm planning on dropping in the club a little later. Saturday night is usually a circus and I don't want to miss it.

No baby, the girl who cut her wrists wasn't Shirley. This girl was psycho and Shirley is too dumb to be psycho. I hope nothing that exciting happens tonight but I won't be surprised at anything. That club has a reputation for odd impromptu entertainment.

It's been a busy day. After I mailed your letter this morning, I went to Bellingham, discovered that the license bureau was closed, noticed the high temperature, bright sun and decided that it was a fine day for golf so I took off for Birch Bay, played 18 holes, left my clubs in the club house and walked back to the base. The 2½ miles of resorts was completely deserted. The sun was setting, the ducks were flapping around above the completely still water of the bay, everything looked beautiful and I was wishing so much that you could be with me so I could fully enjoy the effect that all this created. Occasionally a car would drive by and the drivers gave me funny looks. They must have thought that I was a beach comber or something.

I just spent five minutes starting at your angelic face and letting my mind wander. When I look at our picture I can just about feel you in my arms. Nearly, but not quite.

Right about now the club should be starting to jump so I'm going to clean up and walk down there. 'Til morning baby, I'll be thinking of you every second.

Hi Sweet, It's 8:30 and in a little while I'll be off for Seattle. I made tentative reservations at Lake Wilderness but I haven't seen it yet so today I'll have a look around. If it's nice I'll get things arranged, if not, I'll go somewhere else.

Leopard skin robe—hmmm. And only 20 days from today. Baby, less than three weeks and we'll be married. Time seems to pass slowly but suddenly it's gone. When you read this, we'll only have 18 days to our wedding. Wow, I can hardly believe it's going to happen. In fact when I look at our picture I can hardly believe that those 3 weeks in September were real, but they were and I'll always remember every day of that leave.

I've got to run babe
I love you
I love you
I love you
Your
Baby

p.s. I love you

Monday
18 October

Hi Honey,

I feel like I've got the problems of the world on my shoulders. Yesterday, while I was in Seattle I drove out to Lake Wilderness and checked my reservations. The place is beautiful. We're staying in the lodge. They have cottages but I didn't like them so I reserved us a place in the lodge instead. I won't try to describe it but it's perfect. The only catch is that we'll definitely need a car. Mine hasn't been running lately but it looks like I'll have to have it fixed.

The transfer is out. I may as well be in prison for my chances of getting out of here. Baby, I feel sick when I think about being away from you for all that time. Remember how I used to tell you how I dreaded the time after Sept. I told you that even before I was home. Now it's worse than ever. A year from now I'll still have five months to go. I never really minded the service 'til now. I don't work too hard, living facilities are pretty good and for a single guy it can be interesting, but with you thousands of miles away—honey, I laid awake three hours last night trying to find a solution. It's bothering me so much that I can't think of anything else. I've tried to figure things out systematically, weighed everything involved and I've come to the obvious conclusion that the reason we're doing it this way is to save money—correct? I've tried to figure out how much we'd save. With my allotments, mustering out pay, travel pay, and bonds it will come to approximately $2800 dollars. I've also done some other figuring, inquiring, and probably, foolish planning. Baby, if you were out here we could save just as much. I know that sounds impossible but it's true. Here are the reasons. Rent is low here. Bellingham (pop 35,000) is full of apartments for rent, completely furnished, that have a top price of 50 to 60 a month. Food out here isn't as high as in Chicago because a lot of stuff can be purchased directly from the farmers. I've talked to most of the married A/1c's and the ones without kids are living comfortably, with a car, on $175 a month. Bellingham is 39 minutes from the base. It's not a bad town, and Seattle is 2 hours away. Jobs don't pay as much here as they do in Chicago but they need help in Bellingham and with your receptionist experience there wouldn't be any problems. We could save as much together as we could apart. Time is a funny thing. It can't really be measured. If we were together 17 months would be nothing, it would pass quickly, but baby, it will be an eternity the other way. There are other things to consider of course. All your furniture, the quartet, your job, and being away from the folks. I've thought about all of them and except for the furniture there is nothing I can say. Those are decisions that would have to be made by you. As far as your job goes hon, if Yardley's is going to pay as much as I think it will, you wouldn't have to work after my discharge anyway. The quartet of course is another thing. I know how much work you've put into it and I know how much you enjoy it. And being away from the folks for 17 months wouldn't be pleasant for you either, but, I guess I'm being selfish again, being away from you is no picnic for me. I guess I'm causing you more problems by writing all this but don't worry about it hon. I've told you many times that my main concern is your happiness. That's all I'm really interested in and to me that's all that really counts. Whichever way you prefer is the way I want you to decide, and knowing your sympathetic nature I don't want any decisions made that would be based on being sorry for me. I've never wanted anything that was derived from pity or sympathy. Baby, I want you out here but only if I was sure that you'd be happy and only if I know that you would rather have it that way. We've always agreed to be perfectly honest with each other hon, and if you were with me right now you would have probably said "What?" and I'd have told you all this so that's why I wrote it. And because of the mutual honesty we both want, tell me exactly what you think and as you once asked me in a letter, be perfectly honest about it.

I've got the letter to El on my desk so I'll mention the ring to her. That shouldn't be any problem. When you finish this, how about giving her a buzz and see if she's sent that bond. Time is starting to pass a little faster and I want to get this money angle all cleared up. I didn't mention anything to El about my suggesting that you come out here. As I said, you make the decision and either way, if it's what you want it'll be the right one.

I love you honey and if you should feel a little peeved at me for bringing this up right now and giving you more to worry about, remember baby, I love you. I'll accept any decision you make.

I've already taken two hours for lunch so I'd better close now.

I love you sweetheart, you're all there is.

I love you,

Your baby

p.s. I love you

POSTMARK: OCTOBER 19, 1954

Tuesday
October 19th

Hi Sweetheart,

Yes honey, less than three weeks. Just 17 days from today, two weeks from the day you read this, we'll be together again. That's all I can think of. Time has been dragging but maybe now it'll pass a bit faster.

I had hoped the plane would land a little later in the day but since you arrive at eight I'll make some kind of arrangements. I'll let you know in a few days what to do. If I can I'll get the Varns' to meet you. If not, a friend of mine will be at a base about that time and he could meet you there. I'll arrange something.

The letter I wrote yesterday must have been a little surprising. Honey, you know how I miss you and there are times when I can hardly bear the thought of being away from you for so long. Sometimes I hit such depths of depression that I'm ready for a padded cell. Don't worry about that letter hon. We made our plans so I guess we can stick by them. Having you out here would be too wonderful for words but even if we're 2200 miles apart, distance can't affect our love. No matter how far away you are, you're still my wife, I'm your husband, we love each other and that's what counts. Baby, I do love you so.

Honey, the letters you sent were just what I wanted. Anyone with any warmth in them at all would have OK'd them but not the AF. I guess this outfit just can't be beaten. It's not human. We tried honey but the AF won't be swayed.

I'll write to Gus tonight and ask him for the money. He won't refuse.

If I have my car fixed, we can drive up to see the base. I've got to get a car somewhere. Renting is too expensive and most of the guys with cars that I'm friendly with are married so they need them. I'm going to have mine fixed I guess. It's no beauty but it will run, at least it'll kind of stagger.

Honey, if you miss me as much as I miss you, then we're like two magnets, unstoppable 'til they are together. No matter what I'm doing, whether I'm working, talking to someone, whatever I'm doing, I think about you. How I long for you my wife. When I made the reservations at Lake Wilderness, I said 'Mr. and Mrs. Michael Royko.' Did I feel good!

I told El about the ring and I'm sure that she'll cooperate. I feel bad about it too baby. I didn't realize how things stood when I brought it over that day. I'm sorry hon.

My lunch hour is nearly over sweet. These people are a pain in the neck but they try. Last night I felt so lonely and depressed that I didn't want to write for fear it would sound bad. I'm sorry this is so short hon but they don't give me a lot of time.

El hasn't sent the bond yet. Give her a buzz back babe? Tomorrow's payday so I'll buy the license. That'll be another milestone.

I'll see you very soon my wife
I love you so much
Your husband
Mick

p.s. I love you

[ILLEGIBLE POSTMARK]
Wednesday night
Oct 20

Hello Sweetheart,

It's two weeks from today honey. As you read this, it should be Saturday evening, you've just returned from work, maybe a little tired, it's dark outside the house, and starting tomorrow it will be a week and some days. Two weeks honey. Less than two weeks and we'll be together. Two weeks and we'll be married. Married! Honey, it's all true. It's the most wonderful thing that ever happened. It's a fairytale in real life. Carol Joyce Royko. Carol Joyce Royko. That sounds like music. Baby, can you imagine what it feels like to have a life dream come true? To be on the threshold of a life of happiness—sublime happiness? Baby, you've done all this. You've made me the happiest, luckiest, most fortunate guy in the whole wide world. Oh sweetheart, thank you for being you.

No letter yesterday. I'm sorry honey. I goofed and I've felt terrible about it. I've been up to my ears in work and I just couldn't get enough time off to write. I'm sorry honey, I'll be miserable all tomorrow because you won't receive a letter. Forgive me my sweet?

As you see, I've enclosed the application for a **MARRIAGE LICENSE** [hearts drawn on top]. I'm happy like a fish or something. Take the application to a notary public, fill out the parts listed for female in his presence, someone in your family can act as witness, return it to me and I'll fill out my part, get the license and honey, sweetheart, we'll be all set. Return it as soon as possible 'cause it's got to be on record for three days before they can issue me the license. Anytime next week will be soon enough. Baby, the day is coming soon. Two weeks!

I've written the letter to Gus and I'll mail it tomorrow. He'll probably receive it Monday. That will be the last of my worries.

Honey, in such a short time you'll be in my arms again. All I've been thinking of lately is us at Lake Wilderness. I hope the weather is good. There isn't much to do there. Just a lake, the lodge, some cottages, a few boats, lots of trees and scenery, a nine hole golf course, you and me and no skiing. If I get my car mobilized by then we can drive up here and I'll show you around my home away from home.

I guess I have been neglectful in not writing to the family. I'll sit right down tomorrow and write them all. I promise honey. Sweetheart, this is all amazing. Less than two months ago my big worry was how to become number 1 suitor. In two weeks we'll be married. Honey, it's just too amazing. I'm a confirmed believer in miracles.

Baby, I don't know how I'll stand an eight month separation either. It's sure an unpleasant thing to look forward to. I hate to think about it but it's difficult not to. When I look at our picture together, it seems unnatural to be any other way than together. I feel so incomplete without you. I'm glad you feel that way too honey. We disprove a definition of love that I once read. According to the writer, when two people were in love, one loved and the other allowed himself or herself to be loved. With us it's different honey. We both love and are loved.

I love you my darling
Your husband,
Mick

p.s. I love you

Saturday

Oct 23

Hello Sweetheart,

It's Saturday morning, 11:15, the sun is shining, the day is warm, and in two weeks and fifteen minutes we'll be standing in the chapel together. In two weeks and twenty minutes we'll be married. That's not very long to wait. One month ago I was in Seattle, feeling as low as could be. I guess that time is a cure for just about everything.

Baby, you're right in all respects and honey, how could I doubt that you love me? You're marrying me and that's pretty good proof.

Here are the two reasons I can't have the transfer. 1. The regulation that covers compassionate transfer stated that the ailing person must give evidence of being cured in one year or less or will pass away in one year or less. With cancer it's impossible to really say how it will turn out. 2. Shortage of men. We are losing all our best electronics men here and I'm going to have to take on a lot of jobs that I'm not trained for. We tried honey, but the AF is just too big.

I missed another letter yesterday. I spent the whole day painting the inside of the radar tower and when I got off work I was so beat and felt so lousy I went right to bed. Painting isn't a tiring job normally but I was painting in such a variety of pretzel like positions that I felt like I had been through a wringer. I just woke up a little while ago and I'm going to have to rush to get this in the mail delivery so you'll receive it Monday.

Don't worry baby, your decision was the right one and I love you. Your idea about the Christmas leave sounds good but we'll wait and see. It's hard to plan anything in advance with the AF on my neck. I love you honey. I'm sorry this is so short but the mail is leaving in a little while. I love you, I love you, I love you.

Your husband in two weeks.

Mick

p.s. I love you

Sunday
Oct 24

Hello My Darling,

Honey I miss you. I've been sitting here for a couple hours just dreaming about the future. Not the AF future but the years to follow. I've been trying to picture us together as husband and wife but I'm afraid I can't see us as husband and wife in the commonly accepted sense. When people get married, it seems to me that very often there occurs a period of disenchantment during which they acquire that "married look." Baby, we'll always look like we're just newly engaged or newly married. That must sound like a goofy way to start off a letter but I was thinking along those lines when I started writing.

Yesterday I went to the home of the girl who is going to stand up for our wedding. She has your address and if you haven't yet heard from her, you will in a few days. I guess she wanted to arrange her clothing according to what you'll be wearing. Margo Wade is her name. What about the flowers hon? Orchid? What color? How many? Does she carry one?????? You know, I've never seen a wedding. Have you heard from El about the ring yet? How about the car money? Speaking of cars, we'll be driving a 1950 Ford, just like my Dad's except it's green. Rather than have mine fixed, I'm renting it from one of the guys on the base. It's well worth what I'm paying him. As each problem is taken care of, I feel a bit more relaxed. Let's see, Lake Wilderness, Church, car, people to stand up—that's about it.

We will have the most unusual group of people imaginable in attendance. I'll tell you about them. Joe Kahwaty, a Syrian boxer from Brooklyn, 3 years of college, dark, handsome, and a very good friend. George Shoff, a card shark from anywhere and everywhere. Ermono Gurrucchi, an Italian from Connecticut, 270 pounds, 5'10". Ralph Peterson, best man, electronics engineer from Chicago. Bill Varns, my boss, and another officer who is a farmer from Ohio. Variety? We've got it. Baby, the only thing that they all have in common is that they are all good eggs, good friends, and though extremely different, they are alike in that they are gentlemen. Honey, just twelve more days and they will have the honor of watching the two most-in-love people in the world become the happiest husband and wife in the world. Baby when you receive this, it'll be just ten days. Just one more weekend sweetheart. I love you so.

Within the next few days I expect the bond, the marriage application and a letter from Gus or El to arrive. I'll be glad when all that's done. I'm taking a terrific ribbing from everyone. A day doesn't pass without at least a dozen people asking me how many days of freedom I have left. Fools.

In a way I can understand the surprise of your relatives. Most of them don't know me and had no idea that you were considering marriage again. We did kind of drop a bombshell honey, and our engagement was short but considering the fact that we've known each other for 12 years, I don't think anyone should have any criticisms.

A few more days baby. We'll have six of the happiest days ever.

I love you

Mick

p.s. I love you

POSTMARK: OCTOBER 26, 1954
Monday

I love you. This is the time of night I feel closest to you. It's midnight, I can see you sleeping, all I have to do is close my eyes and I can picture you perfectly and that makes me happy because I know that at this exact moment the picture in my mind is correct. I'm in my room of course. Baby, honest to God, they're playing that song again. I can't describe how I feel right now, loving you so, that song playing. I want to be with you so badly, I want to take you in my arms, hold you, words will be unnecessary. We'll have six days of that honey, six days of complete happiness. It's not a long time honey but I'll be able to stand the thought of the impending separation because I'll have something so wonderful to look forward to that I'll stand anything. You as my wife. Honey, it's still a little hard to believe. Baby, when that man pronounces us man and wife, there is my whole life wrapped up real pretty, happiness assured. Your folks deserve a medal. They deserve more than that. They gave me you and I could never repay them for so wonderful a gift. I'll try though. I'll try by dedicating my life to making you happy and honey, I can't think of a higher ambition than that. I won't be the smartest, richest, or best looking husband in the world, but there won't be anyone who loves his wife more than I love you. We won't ever be rich and that's OK because people who are rich only have money. They won't have what we have. We are rich. We're rich because of our love. I'm the richest person in the world. I can sit back and count my wealth and feel luxurious. Happiness is the ultimate goal of everyone. What is happiness? What else could it be but to love with all your heart and to have that love returned. You've given me happiness honey, you and you alone could do it and you've done it. You've made me see the whole world in a different way. Self confidence I've never had before is now part of me. Success is something I take for granted now because if there is one thing that can't be beaten, it's a team, and sweetheart, we'll be an unbeatable team. What creates success? I believe that it's two things. Incentive and the rewards that come with achievement. You, my darling, are my incentive and your happiness is my reward. Baby, some people are born under lucky stars. My star was cloudy for a while but it's shining brightly now. That night, that wonderful, memorable, historic night you said you loved me was the turning point of my life. You've made me completely dependent upon your love. My whole life is in your hands, your beautiful hands. I love you my darling, my sweetheart, my wife.

It's late honey. I'm going to fall asleep with you in my arms. Good-night my sweet, wonderful, perfect, adorable darling. I love you with all my heart. Could I ever love you more? I think it's impossible. No one could love anyone more. I love you, I love you, I love you.

Goodnight my sweetheart,

My wife.

I love you,

Your baby.

p.s. I love you

Wednesday

27 Oct.

Hello Sweetheart,

As you read this letter you are either preparing to leave for court or you've already been there. Honey, rush me that license application. As soon as it arrives I'll buzz out to the license bureau and get it on file so we can get that license on file.

El's mentioning wedding gifts was very pleasant news, mercenary soul that I am but you were right in telling her that we'll still continue with the loan from Gus. By now he's received the letter I wrote him. Additional expenses came up that I hadn't expected. Since we'll need a car I rented one from one of the guys at the base—$25.00. For six days it's well worth the money. The church will cost, as will gas for the car, flowers, and other odds and ends, soooo, no matter what we receive in gifts, borrow enough from Gus so that you will bring $150 with you. I've tried to figure up expenses and if you bring $150 that will cover our expenses and give us a little insurance. I'll have enough here for the car, church, gas and anything else that might crop up and I'll still have 50 or 60 left. If you bring the 150 along we probably won't spend all of it but I don't want to be worrying about money during those six days. I asked for $125 from Gus and he'll probably cooperate. I still haven't received the bond from El but if she sent it special delivery it should arrive any time now.

Baby, this is going to be difficult for me to write but I've got to do it and I'll explain why. Honey, I don't want to wear my uniform at the wedding. You know how I feel about the air force. If I wore the uniform it would be hypocrisy on my part. I don't like the AF. It's caused me nothing but trouble. It's separated us, it refused to transfer me, and when I'm with you, I want to be your husband, and I don't like to think of myself as a husband while decked out in those blue rags. No one else will be in uniform and I'd feel like a fool. Baby, this wedding is the big moment of my life. Being in uniform would detract from it. Try to understand honey. For 31 months I've worn G.I. clothes, looked at other people in them, hated the sight of them and for me to wear a uniform at my wedding would be like bowing to the AF, accepting it as so big an influence on my life, that I'd wear its symbols at my wedding—Honey, I'm going to wear a suit. I'll be a nondescript looking civilian but I'll feel a lot better. I know that you want me to wear my blues baby, but that uniform would disgust me much more than it would please you.

Ok hon, you stumped me. TWWBMAW? I give up.

Time is starting to pass very quickly. Before we know it we'll be together again. I'm getting that same butterflies feeling I had before my leave. Oh honey, it'll be so wonderful to hold you again. Last night I couldn't get you out of my mind long enough to fall asleep and to put it mildly, I got shook. I must have smoked a half a pack of cigarettes in an attempt to calm my nerves. Baby, you're part of me.

I love you, I love you, I love you
Your baby

p.s. I love you

POSTMARK: OCTOBER 28, 1954
Wednesday night
October 28

My Darling,

The first thing I want you to do is calm down. Relax, stop worrying. I received your letter this afternoon and it was too late to get the letter in today's mail delivery so I decided after reading it to think about the situation before I gave you an answer. Here is what I've decided. If the application doesn't arrive in time for us to be married on the 6th I can change most of my plans. I can change the date at church, cancel the reservations at Lake Wilderness, cancel the renting of a car, and tell the people who were coming to the wedding that the date has been changed but here is what I can't do. I can't change the days off that I've already talked my way into. As things stand now, I'll be off Friday, Sat, Sun, Mon, Tue, Wed and return to work on Thursday. All this time off is not coming out of my leave time and actually it's against AF policy to give anyone that much time off at one time. Varns has done this without the consent of the squadron powers and I doubt if he would change the schedule now. So the best thing to do is—send the application as soon as you can, board the plane as we planned and we'll still have our six days together. The worst that could happen is that the wedding would be delayed 'til Sunday or Monday. If anyone at home wonders about us being together two or three days before we're married, just tell them that I checked with the license bureau and we can still make it for the 6th. If we have to wait 'til the 7th or 8th, no one will know but us and honey it won't matter because we'll be together for the six days just as we planned. Just mail the application and leave the rest to me. And don't worry or get yourself upset. So we have to make a few minor alterations in our plans. We'll still be together, we'll still be married and that's the main thing. I hope that the application arrives in time for us to be married as scheduled but if it doesn't, what's a day or two. As far as I'm concerned you're my wife right now. So remember, no matter what happens, mail the application special delivery, board the plane Thursday and we'll be married while you're here. If not the 6th, then the 7th or 8th. It doesn't matter a great deal hon, the day, the place or who's present. The fact that it's us is all that counts. I'll have a car, we can change our plans to coordinate with our wedding and everything will be OK. It'll just take a few phone calls to cancel the church arrangement, Lake Wilderness, and we'll be set.

Baby, a week from the day you read this, we'll be together. Wonderful? I guess there have been less complicated marriages before but everything will work out ok and before long, I'll be addressing my letters to Carol Royko. We'll have a little unhappiness for a while honey. Being separated is no fun, but after I'm discharged and we're in our house, this will all seem remote and not as bad as it seems now.

You'll probably receive this Saturday, so calm down honey, and everything will be alright. I love you and I'll call Monday night. Remember, we'll just go right along with our plans. I'll see you in less than a week.

I love you
Your baby

p.s. I love you

Friday

Oct 29

Sweetheart,

Your two letters plus the note from Mo arrived a few minutes ago so now I can start being my usual happy, cheerful, bouncing bundle of good will. When I didn't receive a letter yesterday it kind of depressed me and the thought of telling all those people that we wouldn't be needing them next week was starting to become a king sized headache. All morning I shuffled around work like a lost soul, my brain working feverishly. This served to depress and confuse all my associates because of late I have been the happiest guy on two feet. I can assure you that the plans I've been making have been costly, both in time and money. The trips I took to Seattle to arrange for the church, the reservations and to tie all the loose ends together all looked to be for nothing when I read your last letter. I'm glad everything will go according to schedule now.

1. Gifts—Since you'll arrive on Friday, we'll have time to buy the gifts, flowers, and whatever else we need then. I won't be able to get to Seattle 'til then so it'll have to be done the day before the big day.

2. Money—Get the 125 from Gus, stack it on top of the gifts we'll receive and bring the whole mess with you. No matter how much we have, bring it all. We don't want to take any chances on running short.

3. Ring—I'll write El again today, thank Gus for the loan and also get the ring. I mentioned it to her so I'm surprised that she hasn't done anything.

4. Camera—I'll try to arrange for a camera but that'll have to be done in Seattle also. Bring your trusty flash set, and Ralph is bringing his too. We'll have scads of pictures.

Sweetheart, if this were happening 3 months ago, I'd be offered the use of numerous cars free, probably receive a high gift from the boys and be forced to throw a big reception here, but most of the old gang has been discharged and I haven't gone out of my way to cultivate a new crop of friends. As it is I don't anticipate too many gifts here but that's ok. These poor GI's are in bad financial shape.

Honey, it's noon. A week from today, I'll be roaring into Seattle, you'll be waiting for me. A week from the day you read this, we'll be on our honeymoon. Sweetheart, this is wonderful.

I've got to run babe. I'll write again tonight. I love you—love you—love you.

Your baby

In November 1974, I was fifteen and 6'4", and my brother Rob was eleven—and blonde.

POSTMARK: OCTOBER 30, 1954

Saturday Morning

Hello Sweetheart,

I just rolled out of bed a half hour ago after a quiet Friday night. After work last night, someone talked me into a movie in Bellingham. Against my better judgment I went. The movie "Anna" was just the type I try to avoid. Anna, a night club singer meets a nice clean cut lad who wishes to marry her but though she loves him she refuses because she has been having an affair with the bartender in the nightclub. She tells her farmer boy love of this and he forgives her. She agrees to marry him but she can't break the spell that the bartender holds over her and on their wedding day the bartender shows up at the farm house, tries to assault her in the cellar, is caught by the farmer, pulls a gun and loses his life for his efforts. Anna, seeing the trouble she has caused becomes a nun in a hospital and also a nurse. The poor farm boy, when released from jail can't find Anna. He has an accident, Anna's fine nursing saves his life, he pleads with her to marry him before she takes her final vows and she makes the decision to dedicate her life to the church. THE END—I swear, I'm through with movies. The movie, with its ridiculous theme of self sacrifice put me in a bad frame of mind and I was anxious to get back to the base so I could write a few lines. It was very foggy and we were driving very slowly. About a mile from the base we approached a very sharp curve and there stood an airman with blood on his head, a telephone pole broken neatly in half by his car and wires strung all over the road. He's new here and was going faster than he should have in the fog. He had gone off the curve and hit the pole. He was very lucky to be alive. The pole was laying across the hood of his car. We called the cops, and at 1:30 we arrived at the base. Just as we were pulling into the base, another car came flying out. I heard his engine roar down the road then suddenly it was quiet. A minute later a figure came walking out of the fog, blood on his head—another telephone pole. What a night. The fog is still thick as soup and I wouldn't be surprised if we have a few more accidents this afternoon.

The mail should be up by now honey, so I'm going to pause long enough to walk over to the mail room. A letter! I love you sweet.

All the ribbing I've been taking is tinged with envy and respect. You, my darling, have achieved a great deal of fame on this base. It had long been an accepted fact that I was just a free loving bachelor. Now that I'm nearing the end of my single life most of the guys are surprised. Surprised because I've turned into a calm person, surprised because of your beauty, and greatly surprised at the suddenness of our marriage. We'll always surprise people hon. As calmly as everyone accepted everything at home, they can't kid me.

November 1974—The only two people in Monterey Villa who will make as nice looking a couple as us will be our two tall blond kids. We'll never take each other for granted, our love will never stop growing and we'll always be completely happy. I love you.

It's time for lunch so I'll close now. I'm going to run into Bellingham now and buy a white shirt. It is customary to wear one at weddings I've heard.

I love you sweetheart,
Your baby

p.s. I love you

Monday

Hello Sweetheart,

Just received the application, the bond and your letter. Congratulations honey. Just think, one week of being Miss Duckman, Then Mrs. Royko.

I'm busy as heck today so tomorrow I'll take the application to town then Friday morning I can pick it up on my way to Seattle. I'll cash in the bond while I'm at it.

Sweetheart, I'm not sure how much money we have because I don't know the results of my family's wedding gifts but whatever is left over after the plane fare, court costs, clothes, etc., bring with you. I'm having a hard time figuring expenses because of all the little things that keep popping up. Gus has given you the check by now so that's taken care of. We'll probably have money left when you leave so we can probably pay him part of it without waiting for the allotment.

Sweetheart, when you get off the plane in Seattle ask the info desk to direct you to the Olympia Hotel Limousine service. You will be driven right to the hotel, walk in, tell them that you are Mrs. Michael Royko, they will show you to your room and you can wait for me there. Mr. Varns is working Friday and Ed, the fellow at the nearby base is going to be awaiting discharge so I've made reservations at the best hotel in Seattle. For the sake of propriety I imagine it would be better not to tell anyone. You can rest up while you're waiting for me. I'll probably get there about 2 to 3 in the afternoon, then we can check on the camera, buy the flowers and get a gift for Pete. Sweetheart, just four days and we'll be together. No wonder I'm nervous.

Tonight you are having a shower. I know because El told me. El also told me that we'll make lots and lots of money. Great—we can use it.

Sweetheart I've got to run—work—work—work. Remember, limousine to hotel—Olympia Hotel—Nothing but the best for my baby.

I love you, do you know that?

In four days you'll be my wife.

I'll write tonight.
I love you,
Mick

p.s. I love you

POSTMARK: NOVEMBER 2, 1954
Tuesday

Going somewhere tonight? Sweetheart, it's slowly but surely coming true. Four days from today you will be my wife. How lucky can I be.

Last night I had planned on writing a long letter but I received some news that nearly floored me. One of the boys told me that I was next in line for KP and that Sunday would be my first day. I nearly fainted. I got a hold of the keys to the orderly room, found the duty roster, changed my name to a different position so now I won't have KP for at least three weeks. If I had been caught—well, we won't think about that.

I've been working like mad so that the work won't pile up on me when I'm gone and I'll have to limit this to one page.

Don't forget hon, take one of the limousines at the airport. They go to the hotel Olympia and I've made reservations there. You'll be tired so that'll give you a chance to get some sleep. Be careful baby. I love you so. Last night I was awake 'til three, just thinking about you. It seems such a long time since we've been together. I love you so. In three days you'll be in my arms. 'Til then my darling.

I love you,
Your baby

p.s. I love you

"Hello My Sweet Wonderful Wife"

Mike and Carol are newlyweds. The envelopes alone tell part of the story—they are first addressed to Carol Wozny, then after the divorce, Carol Duckman. Now, Carol Royko.

To paint the history of Mom and Dad's marriage as nothing but a rosy extension of these letters would be wishful thinking. By the time Mom died, Dad was atop journalism's tiny summit of superstars, which came stocked with plenty of booze, and bimbos. It was not a place for a family man, and our household was not like the Duckmans', a bright example that showed me what was possible. Then again, it was not like Dad's childhood home either—Mom and Dad might have yelled plenty as they battled, but he was not physically abusive. And they never divorced. Having now mucked around (as Dad might have said) for more than twenty years in the swamp of mediation and severe marital conflict, I have learned that I cannot predict how marriages will turn out. What I do know—what I saw in even the darkest times—is that Mom was always aware of, and could see, the good, even when Dad did his best to obscure it. The letters let us see a glimpse of the Mickey Mom knew, and loved.

Friday, November 12

Hello My Sweet Wonderful Wife,

It's Friday evening and this is the first chance I've had to write. When I hung up the phone Thursday morning, I fell into my bunk and slept for 22 straight hours. I arrived at work this morning feeling fit as a fiddle, all set to tear into my duties and missing you so badly it felt as if my heart would break. When you boarded the plane it was as if my life were coming to an end. I went up to the roof and watched the plane 'til I couldn't see it any more, went to the car and nearly choked myself to keep back the tears. Baby I'm in misery without you.

I drove as far as Everett, about 20 miles from Seattle, then the car broke down. I left it at a garage and caught a bus, arrived here at 4:30 and haven't felt anything but pain since the moment you left me.

It never fails honey. The radio is playing "Always." Not for just a year, but always. Oh honey, I love you so. All day I've been reliving every minute of our honeymoon. Thinking about everything we laughed at together, the few moments of sadness when our tears mingled, and the moments, the many moments of incomparable happiness. No one has ever spent 5 happier, perfect days than ours. I love you my sweet. I love you and I'll always love you.

I spent an hour getting my records changed this morning and it felt great to see Carol Joyce Royko listed in the different places. My wife, my wife, my wife—I can't say it often enough.

Monday I start 6 days of KP. I'm glad it came when it did so I can be free to spend Thanksgiving at the Varns'. I talked to Harvey about the pictures and it'll be a while before he has them developed because there is quite a bit of film left on the roll. I'll try to speed him up a bit. I'm eager to see them.

In nine days I'll be talking to you again sweetheart. I must have sounded kind of goofy on the phone but I was half asleep and could barely hear you. Next time I call, talk loud hon. I don't want to miss a word you say.

I've got the picture of the house on the wall; next to ours.

The boys are throwing a farewell party for Shoff tonight so I'll have to close. 'til tomorrow,
Your ever lovin' husband,
I love you
Your baby

p.s. I love you

That Dad had not yet seen the 1954 John Wayne movie "The High and the Mighty" —and was going to see it only because of Carol's recommendation—suggests that he was not yet the Wayne devotee his readers came to know.

Saturday
November 13

Hi Wonderful,
It's Saturday night, 6:15, and one week has passed since November 6th. It's been a dull day, rainy and boring. I slept 'til 11, ate lunch, read your letter, watched a football game on T.V., ate supper and here I am, happy and yet unhappy. That's a crazy condition to be in but that's just the way I feel. I'm miserable because we're apart, yet I feel great whenever I look at my ring and realize that we are married. Most of my time has been spent in reliving our honeymoon and thinking of how wonderful you are. Every song that I hear on the radio makes me think of you. I can't think of anything else but that's nothing new. After years of having you on my mind I'm getting used to it. It'll be wonderful trying to get used to years and years of holding you in my arms.

Time is going to drag but like everything else, my next leave will arrive and we'll be together. Five months—that's not a lifetime.

Baby, I know what you were going through when we parted because I was going through the same thing. I couldn't see you on the plane but I waited 'til the plane was gone before I left the airport. If anyone had looked closely at me while I stood on the observation roof they would have seen some very unmanly tears in my eyes. Baby this parting is hard to take. It seems like an impossible dream when I think that someday we'll always be together. Even though we are separated by miles of distance, we are really together hon, in our hearts. No matter what I'm doing, where I am, I know it's only temporary and that someday I'll have complete, fulfilled happiness. All I have to do is look at your picture, the picture of our future home and I know that I've got the greatest promise of happiness anyone ever had. Ours will be a wonderful, happy, complete life. The saying "the honeymoon is over" will never pertain to us. Our love will always be fresh and will never require rekindling. I love you my wife. Only 8 days and I'll be talking to you again. I'll hear your voice and I'll feel that we're so close I could reach out and hold you. I know that I can't but it's nice to feel that I can now and then.

By now you've probably talked to everyone at home and they know all (well, nearly all) about the honeymoon. No one can really understand how wonderful it really was but us.

Tonight I'm going to a movie—High and Mighty. I want to see it 'cause you enjoyed it so much.

I love you
Your baby

p.s. I love you

POSTMARK: NOVEMBER 16, 1954
Monday
Nov 15

Hi babe,

I am tired. Absolutely bashed, beat out, and whatever other adjectives can describe being 100% fatigued. At the ungodly hour of 5:30 I started my KP and at 7:00 this evening I finished. I haven't felt so beat in years (except for one evening last week)! I have washed approximately 600 dishes, like amount of cups and desert plates, and silverware to match, not to mention the pots and pans needed to prepare the food for these starving individuals. Throw in a large floor that had to be scrubbed and mopped twice and maybe you can understand why my bones are creaking with such resonance. I've had just about enough of this air force. I'll have this for five more days then two days off and back to the sheltering wing of Bill Varns.

Baby it amazes me that in less than a week I've left a life of Hotel Olympia, Outrigger clubs and such behind me and now spend my hours in the kitchen of a mess hall—such is life.

I haven't mentioned it yet in this letter but in case you were wondering, I miss you. I won't try to describe how much I miss you. That's impossible. How could a person explain how they missed the use of their eyes if they became blind, or the use of their legs if paralysis appeared? I guess the only way I could even try to describe my feelings would be to say that if our separation suddenly became permanent, I would not waste a second in taking my life. It's nothing without you.

Hon, my eyes are falling shut. I'm going to take my old waker-up treatment.

I just finished a hot shower, a shave, shampoo, and I've donned my PJ's and feel 100% better. I wish that I could sit back in a comfortable chair, relax, sit you on my lap and stay there for a year or two. I keep telling myself that all this will come to an end someday, that I'll be a civilian, we'll be together permanently, but God, it seems so far off. Hon, if we weren't married and I had to face 16 months of uncertainty I'd be ripe for a padded cell. Getting married was the wisest thing we could have done. Not only from the financial angle but also because of the peace of mind and added degree of confidence in the future it provides. Babe, I share that feeling of warmth in knowing that despite the many miles that separate us, our love covers the distance. It's wonderful to share a love like ours and to know that all the plans we make are for us. To know that there is someone who thinks of me constantly, just as I think of you. I love you my sweet. Now and forever. Today when I picked up my mail the mail clerk said "here's a letter from your wife." That sounded good. I couldn't get to my room so I read the letter you wrote Friday while I was eating. The guys at the table were amazed at its length and all showed understandable envy. Lucky guy that Royko.

I'll write everyone tomorrow—I promise. I've got to rise and shine early so I'll say goodnight. Someday I'll be taking you in my arms at this time of the evening. Some day.

I love you my sweet wife

Your baby

p.s. I love you

POSTMARK: NOVEMBER 17, 1954

Tuesday

November 16

Hello My Darling,

I'm in my room, the radio is playing soft music. I've just taken a shower, put on my PJ's and feel pretty good despite the K.P. How nice it would be if I could lay my head on your lap and rest that way for a while. Today, while I was working and feeling quite bone-weary, I thought of just that and it was one of those thoughts that helps keep me going.

Someone must have goofed in the postal service because I didn't receive a letter today. I was disappointed when, after finishing the last of the dinner dishes, I dashed over to the mail room, full of hope and anticipation, and was greeted by an empty mail box. I know you wrote Hon, so that's good enough for me. How did I ever spend those many years without you? The thought of never seeing you again seems impossible now. That's something I could face once but never again. You're me and I'm you and I couldn't even attempt to live without you. I love you so much Baby. All day, when I felt so beat and disgusted that I was ready to blow my stack, I'd tell myself that this is only temporary and someday it'll all be behind me and I'll be able to laugh at the world. I'd feel a little better. Believe me hon, there is nothing like KP. I don't mind hard work. Since I've been in the service I've dug many a ditch but that's healthy hard work. Having my elbows immersed in hot, greasy, water is something else. I'm egotistical enough to think that I'm too damn good for that kind of balderdash but these people won't believe me.

I had one happy moment today. While I was unloading clean silverware at the front of the chow line the first Sergeant came in and couldn't pass up the opportunity to crow over me. He held up the line while he told me that KP is fine training, it's not as rough as it once was and stupid statements along that vein of thought. He made the mistake of pausing for breath because then I got mine in. I told him, in a voice loud enough for the whole mess hall to hear, that the toughest thing about KP is talkative old men who find it impossible to eat and leave in silence. With that I walked away amidst loud, loud, cheers from the troops. I've secured my position of #1 on his list but I was there to begin with.

Well hon, there'll be a letter in the morning, I'm sure of that, and in a few days we'll be talking to each other again. I'll call Sunday night and keep trying 'til you're home. I love you my sweet wife. It's a tremendous thrill to look at your picture and say "my wife." In about 160 days we'll be together again. I'll hold you, kiss you, tell you I love you over and over again. It's wonderful to have so great a meaning in life. You are my meaning and no one could have a more inspiring incentive in life. I love you, I love you, I love you.

'Til tomorrow,
Your baby

p.s. I love you

POSTMARK: NOVEMBER 18, 1954
Wednesday night
November 17

Same time, same place, same physical condition. Only three more days of this stuff and I can return to normal working hours. Today was just as rough as the last two have been but the two letters I received, one in the morning, one in the afternoon, make it a much brighter day. Considering that it's been raining for 24 hours, cold as can be, and winds up to 55 miles an hour, you can understand how your letters affect me.

Sweetheart, despite the KP, despite our separation, and despite the AF, I don't remember when I've had more peace of mind and inner happiness. I miss you immensely. At times it becomes almost unbearable but knowing what the future holds for us and above all, knowing that the word is Us. I can almost bust with happiness. Dreams, dreams, dreams—millions of dreams I've had. All have come true or will come true some day. These last 10 months are miraculous. Honey it seems like almost yesterday that I wrote and told you that I love you but actually it's impossible to measure in time because of the happiness we've had in these 10 months. Babe, in the next 16 months there are going to be times that I'll be depressed and miserable. But remember hon, it'll be because I miss you so and I won't let myself stay like that for long. All I have to do is look at my ring, your picture and think back to the days I was in Korea when we both were so unhappy and that snaps me out of it. We're lucky—no luckier people ever lived.

The day you read this, I'll be finishing my KP. Happy day. A good five months stand between me and my next one and by then I'll have some angle figured out. I've got to. I'm getting too old for this balderdash—there's no time for this sort of thing.

Gosh the wind is blowing. They expect gusts up to 75 MPH tonight. I like wild weather but enough is enough.

Carol Royko. Carol Joyce Royko. Mrs. Michael Royko Jr. I feel like waking up the base and telling them how wonderful everything is. I love you. I think you suspect that but in case there are any doubts in your mind—I confess. I think you are the greatest. I can't marry you wench but let's live in sin.

This is crazy. It's 11, I've worked like a dog—2 dogs and I should be dead but I feel as giddy as if I'd just drank two Tiki bowls. Sweetheart how I'd love to hold you in my arms. Just think hon, we'll have another honeymoon in five months. My God, if I go downstairs in the shape I was in that one evening, Bob will—No, I guess he wouldn't but I'd better not develop eyes like I had that Sunday night.

Time for shut eye again.

I love you
I love you
I love you
I love you
I love you
I love you
I love you
I love you
I love you
I love you
I love you
I love you
Your Baby

p.s. Loves you, Mr Babe

POSTMARK: NOVEMBER 20, 1954
Friday
November 19

Hi Sweetheart,

About twenty minutes ago I finished a twelve hour sleep. Last night, after finishing my fourth day of KP I was told by the 1st sergeant that I had to move to another barracks. They want all the radar maintenance men rooming in the same barracks. I moved all my belongings, took a shower and felt so beat that I went right to bed. Today and tomorrow I'm on night KP so I'm free 'til 4 this afternoon, then I'll work from 4 to 2 in the morn. Sunday, your birthday, will be the first day off of two that I get for my efforts, then back to radar maintenance. What a life! I laid in bed for an hour this morning just thinking about the 16 months before me. When I started feeling too disgusted I got up and tried to get my mind off it. Baby, I miss you.

Today is payday and it's also the day I'll receive a letter written by you on Wednesday which is a day you didn't receive a letter. I'm sorry hon, but Wednesday is four days past and since then you've received other letters and day after tomorrow I'll be talking to you.

So the honey-gals have ended. I'm glad you did it babe. Not because I didn't enjoy your singing with them. To the contrary, I was very pleased and proud when I heard you sing, but a babe like Dorothy needs to have her high horse knocked out from under her. I'm proud of you gal.

It's nearly time for lunch so I'm going to run over and get some food, pick up your letter if it's there and then finish this.

Hi Sweet. I've eaten, been paid and here I am with bad news. They haven't started the allotment yet so it'll be January before you receive your first check. The twenty dollars I'm enclosing, I hope will help with the xmas shopping and whatever else we need and next payday I'll try to send the same. We will receive full payment of our allotment from the day we were married but it'll take a bit longer than we had anticipated. I'm not sure how my pay will be affected but in January you will receive the allotment for December and also the one for the portion of November that we were married. Better late than never hon, but leave it to the AF to be late.

No letter this morning but I've got hopes for this afternoon. Sunday's the big day babe. We'll have to limit to 3 minutes cause I'll be nearly broke. What the heck, I keep forgetting that you'll receive this Monday.

I've got to close, Sweet. KP in a little while and I want to take a shower and relax before I start another hitch as a galley slave.

I love you babe. You can't imagine how much I miss you. There are times when I feel like doing something drastic, like shooting the C.O. or something, but never fear—I won't.

'Til tomorrow my baby

I love you

Your baby

p.s. I love you

Timothy P. Sheehan was a Republican Illinois congressman from 1951 to 1959. I know of no relationship, beyond politician and voter, between Sheehan and the Duckmans.

POSTMARK: NOVEMBER 22, 1954

Monday

Hi Babe,

Just finished lunch and read the letter you wrote Thursday. As soon as the statements arrive, which should be soon, I'll submit them along with my request. Hon, I'm not sure but I don't think my request goes to Washington D.C. From here it goes to McChord field, then to Hamilton AFB, then to Ent AFB which is Air Defense Headquarters. It could be vetoed anywhere along the line. Of course if Sheehan presents himself at the pentagon my chances are improved 500%. With the medical statements reading as they do, and a Congressman working for me, I think my chances are pretty good. The main thing is the congressman. The Air Force bows to politicos because they provide the financial appropriations. I wish I had a statement from Sheehan tho, to go along with the rest of them. As soon as you're sure that I've received the statements, get in touch with him. Don't wait for the answer from me. I'll put them in immediately so a day or so after you mail them tell Sheehan to get cuttin'.

You didn't receive a letter yesterday hon because Saturday night I worked my last night of KP and Sunday I didn't wake up early enough to get a letter on the train. The mail leaves Blaine at noon on Sundays and there is no mail pickup from the base so that means I have to get to town in the morning with the letter.

This new development has shook me up. I'm not counting on it but our chances look much better than before. I just hope that his influence makes the difference. Hon, give him all the information on me that he needs. My serial number is AF-********. That's necessary. And the sooner he gets the ball rolling the better. If I had a letter from him to accompany the other requests, I'd be sure that I wouldn't have any interference at the lower commands and that it would get to higher headquarters but if he starts seeing people at the Pentagon, I'm sure that that'll help immensely.

I hope that the statements arrive sooner so I can get this started. Hon, if you've already mailed them and are waiting for an answer from me, then by the time you've read this, I've already submitted them so get in touch with Sheehan. Tell him I'm in the 225th Air Division. The 757th is just a branch of that. God hon, I hope this goes through.

I'm going to cut this short so I can make the mail delivery.

I love you

Your ever hopeful husband

Mick

p.s. I love you

Steve Canyon was a comic book hero from the late 1940s until the late 1980s.

POSTMARK: NOVEMBER 23, 1954

Monday

November 22

Hi Wonderful,

I'm elated. The more I think about the transfer, the more optimistic I feel. This afternoon I spoke to the 1st Sergeant and he said that he sees no reason why the transfer shouldn't come through. I spoke to Bill Varns and he echoed the opinion of the 1st sergeant. I completely re-read the regulation—AF reg 35-59, that covers compassionate transfer and according to that I can't miss. The one thing I noticed in the regulation that bothered me is that requests such as mine go only as high as command level, which for me would be Air Defense Command, commanded by General Chidlow. It doesn't mention Washington. ADC is at Ent AFB Colorado so I think Sheehan might be mistaken. Hon, if you haven't sent out the papers yet, would it be possible to get a statement from him also? If not, send what we have and I think that it'll be enough to do the trick. Of course I could be wrong so having him work from the Pentagon sure can't do any harm and might do the trick. This might be it hon, and if it is, then in less than two months I'll be home, you'll be in my arms and life will be more than perfect.

Baby, do you know what this could mean? O'HARE!!! They will station me as close as possible to home and that's as close as I could get. I'm trying not to get my hopes up but it's such a wonderful possibility that I can't help think about it. God baby, it would be wonderful. We'd be together, live like civilians and save more money—yes, more. $245 from the AF, $120 from your job, and I could work for Yardley's evenings. Babe, it would be—I'd better stop thinking about it. Disappointment will be less bitter if I don't get my hopes too high.

My wife, my wife, my wife, my wife—You're wonderful. I love you so much my sweet. As Dorothy said in a letter I received today—"I'm glad it's Carol. You couldn't have picked a nicer girl. She seems to have everything." I completely agree with my sister. You have everything. You are the most beautiful, sweet, sensible, delightful, fascinating, exciting, dream like wife a man could ever ask for. I love you.

Hon, I'm afraid if Johnny and I met it would result in an inferiority complex for him. He'd see me and think "that's who beat me out?" and his opinion of himself would drop 500%. He probably pictures something out of Steve Canyon and look what he'll see. Ah, love is blind and I'm glad.

I love you babe
Maybe we'll be together soon
Love, love, love
Mick

P.S. I love you

POSTMARK: NOVEMBER 24, 1954

Wednesday Morning

November 23

Hi Sweetheart,

Hon, I'm a bundle of nerves. I'm going from bad to worse. Since Sunday I've been unable to sleep, work, concentrate on anything, and think about anything but the possibilities of a transfer. I'm trying not to get my hopes up but it's hard to do. The 25th Air Division is notorious for the near impossibility of securing transfers but everyone I've talked to is optimistic about my chances. Keep praying hon. This might be our big break. Tell Congressman Sheehan that my transfer does not go as far as Washington. From here it goes to Paine Field for approval or disapproval, then to McChord, then to Hamilton California, then to Ent Air force Base Colorado for the final say so by General Chidlow, commander of the Air Defense Command. Until it gets to him, the commander of the lower organizations I mentioned recommend approval or disapproval and he has the final say. That procedure is known as going up the chain of command. I don't know what effect Sheehan can have upon it in Washington but of course if he knows someone their word could probably be sent to the people involved to give it the highest consideration.

I'm just living from day to day with all my hopes centered on the arrival of the papers. The sooner I get them submitted, the sooner I'll have the final yes or no. Today is Wednesday so that means you are probably mailing them tonight, or mailed them already. I hope they arrive in Friday's morning mail delivery so the Orderly room can get cutting on the paper work. It'll take a month before final approval or disapproval is given. I'm a bundle of nerves. Chances are that if the answer is yes I'll get 755th or O'hare field. That would be so wonderful, I'm afraid to even think about it. Honey, to be near you, to be together. I'm getting myself into a bad state. If the transfer doesn't come through, I'm afraid I'm going to be pretty hard to live with. As it is now, they've given up on getting any work out of me.

God hon, the next two days are going to drag by. I'm spending Thanksgiving here. Just the thought that the papers might arrive to-morrow is enough to keep me here for the day.

Sweetheart, our life is chock full of maybes. Maybe some of them will develop into reality. Maybe this transfer will be the answer to the next 16 months. Sweetheart I hope so. I miss you so much.

So long 'til tonight sweetheart.

I love you

Mick

p.s. I love you

Friday
November 26th

Hi Sweetheart,

I've just left the orderly room where I've spent 3½ hours getting the paper work started. My God, they want to know my life history. We've finally got everything down that they want and baby to quote the first Sergeant, "it's in the bag." To quote the chief clerk, "you can't miss." Sweetheart, I don't see how I can miss. Unless something radical happens, sometime in January, you'll be in my arms. I don't know what base I'll get but since I'll be remaining in the Air Defense Command, that could mean O'Hare, 755th, or anything having to do with radar around Chi. Tonight I'm going to make sure that everything is typed up properly by doing it myself. Your letter, your mother's letter, and the other two have to be typed in ten copies as do all the other things that were filled out here. I'm going to type like mad tonight and I'll enjoy every minute of it. Baby, I'm still trying to hold down my optimism but hon, it looks good.

Sweetheart, do you know what is coming out of the radio? "We'll be together again." Babe, when something like that happens I often wonder if the whole world isn't conspiring to make you and I happy. If this transfer comes through, I'll look back on 1954 as a golden year. As the golden year. Sweetheart, I love you.

Tomorrow all the paper work will be ready and will begin its long trek up the chain of command, eventually arriving at Ent Air Force Base where, I hope, it will receive it's final word of approval. After that?— Near you, babe. I'm not planning on O'Hare sweetheart but if I do get it I'm afraid you'll be faced with the prospect of seeing me every day. Such a fate for such a nice young girl.

One of the things that had to be filled in was a section marked Character and another marked Efficiency. Varns gave me Superior and Superior. Good boy that lad. Sorry, I'll get the Varns address and send it tomorrow. I've forgotten to do that about six times lately. I'm having trouble keeping my mind on anything. Transfers—that's all I can think of. My gosh, if they turn me down, I don't know what I'll do. Now to spend a month on pins and long sharp needles waiting for the powers that be to give their all-powerful word. Keep praying sweetheart. Keep praying sweetheart and maybe it'll all turn out right.

You're wonderful. I can't get over my remarkably good fortune. Sometimes it hits me. We're married. Carol is my wife. Then I feel like I've just reached the end of the rainbow.

Got to type

I love you babe

Mick

p.s. love you

The movie Sabrina was released in 1954 and starred Humphrey Bogart, Audrey Hepburn, and William Holden.

POSTMARK: NOVEMBER 29, 1954

November 29

Hi Sweetheart,

Now for 30 or more days of waiting and biting my fingernails. Despite everyone's optimism, I still place no faith in the AF. The only time I'll be sure of my transfer is when I have the official orders in my hand. For one month I'll be on pins and needles, especially around Christmas, because that's about the time I'll receive the final word. If they say no, I'm afraid I'll be useless to the service from now on.

What a good idea about the Christmas gifts hon. I'll wait 'til I'm home before I give you yours too. That way, if and when I do get home we can have our Christmas. It'll be a few days late, but that's OK.

I was in the club yesterday and I ran into a bunch of Canadians I hadn't seen for about six months. They used to be steady customers and always good for free drinks. When I walked in they invited me to their table. Immediately, one of the wives, they are all married couples, spotted my ring. Since I had never mentioned any chance of my getting married, they were all shocked. They demanded to see your pictures and after seeing you in leopard skin the usual question began, "How in the hell"—I told them that love is blind and I don't understand either.

If only they knew that you married me for my money.

Speaking of money, as you know, after leaving Seattle the car we used on our honeymoon nearly disintegrated about me. I've agreed to pay the owner part of the repair bill so after much arguing and haggling it will cost me $13.00. Sweetheart, you don't have to worry about me drinking, gambling, or running around. After I get done distributing my money I have enough left for 1 beer, a nickel for a pin ball machine, and admission to the latest movie.

Saw "Sabrina" last night. One of the best movies in years though I can't figure out what the big rage is about the actress, Audrey Hepburn. Skinny legs, built-in Dior look, boney shoulders. Honey, you beat them all.

Sweetheart, as soon as I know, one way or another, how the transfer came out, I'll call you. Let me know what hours you'll be working before Christmas because when I get the word, I'll call immediately. Keep praying sweetheart, it seemed hopeless last time but we may have been given a reprieve. You keep praying and I'll keep wishing on matches and we can't miss.

In one month 1955 will be here. So far, 1954 has been the most wonderful year of my life. The transfer would really top it off.

I love you.

Mick

p.s. I love you

Chanute Air Force Base, which Dad refers to as Chanute Field, was located 130 miles south of Chicago, in Rantoul, Illinois. It closed in 1993.

POSTMARK: NOVEMBER 30, 1954
Tuesday
November 30

Hi Sweetheart,

While I was at work today, someone mentioned what they were doing one year ago at this time and it sure gave me a lot to think about. One year ago at this time I was in Korea trying to figure out what to do when I got home in 30 days. You were the center of my thoughts then, as you are now but my plans were a bit different. My problem then was to avoid seeing you, as politely as possible. Now, with the possibility of being home in thirty days how things have changed. In one year, instead of being a silent lover of someone else's wife, I'm looking forward with boundless hope to being with my wife. One year and two lives changed completely. It'll never cease to amaze me.

I can't even get that transfer out of my thoughts when I'm asleep. Last night I dreamed that I was at Chanute Field, rather I had been transferred to Chanute Field and was home. As the dream faded away it was morning, I was slowly awakening and you were sleeping next to me. When I did wake up it came as a shock to find myself in this room. Very realistic. Maybe honey, maybe next month at this time we will be together. Of course maybe we won't. Maybe some cold blooded officer will say "No!" when he sees my request. Keep praying sweetheart. I've got a lot of faith in your prayers.

By now the request is on its way to the desk of some wheel at Paine Field, from there to Seattle, then to Hamilton California, then to the one that will determine whether or not I get it, and if so, where I go, Ent Air Force Base, Colorado. This will take about a month. If it's yes, there will be 3 or 4 days of clearing this base, a couple days on the train, then—home. At the most, it'll be the middle of January. If they say no I'll just have to start counting the days 'til May. That seems so far off. They mustn't turn us down honey. These separations are too hard to take. Being apart isn't as bad as the last moments we're together. It's those goodbye's that hurt the most. Seeing that plane zoom off into the darkness was one of the most painful sights I've ever witnessed. I don't want to have to go through that again.

As each day passes, it'll bring us so much closer to so many things. My discharge, my transfer, my leave, so many things. I love you my wife. I'll never stop being grateful and amazed at how wonderful you've made my life.

I love you with all my heart
Mick

The 755th AC&W (Air Control and Warning) was in Williams Bay, Wisconsin, a two-hour drive from Chicago. O'Hare was on the northwest edge of the Chicago city limits.

El Centro Restaurant was at Central & Elston, a few blocks up the street from the Duckmans' home. Mom and Dad had my eighth-grade graduation dinner there in 1973.

POSTMARK: DECEMBER 1, 1954

Wednesday
December 1st

Hi Babe,

I'm on my way to lunch hour and I just finished pestering the orderly room. Those people are going to get tired of my running in and out.

I had some pleasant news today. Varns is so sure that I'm going to be transferred that he has sent one of the new men in our section down to an administrative school at McChord Field—I'm being replaced. Baby, one month from the time you read this we just might be together again. I'm hoping it's either Williams Bay or O'Hare.—O'Hare preferably. Babe, it would be wonderful. I'd probably work the same kind of hours as I do here, so I could get started in Yardley's immediately. That would be all the more we could save. Hon, if I get O'Hare my total pay will be 245 a month. I imagine we could live on that and save your pay plus whatever I earn in Yardley's. I've reached the point where I'm not only hoping for the transfer, but I'm even specifying bases—and that's bad. Disappointment would be much greater now. For once I'll be optimistic. I'm 99% sure I'll get O'Hare.

Your selection of Xmas gifts was in line with everything else you do. Perfect. Let's hold off on our gifts hon, 'til we're sure one way or another. Then when I'm home we can have our own little Christmas ceremony.

Since you'll be at El's house New Years Eve, I'll call there of course. I'll call a little before Midnight. Only one thing wrong—I've forgot her number. What a memory!

It is a cold, dark, windy, rainy, uncomfortable day. In front of me is a picture of you sitting on Bob's car in the lot. There are over-hanging branches everywhere, it was a warm, beautiful day and apparently you were happy because you're smiling. I was happy too cause it was me you were smiling at. My smoky eyed babe.

What are we going to do my first night home? Shall we go to El Centro's for dinner, to the Clover club for a few drinks and dance, then out to Norwood house for a snack—or shall we sit upstairs listening to music and have Xmas for the new Royko family? This time you'll know exactly what time we'll arrive, where I'll be and even what I'll wear. OK hon, I'll wear the uniform. If I get O'Hare Field, I think you might get tired of the uniform. I have.

Must go now. They're getting all the work out of me possible in my last few days.

Love you babe,

Mick

p.s. I love you

Linell was the name of the dentist Mom worked for as an assistant.

Though Dad was optimistic about when they would buy a house, it would be almost fifteen years before that would happen. By the time I was born in 1959, Mom and Dad were living upstairs, on the second and third floors of the Duckmans' house, which formerly had been the Duckman Funeral Home. Barbara (Eleanor's daughter, later Bob Duckman's wife) recalls the business being in operation from 1950 until 1954, run by Bob, a mortician, along with Fred and Mildred.

This is the first time I know Dad to have gone to church. The other time was when he was researching Boss, his 1971 book on Chicago mayor Richard J. Daley. When I asked him why he was going to church early one Sunday morning—when I was about eleven—he said, in a half-whisper for effect, "To spy on Daley."

POSTMARK: DECEMBER 2, 1954

Thursday
December 2nd

Hi Wife,

Just read your letter describing your activities with Yardley's. There is time enough in the future for Yardley's. Stick with Linell and Marks as you decided to do and when I get home we'll set that company afire.

Babe, I don't think there is an AC&W squadron at O'Hare. When I told you I stood a good chance of being associated there it was because of the following facts. The Air Force is divided up into "commands." The Air Defense Command, which includes jet bases, AC&W , and anything pertaining to intercepting the enemy—The Strategic Air Command, which includes all bombers and long range equipment, and the training command which is self explanatory. I can go anywhere in the Air Defense Command, jet base or AC&W because I work in radio and they have radio everywhere. As you said, O'Hare would be the frosting on the cake but our chances are pretty good.

If I get O'Hare we will be living as civilians, earning more money than most civilian couples and saving more than we expected. Besides that I'd be all set to manage by the time I'm discharged and I'll have to become a manager before the mortgage people would let us buy a house. Sweetheart, if I get O'Hare, we'll be in our dream house right after my discharge. Well, I've got a month to worry about that. Who knows, the transfer may be refused. It could happen. I'll probably crack up after all this optimism if it does. Tonight I'm going to work. They haven't given me a minute's rest since I've been back.

Is your full time work going to continue? Do you realize that if I get O'Hare and you continue to earn $45 a week, we'll be in the $5000 a year bracket without Yardley's—Wow!

Since I've been back I've been asked very frequently what I plan on doing after my discharge. Everyone here had accepted me as a future Hemingway but everyone agrees that I'll make a good salesman. Varns said that I have what it takes and he comes from a family of salespeople. I guess it's cut and dried. You're stuck with a salesman babe. Selling amounts to one thing—the ability to sell yourself to other people. If I can sell someone as wonderful as my wife on the idea of spending her life with an 8-ball like me, then I must be a salesman.

Have you met my wife? I love her you know. She loves me too. I can't understand it but who can explain miracles. They're something that you accept and don't analyze.

Time to saunter over to the Tomain Terrace or Stomach Pump Room as it's sometimes known and get some G.I. cuisine.

Keep praying hon,
I love you
Mick

p.s. I'm going to church Sunday—pleased?

p.p.s. Love you

POSTMARK: DECEMBER 4, 1954
Friday
November 3rd [mistakenly written for December 3]

Hi Sweetheart,

Just a few more days and we'll have been married all of a month. Feel disenchanted?

I've just remembered something. We won't have to use the first allotment check for the Xmas gifts. We'll be getting another $75.00 bond in January and that should take care of it. I'm at a point where I can't get my mind, plans, or anything organized. There are so many "ifs" involved in the next couple months. Someone reminded me of another possible job I might be transferred to. G.O.C. Ground Observer Corps. Civilians do the work on a volunteer basis but they are supervised by airmen and one of the biggest parts of it is radio. G.O.C. headquarters are always in a city. Something else for me to think about.

No letter today but there must have been a good reason. I've finally remembered to get the Varns' address. 5744 60th NE Seattle 5, Wash. When my transfer comes through and while I'm waiting in Seattle for my train I'll stop out and see them again.

I'm running off to town for a movie so I'll finish this tomorrow. See you later hon.

I just rolled out of bed, took a shower and checked my mail. When I walked into the orderly room the first Sergeant showed me a letter that had just arrived. It was from Sheehan to the C.O. recommending transfer. They'll forward it ahead so it'll catch up with the rest of the papers. We can't miss.

I also was greeted by a letter from you my sweet. That Pete. He didn't tell me that he was sending a gift. He asked me for our address so that he could look us up in years to come.

I couldn't be surprised at anything Freddie does. I've seen his type in the service and they all end up the same. Jail or skid row. The best thing for Joyce to do is swear out a peace bond and if he tinkers with the car anymore call the gendarmes. I feel sorry for Joyce, with the kid arriving and everything else.

I hope they rush the papers along. As December comes to an end, I'll be a bundle of nerves. My hands are shaky again. I guess you're the only cure there is. I confess. I married you to stop my hands from shaking.

We're having a section party tomorrow. By the first of the year, everyone who has been here during the past year will be gone so we will celebrate. I hope that if I'm not gone, I'll be at least packing.

Just think hon, we'll be having our third honeymoon in five months.

I love you babe
Your baby

p.s. I love you

POSTMARK: DECEMBER 6, 1954

Monday,
Dec 6th

Hi Babe,

I have the world's greatest hangover. Last night was the long awaited section party. I swear, I'll never, never take more than two drinks again. It seems that Varns, Joe, and the rest of them collaborated on getting me drunk and hon, I'm afraid that they succeeded. I won't go into all the details because my memory seems to be failing me. Never, never, never again. This morning I just couldn't get out of bed. At 9:00 they called me on the phone and I told them I'd be down immediately. I went right back to bed. At 10:00 they came for me. I told them that it was their fault I felt like hell and that I'd be to work after lunch. I didn't ask them, I told them. Forceful kid this Royko.

That letter from Sheehan has created quite a stir. The C.O. is sending him an immediate reply and everyone treats me like a wheel. They must think I'm a politician or something. I don't think we can miss hon.

Babe, this'll be the shortest letter I've written yet but my head is coming off and I've got to eat before work. Never, never again.

I love you
Your baby

p.s. I love you

POSTMARK: DECEMBER 7, 1954
Tuesday
December 7

Hi Babe,

Things are really popping. This morning I walked into the orderly room to see what was being done for my transfer and the C.O. spotted me. "Who do you know?" he said. It seems that Sheehan got in touch with ADC at Ent AFB and this morning a message was received asking for info on my case. The paperwork hasn't progressed up the ladder that far yet so they haven't seen the statements. It said reply with 24 hours. The reply is on its way with a recommendation by the C.O. for approval. I'm pretty sure it's in the bag. I don't know how long it'll take. They'll probably wait for the rest of the statements to arrive before they pass judgment so it'll be at least 2 weeks before anything develops. Right now my big worry is where I'll go. I'm keeping my fingers crossed for O'Hare. That would be just like a discharge. That would be, well, it's such a wonderful idea I don't even want to think about it. I'm planning on being a couple hundred miles away. That way, if I am, the disappointment wouldn't be very bad. I'm not planning on not being transferred. I'm 99.9999% positive. So is everyone else. My replacement is being trained, everyone asks me where I'm going, not if I'm going. The C.O. is sure, the adjutant, the 1st sergeant—Everyone. How can I be doubtful in view of all this optimism? It's just a matter of time hon. This month your allotment started and here is some bad news. An allotment begins only on the 1st of the month so we receive nothing extra for November. The first check of 137.10 will arrive in January, as will my bond for 75.00. That should take care of the Sears account. Since the bond is still effective and my pay is lessened by half because of your allotment, my pay amounted to nearly nothing. After I paid $10.00 on that clothing account I took out, bought some cigarettes and paid half of the Ford's repair bill, my bank account was nil. I forgot all about the twenty I was supposed to send you but even if I had remembered, it wouldn't have been available. Sorry hon, but the bond money should take care of Sears huh?

One month ago today, at this time, we were at Lake Wilderness. Maybe one month from today we'll be together again. We've been married more than a month now—a month and a day. I'm getting old.

Got to run. I've got 5 minutes to eat and get to work. I'll be late. Can't teach an old airman new tricks.

See you soon

I love you

Your baby

p.s. Love you wench

POSTMARK: DECEMBER 9, 1954

Wednesday night
December 8th

Hi Babe,

As you know, you didn't receive a letter yesterday. That's twice this week I've goofed. Sunday, church was the reason. Today it was an alert. At 11:30 I walked out of the office, headed for the barracks intent on writing and getting the letter on its way. At 11:35 the sirens blew. By the time the alert ended it was too late. Tomorrow there's a big inspection so I spent 3 hours polishing up the barracks after work. I'm beat. This is one of those days that would normally drive me into a rage but lately it's pretty hard for me to get mad. The thought of a transfer is enough to cheer me up.

I received two letters today. One you wrote yesterday. That's fast service. First time it's ever happened. Now I won't expect one tomorrow. I shouldn't complain. You haven't missed a day yet. I love you for it hon. Matter of fact I love you period.

The bond we'll receive next month will be for $75.00. We'll also receive a check for $137.00. If I'm at home I'll be paid $50.00 the 5th and $50.00 the twentieth. Of course I may not be paid the 5th 'cause there's a chance that I'll be traveling then. I hope so.

Bob might be right about me being home for New Years Eve but don't plan on it hon. I've seen too much of AF red tape to expect anything but delay and unnecessary time wasted.

This time last year I was on the other side of the ocean, waiting for a ship to take me back to the states. I remember the emptiness and lack of elation inside me. You caused it, though you couldn't have known. Now you are causing all the happiness I feel.

About my Xmas card list. I don't know where most of my friends are. They're scattered all over the world so it's non-existent. Here's something for you to do. Look in the phone book and find Simon Babin. They live on Princeton Ave on the south side. Tell them that you are Mike's wife and find out where Si is. Last I heard, he was in Japan but he may be back by now. They don't know I'm married so you better tell them it's Mike Royko or they could get confused. Si'll probably faint at the news. Other than that my Christmas chores consist only of gifts and I've got a wife who's taking care of that.

Honey, keep praying. If, in a few weeks I'm called into the orderly room and told that I'm leaving, I'm going to fly, not run to the nearest phone and call you. If it comes through it'll be near Chicago. I'm sure of that. Time's dragging, isn't it hon?

I love you so much.

Your baby

p.s. I love you

Monday

Hi Wife,

Only nine more shopping days 'til Christmas. I've decided how I'll spend Christmas Eve. I'll go to bed as soon as I finish work and stay there 'til Christmas day. I'll seal my ears to all Christmas carols, Christmas greetings etc. I'll avoid looking at Christmas trees, decorations or anything that remotely reminds me of the holiday. This will definitely not be a merry Christmas.

It looks like I'll still be able to attend Lenny's wedding. Did you tell them about the transfer? I was the confirmed bachelor in the gang. We figured Lenny would get married first, then Tom, then Si, and maybe someday, me. I was positive that would happen. Woman, you've ruined my plans—but you're forgiven.

This has been one of the most miserable weekends ever. It rained continuously. It was cold, foggy and we had two alerts. I was in such a black mood, I couldn't bring myself to write. Saturday there was no letter and that sunk me deeper into my black mood. Every time I turned on the radio I heard Christmas music and instead of cheering me up it depressed me. I miss you so much.

Babe, I've got a friend who takes care of the leave records. So far, I'm 3 days in the hole as far as leave time goes. He is going to fix things up so that when I leave here I'll be 10 days to the good. If the transfer comes through I'll get about 4 days travel time, take 5 days leave and we can have 6 or 7 days together before I report into my next base.

Nothing like a few connections here and there. I expect some news by the first of the year and should be home during the first week of 1955. If we had known about this we could have waited and been married in Chicago. I myself don't regret anything that's happened but both our families would have got a terrific charge out of our wedding. If I had made as many errors in front of the family as I did in Seattle I'd have brought the house down. Talk about a calm groom. I was so calm I wasn't even thinking about the ceremony.

Soon after I get home, we'll have Lenny and Louise over for dinner.

They will be so envious of our marital bliss that they'll probably elope. Don't forget to check on Si. I think he's due to come back from Japan. Without a bride I hope!

The card, like you, was beautiful. I love you.

Your ever lovin' husband,

Mick

p.s. I love you

Saturday Morning
December 11th

Hi Babe,

I just finished breakfast and I've got about an hour before I start work. We're working Saturdays now. Half the base goes home for Christmas so everything has to be in A1 shape by the 20th. To remind us that it's nearly Christmas they have been playing Christmas music over the PA system continuously from 8 AM to 8 PM. This has one of two effects on everyone. The fellows who will be home beam and feel great, while the other unfortunates, myself included, feel very low. Last Christmas I was on a train but that didn't bother me too much. This time I'll feel much worse. Home means much more to me now. Are you going to put up a tree hon? I don't know why I happened to think of that. It makes a pleasant picture tho. You reading, with a cheerful little Christmas tree lighting up the apartment.

No news on the transfer yet. I don't expect any for quite a while, but every time the phone rings I jump twice as quick as I used to. One of these days it'll be what we're waiting for. They can't say anything but yes. I just can't visualize it. The thing I'm worried about is where I'll be going. Hon, chances are that it won't be O'Hare Field but yet there is that possibility. That would be more wonderful than the AF can imagine. It would be as good as a discharge. About three more weeks and we'll know.

How are you signing the Christmas cards? Donna will be shocked. You are a terrible young lady Carol. First Sonny, then Woody, and now me. Her old flame. Does Gloria—your cousin—know that we're married? I imagine she'll be much more surprised than anyone. Mr. and Mrs. Unexpected—that's us. It still amazes me at times so I can imagine how other people will react.

Hon, I don't have to put on an act. I always look down and out. Being away from you puts a hang dog look on me that won't quit.

It's been more than three months since my September leave and nearly two years since that sad, sad reunion we had. Time may heal everything but I'm glad we didn't leave everything up to time.

It looks like Joyce and Freddy are going to have one of those knock down–drag out marriages. Joyce, to be frank, is psycho. She has probably got more loose screws than Freddy. I think Freddy is just a dumb, crude jerk. Joyce seems to be smart enough, she just needs a little care—Maybe a straight jacket would help. They'll keep that routine up 'til one of them either gets killed or gives up. I hope I'm wrong but happiness isn't in the cards for that marriage.

Keep praying Babe.

I love you

Mick

p.s. I'm your baby

The quotation Mike uses to end the letter is by John Keats.

POSTMARK: DECEMBER 15, 1954

Tuesday night
December 14th

Hi Wonderful,

Your phone call came right at the most perfect moment. I've been feeling terribly depressed too hon and it's hard to figure. I guess it must be that one small chance of not being transferred that's scaring me. I couldn't take it baby. For years I've been living a difficult life. Always looking forward to something or hoping for it but never experiencing it. That was all changed last September and November the 6th but here I am again—hoping and praying that we'll be together soon. It's no wonder we're both a little beat out. For months we were both living for September. It arrived and was everything—more—than we had hoped for. Then it ended and it was November and our wedding and all the plans and changes of plans and a million minor items to worry about. Once again it was wonderful. Then after we both settled down to the loneliness of our next wait—the transfer. The thing that amazes me is that we aren't nervous wrecks. I haven't given it a lot of thought but considering that I had very little money, a rather small income, no leave time, 2200 miles separating us, PLUS the fact that your divorce wasn't final 'til nearly the last minute—everything turned out as perfectly as it did. I haven't figured out how much money we've spent since September 1st but I'll bet if I did, I couldn't account for where it all came from. After all the frantic planning, the long trips both of us made, the partings after the wonderful moments we spent together—is it any wonder that we feel sort of blue and depressed? We're both a little beat out I think. The last few days have taken my nerves and nearly ruined them. Today when you called I had to tell you something that could offer some encouragement after not receiving any mail. It's true—I might be home for Christmas. Last week a message came from A.D.C. on teletype. It requested information on me—my job classification—Squadron's opinion on my transfer and it requested an answer within 24 hours. That was Tuesday the 7th. Apparently they received a letter from Sheehan and hadn't received the rest of the paper work so they wanted some light shed on the matter. Since then—nothing. The first sergeant thinks that they are waiting for all the paperwork to arrive before they make a final decision. If it gets there before the 17th or 18th I may get out in time because that's when most of the administrative personnel go on leave. If it doesn't get there in time then it'll be the first week in jan. before any action is taken. I could have written you about this before hon but I didn't want you to get your hopes up and then be disappointed. It just blasted out over the phone today. You sounded so blue that I had to do something to buck you up. I guess I've been getting lax in my letter writing lately. I've been worrying so much lately that I haven't been writing often enough and when I do write I don't say much. Have I told you that I love you lately? Have I told you how much more you mean to me as each day passes? Sweetheart—honey—I love you with all my heart. I miss you so. At night when I'm lying in bed, looking out at the perpetual rain, sometimes I wonder if you're lying awake missing me as much as I miss you—if you feel as painfully miserable as I do. I know now that I couldn't live without you. Just so many nights like this are all I could take. I've got the future to look to—Without you in it nothing would matter. I long for the day when all this doubt, worrying, hoping, and being apart will be over. In the evening I want to sit with you in my lap, hold you, kiss you, see your eyes get smoky, and fall asleep with you at my side. I want to wake up in the morning and be near you. You look beautiful when you're asleep. I love the way you mumble when you first wake up and look around as if you're not sure what year it is. And I want to have all this with the knowledge that our time together isn't limited.

It's getting late and I feel awful. Another long night will pass and in the morning I'll be full of hope that this'll be the day I'll get word.

I found another nice quotation:
Two souls with but a single thought
Two hearts that beat as one
Mick

"Rudolph, the Red Nosed Reindeer Mambo" was a novelty hit by Billy May in 1954.

POSTMARK: DECEMBER 16, 1954
Thursday
December 16th

Hi Sweetheart,
No news is good news I guess but it's not helping my gray hair any. If, by the time you receive this letter, I haven't called, then I won't make it by Christmas. Saturday is the deadline. If nothing comes by then it'll be impossible to make it home. Actually there's no sense in worrying about a few days. The main thing is whether I'll be transferred or not. Here I

am worrying about when and where and as far as I know it hasn't been approved yet. It seems like ages since I submitted all the papers and started another long wait but it hasn't been too long. I'm sure a hard guy to satisfy. This last year has been so wonderful it's nearly miraculous and so I gripe about a few days.

I checked the morning mail delivery but there was nothing for me—this afternoon I guess. By the time you receive this I'll probably have received word on Si. I've got a hunch that he's back in the states now. He will be the most surprised person in the world.

Christmas music is here in full force. I heard a good one yesterday. A record entitled "Rudolph the Red Nosed Mambo." I'm glad someone did a satire on that. Now if someone will do something about this "Mommy Kissing Santa Clause" dirge, I'll have a much higher opinion of music.

Last night a bunch of us were sitting in the dayroom watching T.V., shooting pool etc., when someone came in and said that the officer of the day wanted the dayroom clean in 10 minutes. It took us 5 minutes to clean it up. We spent the other 5 preparing a mass. We lined the pool balls up in a cross on the pool table, everyone stood around the table with their heads bowed, someone hung two bright curtains over my shoulder and when Captain Tappan walked in I was reading a re-enlistment pamphlet in the same tone of voice used in Catholic churches. Everyone kept echoing amen and crossing themselves. I thought he'd blow his stack because he is Catholic. He was so shocked he was speechless. Finally he said "Royko, you're damn lucky you're being transferred." Half the guys said "Amen." No sense of humor I guess.

My replacement has arrived. I do nothing but sit around the office and drink coffee. If they turn the transfer down it'll sure confuse a lot of people.

Well, maybe tomorrow there'll be news. Keep praying hon.

I love you,

Mick

p.s. Love you

Bob in this letter is Dad's younger brother.

POSTMARK: DECEMBER 18, 1954

Hi Sweetheart,

I'm not sure what time it is. It's Friday night, my clock stopped and it is late. I laid down after work and dozed off and just woke up.

Today has been eventful, sweet. This afternoon a telegram arrived from Sheehan asking the C.O. what is being done to get me transferred. Twenty minutes later a PRIORITY message was sent to 25th Air Division at McChord. A half hour later they phoned the C.O. and told them the paper had left there for Hamilton California on the 10th. After Hamilton it goes to ADC. It should be there right now. Twenty minutes after that we sent a PRIORITY message to Sheehan telling him that. The base brass all treat me like the "golden airman." There are dozens of new guys around the base and already I'm a legend. The guy with the beautiful wife, who knows important politicians.

Hon, do you know that there is only one way a Colonel can make General, or a General can go higher. Congress promotes them. No wonder these boys are jumping when Sheehan cracks the whip. My transfer looks 99.9999 . . . . % sure. I feel wonderful. I received that letter you wrote Tuesday today. Tch-tch—Here I am a devoted husband who loves only his sweet wife, and because of the Xmas letter rush my letters are delayed. I sadly pass Thursday without a letter and on Friday what happens? I'm greeted with a letter that would drive stronger men to drink. Taking a ride with an old suitor. You're a flint hearted wench.

I guess I'll be on my toes tomorrow. There's a chance that ADC might hustle it through. I hope so. This waiting is enough—I know it can't be easy for you sweetheart. You're wonderful. You're my babe.

I've got a roommate now. A 17 year old. Two years younger than Bob. Isn't that something? I'm aging fast. Hear that? My bones just creaked.

Oh to think that we'll be together soon. I can't say "be patient" hon, because I'll miss you each time I have to be away from you, the rest of my life.

Your adoring husband
Mick

Monday

Hi Sweetheart,

Hey, let's get rid of those blues! I just finished reading the letter you wrote Friday. The Christmas rush is holding up the mail delivery so we'll just have to bear it. I didn't receive the letter you wrote Thursday 'til today so things are getting screwed up at both ends. Knowing that you feel depressed serves to make me twice as nervous as I have been. Yesterday it was all I could do to keep from phoning you. I didn't phone 'cause the first thing you'd think was that the transfer was in effect. Nothing so far hon and I'm going nuts. I expected to hear something today but no soap.

Thanks for warning me about the vitamin pills but I'll have to risk life and limb by being home as much as possible. Dangerous wench hm?

I imagine Si will be taking another leave. He's got 13 months left in the navy so I expect to see him before his discharge. It's too bad he won't be home for the holidays.

I took a ride up to Mt. Baker again yesterday with the fellow whose car we used on our honeymoon. We've been hearing "White Christmas" so often, we decided to see some snow. There were six of us and no one who saw the snowball fight we had would have guessed that we were anything but kids, and had all been overseas. My reward for all this is a stiff neck and a cold. A real jim dandy cold. My head aches, neck hurts, and my nose is running so much I think I'll enter it in the Kentucky Derby.

After trying to work me to death, Varns now has gone to the opposite extreme. I'm unofficially relieved of duty. My replacement has arrived. I spend all my time drinking coffee and wandering in and out of the message center, hopefully waiting for a message to arrive that will send me home. Maybe tomorrow.

Last night I stopped in the club after we returned from Mt. Baker and it happened again. One of the guys came up to me and asked to see my wife's picture. I asked why. He said that he had heard that you were beautiful. After seeing your picture he said that you are the most beautiful girl he's ever seen. He's right you know.

Bob's theory on beautiful women may be right but there are excep-
tions—my wife for instance.

See you soon beautiful and cheer up.

Mick

p.s. I love you sweet.

Hi Sweetheart,

Who in the hell ever said that no news is good news. It's a bold faced lie
and its originator should be condemned to twenty years in the Air Force.
This morning has been a total waste. No letter from you and no news on
the transfer. Besides that, it's raining, my cold is colder, so had stew for
lunch and I'm being driven insane by Christmas records. I wish I could
sleep from now 'til the 26th and miss all this "Yuletide cheer." During
the past two weeks I have foolishly allowed myself to consider being
home for Christmas. It's impossible now and I don't relish the thought of
being here alone, thinking about how much better it would be if I were
with you. I'd prefer that, you know. I keep thinking about how Chicago
looks in the winter, especially around Christmas. All the years of going
to school and working downtown have instilled in me a preference for a
big city Christmas. I like being downtown among all the shoppers and
seeing trees in all the houses. This country style Christmas just doesn't
ring a bell. Most of all I like the thought of being with you. You mean
so much to me hon. Last night I was laying awake listening to a church
choir singing all the good Christmas songs and I found it very easy to
picture you in church. That's how I fell asleep—Christmas music and
seeing you in church. I've never even thought about going to church on
Christmas but now—my dear wife, you have revived my spiritual side.
People have been telling me what a changed man I appear to be but they
really don't know. Until we found each other I didn't think I'd ever feel
content and peaceful. I'd have ended up an unhappy wanderer. You've
made me very happy my sweet. I love you very much. Very, very much.

Next week will probably bring some news hon. Maybe by the time you read this I'll already have phoned you. I hope so. I miss you so much. It's pretty hard to fall asleep at night. You've got into my heart and mind and seem to be firmly entrenched. I can't think about anything but you.

'Bye for another day sweet
Mick

p.s. I love you

Neither my brother nor I ever learned—or wanted to learn—how to golf.

POSTMARK: DECEMBER 24, 1954

Wednesday night

Hi Babe,

I just left the weekly propaganda lecture where a chaplain dished out a long spiel on Christmas spirit and love thy neighbor. Today I was generosity personified. I was open hearted. I gave away my golf clubs. This was against my will of course. I spent the day in town, had a few beers, returned to the base and discovered that my clubs were gone. Some of the men got discharged a few days ago and have been hanging around waiting for one of the guys who is driving back east. Apparently one of them thought I was old Saint Nick or something. Hon, I'm disgusted. While I was in town I was listening to Xmas music, everything looked bright—then this. I'm not going to say anymore 'cause I'll just feel worse.

I received two cards today. One from George and one from Chris. George was discharged the 6th of November (wonderful day) and he's living in Pittsburgh Pa. I'll have to drop him a line and let him know about my transfer. With Chicago being the crossroads of the U.S., I'm afraid that we'll be the recipients of many unexpected visitors in years to come.

Soft music is being emitted by my radio. Miss you. I just had a horrible thought. What if my transfer falls through? Something would give and I'm afraid that it would be my sanity. I'm nearly a nervous wreck hon. When I open my eyes in the morning the first thing I think of is—maybe today. By nightfall my ulcers have doubled and it's another day.

Christmas is a couple of days off and then New Years which looks kind of hopeless too. I guess we can't have everything but gosh it's going to be tough spending both eve's away from you. Nearly four months ago we were sitting in the Clover Club and you were telling me of your New Years date with Larson. That had a remarkable physical effect on me. I felt like my body was completely empty. If you'll remember, I played the good sport and said that you should go out. If we weren't married and I had to think about you spending New Years Eve with him I would have probably started my celebrating last week and stayed drunk 'til Jan 20th or thereabouts. Shortly after that, we reached an understanding and you make me a very happy guy when you said that you weren't going to date. Neither of us could have possibly anticipated everything that happened since. This last year has been remarkable. George is the only person who's really seen everything happen step by step and believe me hon, at times he voiced amazement at the storybook aspects of our romance. We'll have a love story to tell our tall blond kids, won't we? I've already decided that they will be blond, tall (of course), smart as all hell, and will learn to play golf before they learn to talk. The first word I'll teach them will be "fore." They'll be happy because they'll be raised in a happy home.

It looks like my plan to spend Xmas Eve in my bunk will be fulfilled. Even if I wanted to go out, which I don't, I'm financially unable. I've paid off that clothing account, got a haircut, and I'm nearly squelched economically. Oh well, someday we'll be rich.

Speaking of my haircut, the barber I patronize is usually pretty good but today I discovered that after 24 years of marriage, his wife has left him. He had been drinking and I now have very few of the waves in my hair that you admire. Never fear, by the time I get home I'll have stopped looking like a shorn lamb.

It's getting late, I'm tired, lonely, miserable, miss my wife something awful and I'd better go to bed.

Merry Christmas my sweet and I hope we never have to spend another one like this.

I love you
Mick

The quote at the end of the letter is from the poem "Bonnie Lesley," by Robert Burns.

POSTMARK: DECEMBER 27, 1954

Monday

December 27th

Hi Sweetheart,

I wish I could write something besides "no news" but that's the tragic truth. It's been 30 days since I submitted all the paper work and still nothing has happened. It looks like it's been delayed by the holidays. Around Christmas there is always a big turnover in personnel due to the men returning from overseas, going overseas, and being discharged. That and the fact that a lot of administrative personnel take Christmas leaves probably explains the delay. After I saw that I couldn't make it for Christmas I began hoping for New Years but it looks like that's out of the question too. Oh well, can't complain too much. Now I'm worried about where it will be. I've nearly got myself talked into O'Hare Field.

Try not to think about it hon. Pick a date, January 10th for instance and think of that as the day I'll arrive instead of hoping from day to day that you'll hear something. This past weekend was nearly the death of me. I stayed on the base, alternated between sleeping and reading and tried to call you Christmas but the wires were loaded with calls so I gave up. I was glad to see Christmas pass. It's the saddest one I've ever spent and I don't ever plan on spending another one away from you.

My cold is nearly gone and I'm sure that by the time I get home I'll be so full of vim, vigor, and vitality, not to mention virility, that you will have to beat me off with a chair. I just thought of something. No it couldn't happen. Well, just in case, I'll bring along some cards.

The time is now 12:30. I woke up about two hours ago and I'm going down to the section this afternoon. My replacement has KP this week and I'll work just to have something to do. Maybe I'll get some news this afternoon. If I do, you'll know. God, I wish that they would give me a reason to call you. I'll tell you what hon, just to keep you from jumping every time the phone rings, when I do call I'll call between 9:00 and

9:30 Chicago time. That way you'll know during the day that after 9:30 you can relax.

Hey hon, if we didn't have this transfer to think about we'd still be counting the days 'til my leave. It's about 120 now. My gosh that's a lot.

I received a letter this morning, the one you wrote Thursday. I guess tonight or tomorrow I'll get some news of Christmas at home.

Last night I dreamed that I caught the guy who pilfered my golf clubs. He came to a fitting end.

To see her is to love her,
and love but her forever
For nature made her what she is
and ne'er made such another
I love you babe,
Mick

Mike's sister Eleanor was married to Gus Ozag.

POSTMARK: DECEMBER 28, 1954
Tuesday
December 28th

Hi Sweetheart,

If time would pass this slowly when we're together I wouldn't object at all but when a person is happy that's when it just flits by. I don't remember six days passing as quickly as our honeymoon did. It's only been 6½ weeks since I saw you board that plane but it seems so much longer ago than that. I hate to think about that evening. It wasn't very pleasant. I'd much rather be the one doing the traveling than the one staying behind.

New Years Eve will soon be here and with it another long miserable weekend. I dislike weekends 'cause there is no possibility of hearing anything. Sundays especially 'cause not only don't I have the chance to check the message center but there is no mail delivery, which makes it twice as rough. I hope I hear something within the next two days. I'd like to be able to call you New Years Eve and give you some real good news. If you haven't heard from me by New Years Eve tho, you'll know we have another weekend to endure. I'll call just before midnight hon. I guess you'll be at El's so I'll call there. When the sirens blow, you can give me a 2200 mile kiss.

I've been having a heck of a time getting to sleep lately. As soon as I turnout the lights my mind starts churning with thoughts of my transfer. Last night I went to bed at 11. At 12:30 I was still tossing and turning. At 1:30 it was better. At 2:30 I finally dozed off but what did I dream of? I think that the Air Force is intentionally torturing me. It's been 31 days since I submitted all the papers. They left 25th Air Division on the 10th. We'll figure that they arrived at WADF on the 12th and allow WADF five days. Give them two days to get to ADC and they'd be there the 19th or 20th. What has been going on since then is something I can't understand but I'm not happy about it. Every time the P.A. system yells for someone I pick up and when they start out "airman first class . . ." I nearly jump. So far nothing.

The weather has been unusual. Usually it rains but isn't too cold. Lately it's been raining and cold too. We're getting everything.

Didn't get a letter this morning but I hope for one this afternoon. I'm anxious to hear about Christmas at the Ozags. A year ago I was avoiding you. Fool-fool-fool.

Keep praying hon, we're not 100% successful yet.

I love you,

Mick

p.s. I love you

POSTMARK: DECEMBER 30, 1954

Wednesday
December 29th

Hi Sweetheart,

Happy (?) New Year hon. Sure It's a happy New Years day. A lot happier than the last one. One year ago I was looking forward to two unhappy years of AF life and then—? Your predicament a year ago wasn't too happy either hon. I'm sure that 1954 won't be surpassed in happiness, suspense, excitement, and wonderful rewards for many years, if ever. It's been a wonderful year hon. In one year, a dream that I've lived with most of my life came true. I couldn't ask for any more than that.

As usual, no news. I wish people would stop trying to convince you that I'll come slyly sneaking into Chicago intent on surprising you. As soon as I hear something I'll be running for a telephone. I doubt whether I'll hear anything this week. You are correct in thinking that some wheel took off for the holidays and left it in his "out" basket. Next week is the deadline. They assured Sheehan that it takes approximately 30 days. As I write this it's 32 so by next week Sheehan may notice the lack of results and send some more telegrams. I don't think it'll be necessary. I expect to be holding you close within two weeks. That's not too long to wait but I'd rather not wait at all. It's pretty tough to be torn from my bride's arms and be thrown back into this insane life. I'm sure Doc Marks would frown upon such conduct. I haven't broken out but it's tough getting to sleep at night. I keep seeing a tall, beautiful blond in a leopard skin robe and that plays hell with my nerves.

The mail delivery is still slow but I expect it to get caught up quite soon. The letter I received today was written Christmas day so the letters that you wrote Sunday and Monday are still floating around somewhere. My writing has been erratic hon but it's getting pretty hard to write. I'd like to be able to sit down and write some good news but I can't and that makes letter writing quite difficult at times. I'll be glad when our letter writing days are over. In the last 10 months, we've had one month together and nine apart. That's not a very good ratio. We'll have to improve on that in the future.

They have me working again and I'm glad of it. Those days were getting too long. I'm a research man now. A big yearly report is due which involves poring over 200 different books and gathering statistics on parts used, money spent, and mass hours expended by this section. I've got so many numbers running through my head I feel like a pin ball machine. It helps keep my mind off the transfer and that's the main thing.

Sweetheart, I'm sure that within 10 days after you read this, we'll be together again. Keep praying and try to keep your mind occupied and before either of us know it, I'll be in Chicago, blanket in hand.

Quick poem;

In '55 I love you more,

than I thought possible in '54.

Love you sweet

Mick

POSTMARK: JANUARY 1, 1955

Thursday night

Hi Babe,

Tomorrow will be New Years Eve and frankly I'll be damn glad that it's over. Christmas and New Years have served only two functions this year. To make us miss each other a little more and to create more tension over the transfer. We were both hoping that the transfer would be effective in time for me to be home for New Years, if not Christmas, but since it hasn't we can wait just as hopefully but not as urgently.

I received three letters in the mail this morning. I felt rich as I was walking away from the mail room. I bolted my food, rushed to the office, pushed the report aside and started reading. A minute later Varns walked in, asked me how the report was coming, noticed what I was doing and apologized for interrupting me. After I read the letters I tore back into that report and worked 'til five fifteen. Then a sumptuous meal of chopped up hot dogs bathed in red sauce, string beans, dehydrated potatoes, apple pudding and water, and I was all set for a nap. It's 10:25 right now and I'm feeling great. My cold has returned, and my back, due to these wonderful G.I. bunks, is aching like mad. To make me feel better, one of the guys in the barracks came in and asked me if I agreed with an article that had been written about golf in a magazine. That immediately brought to mind my golf clubs and made me mad again. It's funny the way I felt about those clubs. They didn't cost me a lot of money and they sure weren't the best clubs that could be had but they represented a summer of what at times was hard work. I felt good when I saw them standing in the corner of my room. Until this summer I had always used that set at Gus's that are to say the least ancient. These were good clubs and had provided me with many an afternoon of fun. I hope that the guy who took them never shoots under 100.

It is now 7:30, Jan 1st, 1955. This letter has covered a span of three days due to my neglect. I just got off work. Hon, it was so wonderful talking to you, hearing your voice, but when I hung up I felt awful. It seemed while I was talking to you, all I had to do was reach out and I'd have you in my arms. You seemed that close. I'm sorry I sounded half inebriated. I purposely restrained from having more than a couple of beers so I would have a clear mind when I called. I hadn't realized how low my liquor capacity had become. Two beers and I was half shot as you probably noticed. After I hung up I returned to the base, put on a uniform, relieved Varns and he went to the party at the Officers Club. An hour later I was invaded by a shrieking group of drunken officers, all of whom wanted to wish me a happy new years. Varns was drunk and feeling very sentimental. He made a long speech praising that multi-talented, industrious, witty, loyal, intelligent young airman, ME. Everyone agreed that I was a fine broth of a lad and they all left, leaving me to guard the great Northwest. The Russians passed up their golden opportunity.

Honey, I miss you so damn much. I could not, absolutely not, stand a long separation. The only reason I'm not half crazy now is because of the transfer. You are all that matters to me and I want you to remember that always. Everything I do, anything I'll ever accomplish, will be done with one purpose in mind. Your happiness. I love you more than you know hon. I can't explain how I feel or tell you how much I love you but believe me my wonderful, sweet wife, no one ever loved anyone more.

I'm going to turn in hon.

Hope I dream of lavender bed sheets.

I love you my darling,

Mick

p.s. Today, tomorrow or Wednesday should bring news.

Canasta was a popular card game at the time.

Monday
Jan 3rd

Hi Sweetheart,

It's Monday, 11:10, I'm waiting for the mail room to open and as the morning draws to a close it's the same old story—no news. If I didn't know better I'd think that they had forgot about me. This delay has got me worried. Knowing the fiendish way that the wheels in the service think, I'm beginning to expect anything. I've stopped hoping for O'Hare Field or G.O.C. Now all I want is the transfer, to be sure that it'll be O.K.'d. I'm turning into a nervous wreck. My hands shake, I have nightmares, when I can sleep. I'm of no use to the Air Force. Last night I was in my room trying to read. I got so jumpy I thought I was cracking up. I finally went to the club and had a double scotch with ice. A couple drunk civilians were there and they bought me a couple of rounds. Shirley came in and bought me a wedding drink. This served to relax me enough to get to sleep. I'll have to get transferred soon because that can't become a nightly ritual. At work today I must have walked in and out of the message center 25 times. It's been about 35 days now and that's enough. God, I hope that by the time you receive this I'll have called you. I know how this must be wearing you out too hon. It means so much. To be together, to get started at Yardley's, to be together, to save more money, to be together, to see our plans take form, to be together. Let's face it. Everything else is secondary. I want you in my arms.

The mail room opened and the letters you wrote Wednesday and Thursday are on my desk. I've just felt my nerves clam down. Your letters affect me that way.

I don't play canasta hon but I guess you could teach me. It would be a case of "Grin and bear it."

Babe, I hope that pretty soon my beautiful wife will be able to tell everyone who asks her, that I am coming home. Everyone I meet asks me the same thing and frankly it's getting on my nerves.

The thought of you, the Christmas tree, and being together is so wonderful it seems nearly impossible. I miss you so.

I repeat—I hope that by the time you receive this we'll have heard something. I don't expect any news today. I don't know why but I just don't expect anything. Maybe tomorrow. Damn. This is nerve wracking.

Tonight, just to be optimistic, I'm going to pack everything I won't be wearing for awhile. I've got to do something or I'll flip my well clipped lid.

It's nearly time for the mess hall to close so I'll have to go hon.

Keep praying sweetheart and maybe soon we'll fulfill Rosemary's words.

I love you,

Mick

POSTMARK: JANUARY 4, 1955

Tuesday

Jan 4th

Hi Babe,

This is starting to get me down. Another morning has passed and still no news. I went in to see the 1st Sergeant this morning and asked him what could be causing the delay. He didn't know so I suggested that he send a message to ADC. He refused as I expected because he's afraid of getting some higher ups mad. It's been 37 days now and that should be enough. I wish that something would happen. I'm a bundle of nerves and I'm getting worse every minute. Last night I woke up four times and had a heck of a time getting to sleep. I was sure that by now I'd have heard something. I didn't expect to make it home for Christmas but I did have hopes for New Years and I was sure that after the 1st I'd be on my way. Here it is the 4th and not a word. I hope Sheehan has noticed the time delay. A couple more days and I'll be getting panicky. You'll be reading this on the 6th. If you haven't heard from me by now you can be sure that I'm half way into a padded cell. I can't understand what could be causing the delay. Maybe the AF figures that if they ignore me I'll forget about getting transferred. I don't know. Over the last weekend I was positive that I'd know by now but I'm wrong again. Maybe Sheehan is working on it right now. I hope so. Not knowing whether it's even being looked at is the worst thing. It could be lying in a basket somewhere under a huge stack of other items. If only I knew what was being done.

I just checked the mail room and my box was empty. It's only four hours to the next mail call so I'll have to be patient.

If nothing comes this afternoon I'm going to ask the C.O. to send a message to ADC. What the heck, the guys on top can't be so inhuman that they can't understand what tension they are causing. This could go on for another month and I'd be expected to sit here and be patient. If they decided to stall it off there isn't too much I could do about it. I guess Sheehan is the only one who could help then. I hope he hasn't forgot about us. Babe, I guess you can tell by the things I'm writing just how mentally confused I am. My mind has been whirling with all the possible disasters that could occur. Every time a phone rings, every time the P.A. system starts, I nearly jump out of my skin. I distrust the AF immensely and would put nothing past them. Maybe they are stalling or something. This delay just doesn't make sense. I hope that by the time you read this, you've heard from me or Sheehan. I'm powerless to do anything here. I hope Sheehan doesn't let us down.

I'm going to eat hon. I'm sorry that this had to be so short but I'm incapable of thinking of anything but that transfer. Keep praying hon.

I love you,

Mick

Mike finished his last letter to Carol on January 5, 1955. That day's Chicago Tribune carried a brief story with the headline "Labor Federation Backs Daley in Mayoral Primary." Mike would edit and write for a base newspaper at O'Hare in 1955 as Richard J. Daley was being elected to his first term as Chicago's mayor. The collision course was set.

Carol, it turned out, was the one to finally deliver the news Mike was so desperate to hear.

Hello Wonderful,

Hon, it's been about two hours since I hung up the phone and it just occurred to me that I didn't sound very excited when you gave me the news. Hon, I've been in such a state of mind in the last month, hoping for O'Hare and yet not really expecting it, that when I did hear the wonderful news I was too shocked to really offer any kind of reaction. When I walked into the orderly room, the 1st Sergeant asked me what I wanted—I said "huh?" He looked closely into my face and said "What the hell is wrong?" I was in a daze but I told him that I was going to O'Hare. He asked me how I know and I told him. The two of us marched into the C.O.s office and told him. I'll be home soon hon. As soon as the squadron gets word, I'll go to Paine Field, pick up my orders and I'll be on my way. Hon, if this was a movie it would be nearly over. The happy ending would occur when I arrived at the train station. This is much better than a movie since we have a lifetime ahead of us. Baby, I'm still in a daze. This is so wonderful I can hardly believe it. I'll walk into the apartment, set my bags down and that's it—I'm Home for Good!

As you can tell by the letter I wrote earlier today, I was getting kind of "shook." I was laying down in my room when I heard the PA system say "Airman First Class"—I was on my feet—"Royko"—I was running down the hall—"call the switchboard"—and the phone was in my hand. Babe, when you said "O'Hare" I got weak in the knees. The whole base knows by now and everyone will be very relieved. I haven't smiled in a long, long time. They can call me smiles from now on. Hon, you'll receive this Friday. Don't write any more. I'll be home by then. I'm going to do some packing (that'll be fun) and finish this tomorrow. See you very, very soon sweetheart.

Hi Babe, It's been two hours since I finished that last paragraph. I've packed all my "G.I." stuff and I'll leave the civies 'til the last minute. I've been going through my desk and trying to organize all the letters I've received. I'll bring them home but I don't know where I'll put them. I've been reading them as I go along, at random. Here's one in June. "Sure

I could fall in love with someone else while you're gone, but that could happen if you were living next door." Oh cruel heartless wench, why doth thou torment me so? (Royko—2nd Act) Here's a three pager in which you discussed the weather, Villa Venice, and the Edgewater—So, everything didn't pan out. Here's one written in May in which you were wondering what I was doing while you were at a movie. It was Saturday night so I was drunk. I don't remember, but I must have been. Here's a sweet one written in July in which you told me I was wonderful. You are wonderful too hon. Reading these letters makes me realize just how unbelievably lucky I am. One year ago I was so depressed, so down hearted, so hard to live with, my whole family was kinda glad to see me leave. In a year my whole world has been turned upside down. Thanks to you babe. I love you. Coming home will put butterflies in my stomach just like it did in September and November. I love you so much. I'll never stop loving you or telling you that I do.

Hi babe. It's Wednesday night and I'm going to finish this so you'll get a letter Saturday.

I didn't get any news today but it didn't bother me 'cause now that I know I'm going, and where I'm going, I can stand a few days wait.

Everyone has been congratulating me and saying that this is as good as a discharge. They are absolutely right. This is as good as a discharge. I don't know what kind of work I'll be doing at O'Hare but anything will be OK. O'Hare does create a few problems that I hadn't planned on, the main one being the necessity for a car. I've been trying to get all the financial figures organized in my mind but it's getting confusing. By now you should have received 137.10 and the 75.00 bond that will arrive at El's house. That's $200. As you can see, I was paid so here is 40 more. I'll have about 15 days at home before I have to report to the base and that will give me time to get "unshook" and also enough time for us to get financially organized. Once I report in and get paid at O'Hare, I'll get a total of 245 a month. I have absolutely no idea what it costs for two people to live so I think the easiest way to settle that problem is for you to take care of all the money. I won't be able to start in Yardley's 'til I get squared away at O'Hare. If I get into radio work I'll be working goofy hours and that would make it tough to demonstrate. I hope they don't need me in radio there so I can try for a job that involves only day work.

As soon as I find out when I'll be home, I'll call you and unless you are working, you can meet me. If you are working hon and can't be there, call up Bob (Royko) and maybe one of them can be there with a car. Cab fare would be high. I expect to be home the early part of the week. Sooo we can make next Sunday's dance instructions at the Ozag Studios. That sounds like fun babe tho I've never thought of myself as doing a Mambo.

I'm going to close hon. Just a few days and we'll be together.
'til then,
I love you always
Mick

TELEGRAM
1955 Jan 14
Everett Wash
Carol Royko
5408 North Central Ave

Arriving Sunday at two. Great Northern RR
Love
Mick

WESTERN UNION
TELEGRAM

The filing time shown in the date line

⸻ CS398 PD=

=CAROL ROYKO=

:5408 NORTH CENTRAL AVE=

CLASS OF SERVICE	WESTERN UNION (37) 1201	SYMBOLS
This is a full-rate Telegram or Cablegram unless its deferred character is indicated by a suitable symbol above or preceding the address.	W. P. MARSHALL, PRESIDENT	DL=Day Letter
		NL=Night Letter
		LT=Int'l Letter Telegram
		VLT=Int'l Victory Ltr.

The filing time shown in the date line on telegrams and day letters is STANDARD TIME at point of origin. Time of 1955 JAN 14 AM 5 45 at point of destination

⸻ CS398 PD=EVERETT WASH 14 232PMP=

=CAROL ROYKO=

:5408 NORTH CENTRAL AVE=

ARRIVING SUNDAY AT TWO GREAT NORTHERN RR LOVE=

:MICK=

THE COMPANY WILL APPRECIATE SUGGESTIONS FROM ITS PATRONS CONCERNING ITS SERVICE

le by a graphologist in wr

e slope of the lines of a p

s the mood the person is wr

I'll be writing ~~stop~~ virtual

o me a great favor. Dont stay

me letters. Dont misunderstan

e the greatest thing thats

but your schedule sounds so

dont want you losing slee

Write them but do it wh

awake. ~~tired~~ No one is completely.

me the one person in this wor

alive and healthy.